Liberation

find *your* way, find your freedom

A BOOK FOR THESE TIMES

Emma Eker

Published in the UK in 2021 by EvolvingPublishing

Paperback ISBN 978-1-8383197-0-0
.epub eBook ISBN 978-1-8383197-1-7
.mobi eBook ISBN 978-1-8383197-2-4

Cover design and typeset by Spiffing Covers

*I dedicate this book to my mother and father,
Janice and Richard Eker, who have supported me
and loved me so very dearly throughout my life.
You are truly beautiful human beings and I love
you with all of my heart. Thank you does not do
it justice.*

CONTENTS

Acknowledgments

There are many individuals whom I wish to thank, too many to list here. There have been hundreds of people who have been an integral part of my journey, whether they know it or not. There are the many friends, past and present, the wise 'teachers' and guides who have pointed the way and those who have written the books that have been my constant companions throughout my life.

To the friends (both old and new) and to the family who have travelled with me, holding me in my most difficult times and sharing in my joy, you know who you are and I thank you with all of my heart for your beautiful friendships and your unwavering support. I love you all.

Above all, I offer deep thanks and heartfelt gratitude to the field and force of life, the benevolent energy that wraps each of us in a loving embrace, urging us forward on our path. I am continually astounded and humbled.

They asked her, "How did you free yourself?"
She answered, "By embracing my own power."
Yung Pueblo

Introduction

Life is a fascinating journey and, in my case, an adventure of extremes. It seems I've spent my whole life trying to get 'there'. Destination still unknown. It has been an interesting ride, one that has not always been pleasant, smooth or indeed comfortable, but entirely necessary to the process of 'unfoldment', re-membering and be-coming… me.

A defining moment in my life occurred in 2006 when I found myself in rehab aged 28 following a breakdown whose time had come. It had been building for some years – maybe since forever – and finally in March of that year, I crumbled and the game was up. It was the beginning of a new way of being for me and the entry point for a new phase of my life to begin – it provided a doorway that would ultimately lead me home.

In order for me to search for a solution, there needed to be a problem and, in my case, it showed up in a few ways, but primarily as addiction. It was a slippery slope that started in childhood – the desire to fit in, the longing for connection, the search for identity and the unanswerable questions…

Many of you will resonate strongly with my story for we all inhabit planet Earth and our struggles are similar. We are all looking to find meaning and make sense of who we are. In this book, I share some of who I am and some of my journey – the confusion and bewilderment, the suffering, the addiction, the isolation, the loneliness of the search and the journey back home… We're all doing our best to navigate our course and find our way. Wherever you are, you are not alone. We're all in very good company.

If traversed 'well' with a sincere desire to come to know the Self, there is an incredible upside to the journey – there are precious gifts in the suffering. Disappointment and heartache can be signposts, golden opportunities that can ultimately lead us to freedom. Our pain can be our doorway to joy. Indeed, as the great Sufi poet, Rumi, said, "The Wound is the place where the Light enters you."

The journey has, at times, been incredibly challenging for me and deeply painful, but it has also been filled with magic, with synchronistic happenings that continue to astound me and this human experience now feels exciting.

All experience is an opportunity for growth if you're interested in looking in that direction and, gratefully, I am. I have accumulated a wealth of understanding of this process of be-coming (me), which has been fundamental and more than a little helpful in navigating life's pitfalls. Everything I have been through has brought me to this moment and I am in awe of life.

I share with you that which has made sense to me

along the way, allowing me to find an element of peace in the madness, a place within myself that is my sanctuary. I want this for you too, truly I do.

Is life still challenging? You betcha! Would I change anything? Not a thing. I know who I am and I love what I know. I am human so I have my moments (sometimes considerably long moments), but with its continual surprises, I see that life is perfect and there is a greater plan for each of us if we'd just get out of our own way. I have an unwavering commitment to this path and it is my soul's desire to help others to re-member who they are and to help make this journey of life a little more joyful.

With a profound change of worldview, we have the ability to see differently, to develop and nurture our relationship with life and cultivate faith in the unknown. Trusting life to take us exactly where we need to go as we cultivate a deep 'knowing' that, regardless of our circumstances, regardless of our pain, our disappointment, our confusion, our turmoil in the moment, all is happening perfectly. We are able to forge a deeper connection with the Self (the part of us that 'knows' and guides us through life) and therefore, within this relationship, together with our trust in life, we can enjoy whatever comes our way.

So ultimately, this book is about trust – trusting the magical adventure that is your life, designed specifically for you, perfect for your incarnation in this lifetime. It is about getting out of your own way, letting go and letting life live you, holding your head up high and declaring 'this is me – you're welcome!', looking yourself in the eyes and loving who and what you see, regardless of any perceived ideas of where you 'should' be or any 'difficult' life circumstance you're navigating.

Let this book be a guide and companion, providing comfort through the challenges and difficult times, allowing for a deepening into your potential and an awareness of what's possible. Together we're embarking on a journey that will allow you to see your beauty and own your power. You will step into the grander version of yourself and create a life you love, allowing your light to shine and making magic.

Even when you don't know, you *know* – we just haven't been taught that we have all the answers residing inside of us – we just need to listen. Even when you feel alone, you're not. When you feel life has forgotten you, it hasn't. When life looks like it's all going wrong, it's all alright.

You have the ability to let go – of all the thoughts, constraints, misunderstandings and beliefs that do not serve you which have thus far stood in your way... up until now. Let go to gain, give up the fight to win, move away from what you 'think' you know in order to see the truth, come out of the mind and back into your heart, allowing it to lead. We are not in control anyway; there is an intelligence to life. None of this is up to us, which is great news – we can breathe a huge sigh of relief!

It's time for you to re-member and to be-come you – give your Self permission to be visible in the world and finally allow yourself to be happy, empowered, loving, joyful, radiant, free and in alignment with the divine truth that lives within you, running through your body and coursing through your cells. Ultimately, we are here to say YES, to you. Here's to your liberation! Happy Birth-day!

And with that, here is my story.

PART I

A Bit About Me

The Start

I have always asked questions. I have always wanted to know. As a small child I remember staring out of my window at night, gazing into the black sky whilst I wondered – where, oh where does it all end? Who are we? Where are we? Who's out there? Where does space actually stop existing? And then what? What happens when we reach the edge?

These thoughts baffled me. I often felt the need to divert from this train of thought, as I truly had nowhere to go with the questions, let alone my idea of the answers. The wonder, awe and bewilderment these musings provoked within me seemed far too big for my little mind to contain – if I kept looking, surely my brain would combust! But there it was, the precedent had been set – I was a searcher. I was questioning as soon as I knew how and it hasn't stopped yet. I am certain it never will.

Life was 'normal' growing up. I lived in a house in a suburban road in north-west London, UK, with my mum, dad, sister and various cats at different times. I moved through the schooling system in the 'right' way. I was taught right from wrong, correct manners, my please and thank-yous, what to wear, how to dress, who to be friends with, the way life goes, that life is tough (you've got to work hard in a job you don't enjoy in order to get what you want), that you can't do this and you can't do that and much more about the nature of life and what it means to be human. Most of which I wouldn't have chosen were I to be the designer of life – incidentally, it turns out that I am… more about that later.

As for my personal identity, I understood from my outside world that I was naughty, a little aggressive (with a satanic temper, apparently), that I spoiled happy occasions and was generally very difficult to get along with. As one can imagine, this is not an ideal sense of self to grow up inside of and to brandish in everyday life and, needless to say, I didn't feel great about myself.

As a caveat, I clearly see that I learned to give people the exact 'me' that they expected. We tend to hold gospel to that which we're told from a young age and it becomes our identity (who were we to know differently?) and we wear our labels as badges of honour, no matter how crappy they feel.

As someone who's interested in understanding 'the journey', be it psychological or otherwise, I have often considered what set the precedent for my breakdown and journey into addiction – be it OCD, co-dependent relationships, food (under- or over-eating), drugs or alcohol. It's an opportune moment to tell you that my longest relationship to date has been with cocaine. We hung out together for 11 or so years and, in hindsight, it potentially wasn't the best choice of partner. Regardless, I have no regrets… more on this later.

So, to the 'cause' of my foray into addiction and my descent down the spiral, there are a few suspects…

Fitting In

My feeling is that I was generally uncomfortable in my own skin. There was lots of 'fitting in' to do and I was constantly contorting myself into a shape that was not me. I was a strong personality with anger being a very familiar emotion for me. I have been told that I would regularly tantrum from a very young age to the point of passing out – I guess my little self just couldn't deal with the rage that I felt – I simply couldn't contain it. My mother was concerned at first (who wouldn't be?) but as with most things, you get used to them and I always came round quickly after the intensity subsided. The body is incredibly intelligent and it took me off-line whilst it recalibrated.

Who's to say why I was experiencing such intense emotions from such a tender age? It is what it is and, although I absolutely cannot say for sure, I have always been fighting the status quo, fighting for justice, for what feels right and sometimes it just felt too much.

This feeling of fitting in has been a familiar thread in my life. As I mentioned, I am not sure where or when this materialised or at which particular point I received the message that my natural shape was flawed, only G-d knows the starting point, but I have often considered the impact of systems and how instrumental/detrimental they have been to my sense of self and wellbeing.

We're brought up in a society where there are hard and fast rules and a protocol to adhere to, a 'right way to be' and a correct way to behave and if, like me, you receive a message from a young age that you're 'too much' and it is simply not tolerated, the child will find ways to adapt that are acceptable. To one's detriment.

You see, if I consider who I was before I forgot (that is, before I was shaped by environment, societal protocol and the like), I have a sense of being a carefree, creative, highly emotive and sensitive individual, potentially leaning more towards the arts with a strong desire to express and to feel my way through life, rather than to think, rationalise and use logic. Indeed, I believe this is the case for the majority of children before we reach a stage of being that barely resembles the truth of who we are and what is possible.

It is important to mention at this stage that with the message of 'I'm too much', I learned to dim myself down. This dimming down meant that I moved through life as a lesser version of myself, a less shiny model. And when you're not being true to yourself, when you're hiding, it's a lonely place to be and it's hard to forge deep and authentic connections when the you that shows up in the world is a false self and not the full picture. I learned to swallow myself down, that is, to stuff down my feelings and emotions from a very young age.

We all need to be met on an emotional level, we need to feel that others love, understand and accept us, for all of us. I did not have the experience of being affirmed at this level, although this was not through a lack of love, interest or desire, but more from others' inability to do so. People around me were not so savvy in this area; I was not surrounded by a high level of consciousness or emotional literacy. I was seen as 'difficult' and the feelings that I didn't speak out loud, which lay underneath and behind the outbursts, went undetected.

This dimming down and fitting in was only exacerbated by the schooling system, which (especially at my time of growing up) favoured learning in a linear, cognitive capacity rather than leaning towards creativity. I cannot claim to know a huge amount about the workings of the brain, but I am aware that the right brain deals with creativity whilst the left brain leans towards logic. This differentiation is necessary to mention at this juncture, for I believe it to be an integral part of my journey and I have no doubt others will resonate with this battle also – being vs doing.

When one exists more within the right brain, creativity is expanded, intuition is strengthened and we use our emotional intelligence to navigate our way through life. On the flip side, when we exist within (and give credence to) the left brain, we will tend to think things through and rationalise our reality, dismissing our inner knowing and hunches, moving away from imagination and the invisible world, to trust and rely on the five senses and the 3-D world to guide us through life.

This differentiation is important to highlight as I sense strongly and deeply that the troubles began when I came out of a heart-based/feeling way of living and existing and into a very mind-identified, logic-based and rational existence. I was giving onus to the intellect and to the external world (rules, regulations and 'right' ways of being), thus ignoring (indeed, no longer hearing) the internal whisperings of my heart.

Simply, I adhered to 'shoulds' and accepted societal ways of being rather than following my inner wisdom and internal guidance system, which I have now come to see as much more trustworthy than that which takes place in my head. In the world of form (3-D), it seems the world of the formless (imagination, intuition, etc) is not so readily accepted. What we can see and touch is trusted much more than what we feel and intuit.

I do not walk through life pointing fingers of blame for what has been and for that which now lives in the past. It is what it is and nothing was done maliciously. In many areas of the world, there's a protocol we follow as human beings that has been adhered to for centuries as the right way to live and behave and no one has really questioned whether this is indeed right or beneficial. We're caught in a system and doing our best, it's just not conducive to what is actually beneficial and possible with regard to the full flourishing of a human being. Who we think we are is learned information and, to my mind, we're all OK until we're taught otherwise and to think we're not.

There was never anything 'wrong' with me (as we are all born as G-d intended) and I would've found my own individual shape and flourished accordingly if I hadn't received less than helpful messages with regard to my identity, whilst being poured into a mould that was not the shape of my natural Self – that is, placed in the schooling system, favouring mind-based intelligence across the board, rather than creativity and individuality. I was taught to 'work out' equations, colour inside the lines and to wear a uniform that kept me… well, uniformed. I definitely did not question the status quo. I guess I didn't know there was a choice – not an achievable one at this stage anyway.

As I type this, a memory has come to mind of a fellow pupil in my infant school. We were gathered on the carpet for reading time and I distinctly remember this little boy being comfortable sitting with one leg crossed on the ground and the other foot flat on the floor with his knee tucked into his chest. Thing is, it wasn't right. The protocol was to sit cross-legged and I remember many occasions when this boy was reprimanded for sitting badly.

For me, this highlights the struggle of being taught that we need to be like everyone else, that there is simply one way of doing things and, to my mind, it makes absolutely no sense. What felt comfortable and natural for his body was deemed wrong. His natural leaning was not acceptable at reading time and therefore he had to fall into protocol and change his shape, which he really struggled with – he just couldn't sit comfortably cross-legged. He was admonished and made to feel wrong for doing what was natural to him and for his body.

This may seem like a minor detail and somewhat irrelevant, but it's a neon warning sign for me and a subtle little message that we need to fit in and be like everybody else in order to be accepted. Maybe you'll tell me this is harmless and perhaps this particular incident was, but a lifetime of fitting in and receiving messages that your natural inclination is 'wrong' is going to have detrimental consequences.

Even now in the typing of this manuscript I am having to fight against the logical part of me that feels like this is all up to me, that the pressure is on for me to create something perfect for the reader as I feel the fear (the old learned story) that I will not be able to deliver accordingly. It's a battle between the taught way of working through my left brain vs trusting the creative process and allowing what needs language, to find its way onto the page.

We've forgotten that creativity, problem-solving and great ideas come from surrendering, daydreaming, letting go and allowing the mind to wander rather than sitting in the 'right' position and working it out with logical straight lines. There's such a huge distinction here and one that is becoming more and more obvious to me as I move through life. The former way of creating would have felt effortless and easy for me had I not been taught otherwise – namely, to think, think, think rather than to simply feel, allow, let it flow and express.

If you converse with any creative mind, they will tell you that their ideas came out of 'nowhere'. There is a famous poet who actually speaks of having her poems come *to* her, with her only job being to take these words from the invisible world of thought and potential and transfer them onto the page and into form for the world to enjoy.

This is true of songwriters, artists and musicians. Creatives often see that their creations already exist in the realm of potential and view themselves merely as vessels/channels for the expression of the music, art or idea. They do not always take the credit – they trust the creative process, which is 'beyond them'. Namely, they do not produce their work from the thinking, logical and rational mind, but they 'make space for' and 'allow' that which has thus far lived in the world of the form*less* to take form in the 3-D world.

Some of the most brilliant creations, ideas and solutions to world problems have come into play this way. For instance, Mozart was four or five when he started composing music and I'm pretty sure he hadn't spent the first four years of his life in intensive music academy! Where did his compositions come from? He most definitely wasn't 'working them out'.

Memory is somewhat unreliable and my mother will often tell me that I enjoyed my time at school, it's just that when I think about this time overall – with the human tendency towards selective memory syndrome – I remember feeling like it was a constant attempt to fit in, thus moving away from who I actually was towards a distorted version of myself. For this reason, and the reasons highlighted above, in my earlier years, I had no idea who I was. I had forgotten.

Another memory visits me of baking cakes for friends' birthdays whilst at senior school. I did it often and let it be known, that whilst the process of creating those delicious chocolate cakes was enjoyable for me (and I'm really rather good at it!), the intention and sole purpose behind this seemingly altruistic and generous offering was my need to be accepted and liked – to be 'in favour' with the popular girls. Funnily enough, I actually think that I was one of 'the gang', but I simply didn't feel good enough and felt I had to keep earning my place.

I spent my time trying to impress the girls around me, those who (to my mind) were 'better' than me. I attempted to cement my place by attracting attention and audience, performing as Clown in order to make people laugh, 'acting up' in a bid to be perceived as Rebel or becoming Bully to be seen as strong. I was constantly distorting my shape in the interest of gaining affirmation and moving myself up the leader board. I was constantly looking for external validation.

To highlight my inability to discern my preferences at this stage, I can remember that whilst many of my fellow school goers had the latest celebrity stud adorning the fronts of their lever arch files, I had absolutely no idea which music I favoured and which current boy band I should be drooling over. I simply liked whatever my peers liked and would engage in lengthy conversations about whoever's smiling face or smouldering glare was staring back at me from the magazine cover!

I didn't know myself well enough to gauge my preferences and I certainly did not have a strong enough sense of self to admit that, in fact, I had no interest whatsoever in being involved in discussions around pop music or boy bands. So far removed was I from any type of personal identity that I think it's safe to say I wouldn't have been able to spot my opinion or preference in a line-up!

The Status Quo

I felt very secure in my home and within the body of my family and my parents have always been wonderful, incredibly generous, good hearted and well meaning people. But as with the rest of society, they too were doing their best within their level of emotional capacity and their desire to fit in with correct protocol and adhere to the status quo.

They taught me the rights and wrongs of the world (as they believed them to be), ideas of how to live, what's acceptable/unacceptable and 'right' ways of being/behaving, etc. Most people are innocently following the herd in blind compliance with the 'way it is'. Again, it's no one's fault – it's just the way it's been. How many people actually stop to question protocol and the status quo from the 'powers that be'? As children, we're looking for guidance, to have our feelings and emotions validated and taken seriously; we're looking to understand and be understood, needing to make sense of the world and our place in it and we are easily moulded. Why would we dispute the information we receive from our elders? How could we discern that we may have been misinformed?

The problem was, much if not all, of these 'correct' ways of being were incredibly unhelpful to me and much of my internal world went unnoticed or was misunderstood. The 'way things were' was oftentimes unsupportive of my best interests and simply did not feel right to and for me – they were in no way aligned with or based on any type of 'truth'.

I lived under an illusory idea of how the world works (the state of 'normal') that was not conducive to my personal freedom and self-expression – in this, I am not alone. I learned it was somehow wrong to be me. That I needed to be someone else in order to fit in and be accepted, and no one, least of all me, was aware of how this prescribed way of living – the contortion of my natural shape and the swallowing down of my truth – was to impact me on an individual level, inside and out.

If my parents had had an inkling as to how I was feeling growing up, they would have pulled out all stops, but there was a disconnect between my emotional world and theirs and I wasn't sharing what was taking place inside of me. This was all going on outside of my conscious awareness and, even if I'd noticed it, I simply didn't have the language to share it. At a young age, I wouldn't have had the foresight to put words on what was taking place invisibly and outside of my eye line.

As human beings, we are always looking to make meaning and we receive messages both verbally and nonverbally. I have a strong memory of sitting on the carpet in the front lounge of our family home in front of a colouring book. I was doing as children do and using each colouring pencil in a completely non-linear and messy fashion – playing, enjoying and splashing colour every which way onto the page. I showed my handiwork to a family member, who lovingly, but in no uncertain terms, told me I needed to colour within the lines, for that was the 'way to do it'.

A little disappointing for the younger me perhaps, but I did an about turn and tried my hardest to trace around the inside of the borders in straight, exacting lines. It was frustrating for me and I couldn't get it 'right'. I therefore found a page in the colouring book that my older cousin had completed (perfectly within the lines) and attempted to take credit for her efforts instead.

Again, this situation seems pretty harmless in and of itself, but it is yet another message that order is favoured over 'mess', that for things to be right they need to be perfect and must exist within the boundaries already marked out, that there's a certain and correct way to do things. For me, this was another step further away from my creativity and self-expression. I had received the message – to be accepted, you must literally 'stay within the lines'. It's all loving, it's all innocent, it's happening all over the world… and it's a travesty.

I am sure my experience is representative of much of society. We're all looking to 'fit in' and to make sense of who we are as individuals and we all come to the party, innocently enough, with our invisible and, for the most part, unconscious 'stuff'.

With me being an incredibly sensitive and highly intuitive child, I was not only picking up on what was said and modelled to me, but I was also taking in that which was unsaid and invisible – other people's fears, unmet needs, feelings, judgements, energies, etc. We are forever making meaning and, as a child, it is difficult to discern between what is 'theirs', 'his' or 'hers' from what is 'mine'. It's difficult enough now I'm an adult, so I understand why children can feel so confused and disheartened, oftentimes seeing themselves as the cause of suffering, much of which has absolutely nothing to do with them and identifying with so much that simply isn't theirs.

Family Dynamics

It's hard to marry the two different images I have of my dad. I have memories of us on holiday when my dad was always involved in the fun – building sandcastles with my sister and I, throwing us over the waves in the sea, which I absolutely loved. He was always up to something, a real joker.

We often holidayed in England and on the drive to or from the destination, he would be steering the car with the back of his hands on his lap (which my sister and I couldn't see) and he would tell us that Horace was driving. We found this fascinating and magical! We would often shout, "Dad, let Horace drive!" He always had such a light-hearted, playful and childlike manner.

There was another occasion when we had returned from a holiday in Italy and, unbeknownst to us, Dad had purchased a 'Smurf village' – *The Smurfs* was a popular cartoon that aired on TV whilst I was growing up. There were little plastic Smurf characters with miniature props to create scenes of the Smurfs engaged in different pastimes. There was Sailing Smurf, Fishing Smurf, Mummy Smurf,

Relaxing Smurf on a hammock (my favourite), Smurf at school, Teacher Smurf, etc.

Our lounge had two entrances, one from the hallway and one from the TV room. One evening, Dad locked both doors to the lounge with himself inside and drew the curtains so that we couldn't see what he was doing. I ran around from the hallway to the TV room trying to catch a glimpse of the internal goings-on, but to no avail. I kept asking my mum what was happening, but she wouldn't tell.

After what felt like an age, Dad drew back the curtains and opened the sliding glass doors and there, spread out over the dining-room table, was an entire Smurf village. I was in awe! I was delighted and my excitement knew no bounds – it was a wonderful sight to behold. There were so many of them covering the whole surface of the large table. And to think, Dad had brought all of these little Smurfs home from Italy without our knowledge and spent hours setting it up in anticipation of our sheer delight. That's my dad.

Family photo albums were another of his creative pastimes. He would take hundreds of photos of us on holiday, come home and stick them all in albums. This took him hours as he sorted through the pictures, arranging them in some kind of order with handwritten captions placed by each one, creating a story that was always funny.

These albums are priceless to me, even more so today as time moves on and I look back over the years. And this is a gift that my dad gave to us, wonderful treasures for all the family to cherish. When I imagine the love he poured into this act, I feel overwhelmed. Again, that's my dad. A truly awesome and great human being.

Then there's this other version of my dad that I hold in my mind who is a completely different character, a version that bears very little resemblance to the dad of above.

As I grew up, I became more insular and withdrawn and the lack of emotional connection between us became more apparent. The difference between how I showed up in the world and who I was inside created a gulf between us – a huge disconnect. I can only assume he did not know how to relate to this version of me. As a result, I came to regard him as stoic, our communication feeling business-like. He was physically there but in some ways, a stranger to me – I never seemed to be able to get *inside*. For many years it was difficult to hold these two very different versions of my father. Not to mention confusing and painful.

I remember how incredibly difficult I found dinner times. On a Friday night we would eat together as a family and this time together felt suffocating to me. If my mother and sister left the table at the same time, leaving myself and my father alone, I would feel rising panic. My senses would be on high alert and I'd feel awkward and anxious, willing their swift return.

I didn't know how to relate to my father. I had nothing to say. I couldn't find any words or any type of connection with him that was not forced – it was torture for me. I would sit in silence, increasingly desperate to run away, but unable to leave. No one around the table was going through anything that bore even a tiny resemblance to my ordeal; this was simply my internalisation of events.

For years after I would struggle with dinner scenarios. I built up a negative connotation with regard to sitting around a table. I would be scared that conversation would lull and fall into silence and all participants would be sitting around feeling awkward, whilst my innards and intense anxiety slowly consumed me.

Prior to any 'what-could-be' awkward dinner situation, I anticipated the occurrence of uncomfortable silence, a loss of my words, being questioned and finding myself drawing a blank, stuttering, talking nonsense or being unable to speak. It was a huge fear of mine – I didn't trust my ability to talk freely and eloquently in the company of others. I found my brain unable to function under the pressure and I'd panic, which made it worse.

I understood that 'making conversation' was something you did and were good at, rather than communication being about... well, just being me – present, listening and organically responding. At this point, 'me' was a long way off in the distance and moving further away. My ability to converse became an extreme effort and therefore I was never able to simply relax around the dinner table or around people. It was much easier to be on my own. I felt trapped. There was nowhere to run and only so many times I could visit the loo!

My dad had a very dry sense of humour and in my teens I was embarrassed by this 'weirdness'. I was used to it, but not everyone knew how to receive him, not quite understanding the meaning behind the 'jokes', unsure whether he was being serious or not. I imagine it was quite unsettling (at least, it was for me) for my friends who were teenage girls to be met with this deadpan humour with no idea how to respond. I was never quite sure if he'd say something in jest that they would misconstrue, view as a reprimand or verbal affront and would therefore no longer want to visit my home and I/my dad would be the topic of ridicule.

I realise this situation was merely my perception as I had cultivated a sensitivity to it. I felt so awkward and uncomfortable that I simply assumed others would too – classic projection. If I checked this out with those same friends today, they may have no recollection of anything 'out of the ordinary'. The point is, this was my reality and therefore my experience. As I type today, I have a very different vantage point and therefore a completely different understanding and relationship to this time in my life. Back then, my experience of the relationship was challenging and it had knock-on consequences.

I guess, as I retreated into myself, it was harder for my dad to understand me and relate to me, but then I wonder if I retreated due to the dynamic. I'm not sure if I changed as the years moved on, if he changed in relation to me or whether the change was within him. He had become more serious, more burdened with life, his working life being a noose around his neck, weighing him down, as responsibility lay heavy on his shoulders. I do not need to understand every detail and the 'why' something happens, I merely relay my experience to give you an insight as to how my internal world was being informed and shaped and how my lens was being sculpted.

I used to attend a youth club on a Sunday and my mum would drop me off and pick me up in the afternoon. On occasions, she wouldn't be able to make it and instead, she'd send my dad to collect me. When I walked to the entrance of the club and saw my dad standing there within the group of mums and dads, the panic set in as I anticipated the journey home.

The distance from the youth club to our family home was minimal, only minutes away, but those five or so minutes in the car felt like hours to me as I once again scrambled to fill the silence and dispel the (my perceived) tension. My whole body was stiff, in fight or flight mode and I'd stop breathing. Once again, I felt an overarching sense of responsibility to fill the silence, together with an inability to do so.

I'd stare out the window, willing red traffic lights to turn green, longing for the driveway of our family home to come into view. And I am almost certain that my dad was totally oblivious to this, having an altogether different experience. He was probably enjoying a leisurely drive home on a Sunday, fulfilling his husband/fatherly duties and enjoying his day away from the office. He would be horrified to learn that in this unremarkable and 'everyday' situation, his daughter was having a cardiac arrest in the back seat of the family Volvo!

The effect of this and other situations in my life materialised as an inability for me to withstand any type of discomfort and it moved with me for many years of my life. I couldn't trust that life would flow without my meddling and I felt an overwhelming sense of responsibility. I constantly stood at the control panels with octopus arms, managing all the events of life. I had no idea how to simply flow with situations as they materialised and, once again, I felt trapped. I was always looking for an escape route – a way out, an exit or a place to bolt.

Please don't get me wrong here; my dad is up there with some of the best people I've ever met. He is good through and through, kind, generous, charitable, a stickler for doing the right thing with incredibly high ethics and a strong moral code. He's also incredibly intelligent to boot, it's just that I had my own experience of our connection; I was the one making meaning, which became my reality.

As a child and a teenager, I was desperate for a deep connection, not just with family, but also in life. So whilst I wanted for nothing and I felt outwardly safe and secure in our family home knowing I was loved and cared for, my inner experience was that of feeling unsafe (in constant fight or flight), unknown and misunderstood.

I lived in my own bubble disconnected from others,

which was detrimental for me – it would be for anyone. I just couldn't get under the surface, couldn't find my way 'in' to the people around me. Growing up, this occurrence (my level of disconnection from Self and others) was somewhat unconscious for me. I really wasn't spending a great deal of time mulling it over, but it was always there in the background playing itself out. I wasn't aware of how much it had affected me until years later.

The world I lived in wasn't such a great mirror for me. Most people around me did not model or practice Self-love. It just wasn't a 'thing'. You just got on with life, as life was 'meant' to be lived. There wasn't space for (or any notion of) self-improvement/evolution. On some level, I took on this idea of 'normal', aware that I needed to follow the herd and wear a mask for the outside world in a bid to be accepted. And having come to believe that my shape was flawed, that I needed to be something other than myself, I learned to hide the truth of who I was and it is important to say that I was raging about all of this. I didn't consciously understand this growing up, but I saw it in later years. I was angry that I had taken on all of these misunderstandings with regard to the world I inhabited and who I was. Angry that I'd had to hide my Self, my true colours – my light.

No one ever told me that who I was was perfect, that I was capable of achieving anything my heart desired and my lack of self-confidence and the swallowing down of my truth brought with it a feeling of low-grade depression that followed me in my day-to-day life. And I won't be the only one who identifies with this experience, not even close. In fact, those who have been held in a conscious manner are unfortunately in the minority.

Interesting to note, I have a vague recollection of wondering when I would be old enough to use the words 'I feel depressed' and it be acceptable. It was as if this were some kind of accolade to aim for – what a lofty goal! I'd heard so many adults say this, that I believed it to be the norm, something worthy to work towards. I was genuinely considering as a very young child, 'at what age can I utter these words aloud and have them be taken seriously?' My G-d, did I ever find out! Another case of 'Be careful what you wish for'. Again, I am not pointing the finger of blame at any particular person or body; I am merely documenting (what I recount to be) the truth of my experience in response to life situations and circumstance.

I'm Not Good Enough

If I go back to how I felt as a young girl, before my entry into the schooling system, I remember feeling that my sister was favoured. I always felt that she was prettier than me, cleverer than me and generally 'better' than me. There are countless situations that gave me all the evidence I needed to come to this (incorrect) conclusion but, nevertheless, my conclusion it was. In life, we will always make meaning of the situations we find ourselves in, even if our interpretation is a long way off from the truth.

I can remember being on a family holiday abroad and desperately wanting to hang out with the older girls – pretty standard, really. It was evening and we were gathered in a large group, lots of families together and I wanted to sit on the lap of one of the prettier, older girls. Thing is, her lap was already occupied by my sister and I felt I couldn't get a look in. I actually remember coming around from the back of the chair this older girl was sitting on and moving to her side in a bid to gain her attention. My efforts to be seen, wanted and accepted were in vain as I remained unnoticed. Enter confirmation of the message – 'I'm not good enough'.

Another example – it was possibly my 10th birthday. My mother had organised a party at home and all members of my junior school class were invited. I was excited as any child would be – parties promised fun, cake, presents and all attention on me! I vividly remember being in my sister's bedroom before the start of the party and sitting next to the piano (the only place we could find to house the little piano we practised on) and spying a My Little Pony toy still in its packaging, perched on top.

I asked my sister whose it was and she told me that our next-door neighbour had brought it for her. Now, looking back, this was very caring of the neighbour, giving my sister a gift to ensure she wouldn't feel left out on my big day. Thing is, I coveted this My Little Pony and I desperately wanted it to be mine; I was aware that this situation had never occurred in reverse – I had never been given anything on my sister's birthday. I remember the shock I felt at this revelation, it reverberated in my body. I was in a state of disbelief. To my mind, this was the 'best' present, better than all the gifts I'd received and it had been reserved for my sibling... on my special day.

And there you have it. I'd reached a conclusion (albeit an inaccurate one) and another message for me – 'I'm not good enough/not as important as...' As I say, it clearly wasn't the truth, both the meaning I'd made from the giving of the gift and my felt experience, but that's what I'd internalised and I felt my sister had stolen the limelight.

Another memory visits me of myself and my sister sitting on my parents' bed early one weekend morning and my mum asking if we knew the months of the year. Now, I'm two years older than my sister and I drew a blank – I just didn't know the answer – but my sister... well, she reeled off those 12 months perfectly, effortlessly and in record time. I was once again left feeling embarrassed, stupid and concluding that 'I'm not good enough/not clever enough/my sister is better than me'.

Why is any of this relevant? Because all these experiences, rightly or wrongly, became my foundation/ my lens and led me to believe that who I intrinsically was, was below par. I simply didn't make the grade, which became a belief system that I carried with me (not always consciously) throughout my life, always running in the back of my mind. This feeling felt 'true' and it underpinned everything.

Sensitivity

I was a highly sensitive child who felt a lot of fear. This has been with me for much of my life and has played out in many areas and on many levels.

When I was a very small child, I can remember being full of angst when my parents ventured out of an evening. I have spoken to my mother about this over the years and she assures me that she and my father rarely went out on a weekend but when they did, I would worry about it throughout the day and the thought of their impending departure would fill me with dread. I would sit in their room as they dressed for the evening, asking when they would be home and how long they would be gone. Whether my grandma babysat or we had a sitter, I would be on edge all evening, not wanting to go to bed until my parents were home, safe and well.

When the inevitable happened and it was bedtime, I would lay in my bed fighting sleep until I heard the key in the front door, which signalled my parents' return. Only then would I allow sleep to take me. If it was my grandma who babysat, she would sleep in the spare room and if she had gone to bed before my parents had returned, I would watch her sleeping, monitoring her breathing, scared that she would die and my sister and I would be left alone.

Another strong memory comes to mind of me as a young child, lying in bed and sensing the walls of my room moving towards me. This felt so real to me that I would call out to my mother, father or the babysitter and tell them, "The walls are caving in on me," and ask them to feel for themselves. Of course, they felt nothing. But for me, this was happening. I would have laid my life on it; it wasn't up for debate.

I wonder how odd this must have sounded to those I'd called to my aid, but I didn't consider that back then. I wasn't concerned with the strangeness of my perceived observations, for I was much more concerned about what would happen when the walls came close enough to trap and potentially squash me. I can only imagine I was feeling suffocated even then. Either that or I was having some pretty convincing and lucid hallucinations! Interesting though, how these occurrences are plausible to the young mind of a child, before they are told that these, among many other things, are impossible. I myself didn't find this odd at all – the walls moving towards me were as real as the sky is blue. This was my experience and I was simply pointing to it.

Even when my parents were home, I could feel petrified through the night. If I hadn't fallen asleep before all lights went out, I would lie rigid in my bed, scared stiff of ghosts and spirits. I'd sit bolt upright in bed, a rabbit caught in headlights, listening like a hawk for every noise or movement. For years this went on and I would regularly creep into my parents' room and sleep on the floor. I needed to be near them, I simply couldn't be alone.

This was such a familiar occurrence that oftentimes my dad, who rose early in the morning for work, had to be careful not to trip over me! I must be honest and tell you this wasn't reserved solely for my childhood years. I could be found sleeping on the floor next to my mother's side of the bed even in my 20s. When the morning light came, I would take my pillow and duvet and make my way back into my own bed, usually exhausted, but so very relieved and grateful that the night had passed without event and the fear had left me.

Sensitivity has been with me all my life and not solely in regards to people (picking up on energies, that which is unsaid, feeling disproportionate upset in relationships when things go 'wrong', etc). I am also incredibly sensitive physiologically. I have a record speed response to drugs/meds/alcohol and heightened responses to life in general, compared to others. I have suffered with digestive/gut issues, acute sensitivity to noise/loud music/crowds, etc, experiencing an over-stimulation of my senses that I simply found 'too much'.

To witness any type of suffering, human or otherwise, has also been too much for me to bear. To see someone in pain, whether in life, through a TV screen or in a newspaper can affect me considerably. Even thinking about someone's suffering can affect me to varying degrees.

Human greed and unconsciousness have also been something I have grappled with throughout my life, feeling sickened and shocked, angry and hopeless when faced with certain human behaviour – the mass killing of animals for fashion or food, with a huge percentage of it making its way into the garbage, the devastating and unnecessary waste of life to meet the demands of human greed and desire has been unbearable for me. Baby calves being kept in tiny, isolated boxes away from their mothers to produce veal (their inactivity keeps muscle production to a minimum and their meat tender), textile industries leaking dye into rivers where children bathe and drink, slavery, sex trafficking, the culling of rainforests... the list goes on, together with my aching heart. I feel like screaming into the abyss, "WAKE UP!"

I have had to censor what I allow into my awareness and space in a bid to protect myself from the pain I experience on the back of hypocrisy, injustice, unconsciousness, abuse, poverty, suffering, etc. It has been overwhelming. I have wanted to wrap my arms around the world and rescue all those suffering, especially children. It's been 'too much'.

Just so you understand the level of feeling I can find myself in, it is even difficult for me to watch the children's animation, *Finding Nemo*. The thought of that little fish alone in the big sea having lost his parents can finish me off! There was a visit to the cinema with my sister to see a box office hit which, unbeknownst to me, featured a suicide and a subsequent heartbreak for one of the characters. Needless to say, I was inconsolable. My dear sister was genuinely worried for my state of mind and my ability to drive home! It took me two or three hours to move through the upset. This was the evening prior to a new work position and the following morning I awoke looking and feeling like I'd been punched in both eyes!

So you see, my sensitivity is high and I share this with you so you may, on some level, have an inkling as to how I have walked in this world. And I wonder how much this sensitivity has affected me throughout my life, how much I have unknowingly picked up on and held the pain of others around me, finding this level of feeling too much to bear or mistaking it as my own.

I wonder how much I suppressed and shut down this sensitivity (also a huge gift – more on this later) to avoid being overwhelmed – I'm pretty sure it's been a protection mechanism. Potentially in my younger years I wasn't able to hold the space for it, swallowing it down, too painful to experience. I am also aware of how misunderstood I have been on the back of this level of feeling (Emma, you're too sensitive, don't be so silly, you don't need to take it to heart, just let it ride over you, let it go, etc) and how much I have had to apologise for myself when I have reacted from my level of hurt (others being unable to understand my level of upset), walking in the world feeling like an open wound, desperately trying to avoid all the salt! I have come to a place where I can now understand this gift and use it for good as I make my contribution to life and offer myself fully in service.

I'm Alone/Unattractive

Another memory that has visited me over the years is being outside in the garden of my childhood home on a warm summer's evening. The sprinklers were on, my mum was hanging out the washing and I was bathed and in my nightdress, ready for bed. There were houses backing on to ours that belonged to other families with young children who I knew well and we had interconnecting gates that allowed us to run in and out of each other's gardens. The neighbour next-door occupied the corner plot and had a huge garden and us children would be allowed to play there. It was a beautiful space due to them being keen gardeners, and being allowed to explore and run free was a real adventure.

On this particular evening, some of the children had grouped together and made their way into this garden. I could hear them running and laughing and although I cannot recall the exact words they were shouting, I felt a little taunted, excluded and alone.

I was wearing a flowery nightdress with frilly short sleeves, which only added to my discomfort as I distinctly remember feeling awkward and unattractive – pathetic, even – in my babyish night-time attire. I felt aware of my mother's presence in our garden and hoped beyond hope that she couldn't sense how upset and ugly I felt inside, hoping she hadn't noticed that I'd been excluded by the other kids. I pretended to be absorbed in play, slapped a smile on my face, swallowed down the upset and pretended everything was OK. I wanted to protect her from my hurt and save myself from having to talk about it aloud and admit how I felt. I would deal with it on my own once I was in the privacy of my bedroom – only then I would allow the hurt to surface.

I was once again skipping over something important, smiling through pain and feeling the intense desire to escape and run away, no language to convey my feelings. I remember the acute level of self-disgust I felt inside of myself, especially in that long, unattractive, floral nightdress – I felt pathetic. Fundamentally, I didn't feel good about myself and who I was. And even at this point I wasn't going to give voice to my internal world; I didn't let people inside – my pain was for me alone. I didn't feel I had the forum to be transparent with my feelings in front of others.

The above scenario and felt sensation in my body has been all too familiar to me throughout my life. Looking back on my younger years, it's hard to remember myself outside of this identity. I spent much of my life feeling awkward and self-conscious, an outsider, and pretending this wasn't the case – pretending that I was confident and secure within myself whilst I desperately wanted to fit in, to be a part of/accepted as one of the popular girls.

This feeling of unattractiveness and discomfort with my body and in my clothes manifested on many occasions. I would only wear certain items of clothing that felt comfortable for me. I hated the majority of the clothes in my wardrobe, even though I had picked them all and, gratefully, had many items to choose from.

As a result of not knowing my own mind or my preferences and desperate for approval, I vividly recall picking out clothes that I thought others would like. I would shop with my girlfriends in mind and only choose the items I believed they would deem acceptable, articles that were trendy and 'in fashion'. On the occasions that I *did* like something 'out of the ordinary', that fell outside of what my friends were wearing or what was acceptable, I would place it back on the rail, lacking the confidence to wear it in the public domain.

I remember my mum collecting me from a friend's house and, in her embarrassment, apologising to the mum, saying, "She does have other clothes," as I was wearing the same black jodhpurs and jumper that I wore every time I played there. I felt horrible in everything else and I remember it being the only outfit I felt comfortable in and would wear and wash it on a loop.

I could be found wearing a hot woollen dress in the summer because nothing else felt 'right' that morning. I even wore my school uniform to the library with friends on study leave as nothing else I put on that morning felt good – everything I had tried on felt uncomfortable. I remember dressing that morning and, as I viewed myself in the mirror, trying on item after item of clothing, I felt revolting and pathetic in everything I tried on, so my uniform felt like the easy option.

I remember walking to the library a little while after my dressing frenzy, anticipating my friends' surprise that I was in uniform outside of a school day. I felt embarrassed and stupid turning up like that as my peers were all in their weekend clothes. During my walk, I kept imagining what I'd say and how I'd be flippant about it and laugh it off. They were, of course, more than a little surprised to see me in my navy school skirt, burgundy jumper, white shirt and tie, but I made the excuse that I'd wanted to dress for the occasion, namely 'study', and that the association of my uniform would help me to concentrate. I actually think they believed me – why wouldn't they? What other sense could they make of my turning up in uniform?

To recall the events of that morning can still pain me today. I remember how frustrated and upset I'd felt getting dressed and how many items of clothing I'd put on and ripped off. I remember how dejected I felt walking to that library, angry and sad that I couldn't dress myself and that all my clothes felt horrible. So horrible in fact, that I'd rather wear a synthetic jumper and skirt teamed with a constricting shirt and tie than anything else I owned.

Nothing felt right, but more than that, I didn't feel 'right'.

I felt awful inside, uncomfortable in my own skin and in my body. I acted out, was a difficult child and I wasn't always particularly nice to my family or the people around me. It's not possible to act in love when the most prominent feeling a person feels is intense dislike for themselves, verging on self disgust. I didn't want to cause hurt or harm another in any way; I just had no way of managing my emotions and the intense discomfort I felt inside.

I felt misunderstood, angry, deeply sad and I raged. If I could have put language to my feelings and if I'd had emotional intelligence at this stage, I would have told you how much pain I was in and how much upset I was carrying inside. Unfortunately, this was not a language I knew and so my pain came out sideways, usually with insults, door slamming, shouting, rage, screams and tantrums. I regularly felt as if I wanted to rip my insides out. I simply felt disgusting inside.

I want to assure you that this was not all of my life. I had lots to be incredibly grateful for and at times I felt great. For the purpose of allowing you to understand my journey into breakdown, it is necessary to highlight these points, since I would never have followed the path I took if the overriding feelings I experienced were joy teamed with a positive self-image.

And again, I want to reiterate that this internal sense of self was coming from me. It came from my interpretation of life events and had nothing to do with anyone around me. Yes, societal protocol had not helped in the individuation of my self. Free expression was not highly encouraged, but my felt experience was coming from me; my interpretations of life and any coping strategies I developed on the back of this were my personal response.

It makes sense to me – in fact, it is wisdom – that I turned inside of myself in order to gain a sense and level of control when the 'outside' felt so precarious and uncomfortable for me. The experiences in my life thus far were innocent enough and I was surrounded with a lot of love and good intention; only *I* came away with negative connotations of my capabilities, of who I was as an individual and how I was perceived in the world. I'd developed a warped way of living in what seemed to me to be a very warped world. It was too difficult for me to live in constriction, so far outside of my truth and natural shape, so it's no wonder I turned inward on a path to self-destruct.

Now, let it be said, there were many other experiences happening around me at the time of the above examples (other things I could have focused on) and many other conclusions I could have reached that would have dispelled the meaning I made (which became the story of my life and my lived experience); but unfortunately, this way of seeing myself just gathered momentum over the years as I honed in on what was 'wrong' with me. I developed a distorted lens through which I viewed my circumstances and therefore I was always on the lookout for evidence to back me up and support my limiting belief systems. And believe me, I found them.

Is it necessary to attempt to list them all? Not really, for the importance is not in what happened, but in my felt experience and, therefore, conclusion of who I intrinsically was and the unfairness of life that I had made concrete, which became an identity I wore like a heavy coat.

I feel trapped. I need to run

My journey into senior school brought with it its own 'struggles'. My parents have always wanted the best for me and this included ensuring I attended a 'good' school to provide me with the best foundation for achieving my potential. I have always been bright but as I have mentioned, this didn't always show up in the 'intelligence' sense of the word and I wasn't a natural A-grade student.

So, to give me the best chance of 'success' in passing the 11+ entrance exams, I was tutored on a Saturday by a teacher who lived in our area. This was nothing short of torture for me. The last thing I wanted to do on my weekend was to study and be assessed in a stuffy room with a bunch of other kids all doing the same. I struggled with maths equations, problem solving and essay writing and I counted down the seconds until break time when I could sit in the garden and eat my lunch, only to count down the seconds again until pick-up time and my subsequent escape. I am also sure I took many more toilet breaks than was necessary in a bid to grab a few extra seconds of precious freedom.

This experience wasn't just reserved for tutoring. My father is incredibly intelligent and in a continued bid to ensure my success and secure my place in a 'good' school, with a loving heart and altruistic intentions, he would sit with me whilst I worked through old entrance exam papers.

Although this exercise was seen to be for my highest good, it was torture once again. The questions felt impossible to me – they read like double Dutch. I just couldn't 'get it', making the same mistakes again and again. Although my father has never raised his voice to me and is beyond calm and good-natured, I registered his frustration and my heart was in my throat as he patiently waited for me to come up with the correct answers. I desperately wanted to 'get it right' and I just couldn't. My brain didn't naturally work this way and this only added to my felt sense that I wasn't clever enough. I was continually swallowing down my intense desire to run and a sometimes overwhelming level of anger. I felt imprisoned and I was raging and screaming inside.

There was a family holiday that took place in the summer before said entrance exams and the dreaded exam papers came with us. Each day, after lunch, we would go to the room, sit around the table and continue our work. Although only for a very short period of time, these study periods felt never ending for me. Not only did I feel gutted to be taken out of the sunshine (insult to injury – where my sister was gaily running free!) and away from the swimming pool, I was once again faced with maths problems that felt far too difficult for my mind to solve and made absolutely no sense to me – more torture as I read and re-read the maths questions over and over and over again and they just wouldn't sink in. I was desperate to bolt through the bedroom door. I felt feral, but to no avail. The familiar panic and uncomfortable feelings would arise once again. I simply didn't know how to 'be' and I felt unable to deliver.

I knew that my dad wanted me to get these answers right and I believed that in order to please him I needed to be 'clever' and, once again, I found myself lacking. What could I do? My brain didn't operate like this, it wouldn't play ball and therefore I felt I had disappointed him. I am sure he felt incredibly frustrated, as for him these maths problems were easy – second nature.

The funny thing is, my parents probably won't even remember this occurrence and would be shocked to know the extent of my discomfort, but as I am trying to highlight, situations do not necessarily need to be 'bad' in order to have a 'negative' effect. Indeed, the intention can be pure and loving, but we are always only having our own invisible internal experience and, altruistic or not, for me this sucked.

I had exactly the same experience with Hebrew school on a Sunday. Just re-read the above, swap my father for a Hebrew teacher, the Saturday tutoring or family holiday to a Sunday morning and you'll have the exact same story. And yes, I spent a substantial amount of time in the toilets there too! I am now wondering if my escape into institutional toilets is where my IBS-type symptoms stemmed from – the association of freedom and relief being found in the loo!

Bottom line, I felt intellectually under par and was continually attempting to contort my shape from its natural inclination into what was rendered necessary and 'right'; from creativity, free expression, intuition and *being*, into logic-based intelligence, working things out, control, analysing and *doing*. I was always fighting an intense rage and a strong desire to run. I had been running from my Self for so many years and I'd be running for many more years to come.

With all the above being said (and with these examples being only a drop in the ocean) I moved through life feeling really rather awful about myself. I learned to stuff down these feelings of internal disgust, upset and dislike of who I was and just got on with life. When it came to walking out of the school gates for the very last time, how on earth was I to make a decision on important life matters such as what I wanted to be when I grew up? I had no real sense of who I was – I couldn't even tell you my preferred crisp brand. Mind you, with my obsession with food as a control mechanism, I could potentially tell you the calorie and fat content!

I had absolutely no idea what I wanted to do with the rest of my life and I don't recall ever having a conversation with regard to further education or university. I'd had enough of the 'system' and I wanted out. With no concrete idea, I was so far away from formulating a plan and making a decision that seemed right for me that I simply went with whatever turned up.

I liked my beautician, so I did a beauty course. I didn't finish it. I went to a reflexology course open day, decided I'd give it a whirl, my Mum sent the cheque and then I realised it was on a whim and we promptly cancelled it. Finally, I ended up enrolling on a six-month secretarial course (just to do *something*), which unbelievably, I did see through to the end and promptly took the first job that came my way.

There was absolutely no plan, no idea of what I wanted to do and not even a whiff of what would make me happy. The proof being that at last count I deduced that I've worked in around 32 full-time jobs, with that figure excluding many temporary work contracts. I pretty much detested them all. Clock-watching was a regular occurrence for me, with long stints in the toilets (oh yes, I was in there again!), staring helplessly into the mirror, feeling trapped and wondering how I could escape. There it was again, the familiar theme in my life – wanting, *needing* to run away. I simply couldn't sit with the feelings of confinement; it has always felt unbearable for me.

Some work positions lasted a few months, some a couple of years, with a few places of employment lasting mere days. It's astounding to me actually, that even at that stage of my life, I had no idea what I was doing (I didn't really contemplate it), where I was going or what I wanted.

I could be found working at loss adjusters, building construction companies, media agencies, recruitment firms, fashion/TV companies… the list goes on. There was simply no plan and no direction. My behaviour was completely erratic as I blindly fumbled my way through life, grabbing onto whatever driftwood came my way. I was scattered, aimlessly floating in a boat without paddles.

At some point, I moved into working as a PA (personal assistant) in the advertising industry. Whilst this too was mind-numbingly boring for me and I absolutely detested the long train journey into town and the never-ending hours seated at my desk behind a computer, once again watching the time tick by, it was, however, a 'fun', young and hip industry and there was a huge drink and drugs culture.

Long, boozy lunches were commonplace and pretty much an accepted occurrence. For the most part, Friday afternoons at work were a write-off – it was standard that 'lunch' would continue into the evening and possibly into the early hours of Saturday, with all manner of carnage ensuing. This was good news as far as I was concerned – another opportunity to escape from my reality in some dark club, pub or bar with some degree of anonymity, being with work 'friends' rather than those from my home environment. With that, it's probably an apt time to talk about my experience of addiction and the downward spiral that brought me to my knees.

Where Did the Addiction Start?

I will talk about my experiences with addiction, but it is important to note that the painful feelings I were attempting to 'get rid of' – loneliness, anxiety, heartbreak and self-disgust to name but a few – gathered momentum over the years and have fluctuated. That is to say, these felt sensations were not consciously with me every moment of every day, but they were always operating in the background of my life, residing just under the surface, ready to visit me at any given moment and have been very familiar 'friends'.

As I have documented, I had been hiding the real me for as long as I could remember and had never truly felt understood. This swallowing down of my Self (and I use a capital S for the essence of me, rather than the personality construct/our identity) meant that I often felt ill and tired as I felt exhausted with constantly 'trying' so hard, fighting, ignoring my internal whisperings and fitting in – I was totally out of balance, which is the very meaning of *dis-ease*.

I was constantly monitoring my behaviours and

the words I spoke in a bid to be liked and accepted and continually grappling with my extreme emotions, reactions and anxiety. I don't think one can understand how detrimental this is unless you have travelled this path (which unfortunately, too many of us have to varying degrees).

As I looked back over my life, although I now know that all happens perfectly, the extent of my suffering felt tragic. The depth of loneliness I experienced on the back of being a version of myself that has not been representative of who I truly am, is hard to put into words. It's deep, it's painful and it physically hurts. At times (too numerous to mention), my heart ached with a grief and loneliness that one experiences only with the death of something precious.

Was this loneliness and internal pain so unbearable when I first attempted to 'get rid' of it through addiction and obsession? I'm not so sure, but it's safe to say that some level of internal suffering must have been taking place for me to feel the need to control my internal world (that is, the pain inside) with the external.

With that being said, my first memories of 'addiction' started with OCD (Obsessive Compulsive Disorder). The definition of which is '...*an anxiety disorder in which people have unwanted and repeated thoughts, feelings, images, and sensations (obsessions) and engage in behaviours or mental acts in response to these thoughts or obsessions. Often the person carries out the behaviours to reduce the impact or get rid of the obsessive thoughts, but this only brings temporary relief. Not performing the obsessive rituals can cause great anxiety.'*

If I trace this back, from a very young age I remember trying to control my environment in an attempt to feel safe and comfortable. As a young child, I would go to bed at night surrounded by particular toys and dolls arranged in a certain order on my pillow. I would not be able to relax unless each toy was accounted for and in its exact position.

This may not seem like a huge deal to the reader, but for those who have suffered with this affliction, the ritual needs to be 'perfect' and the perfection is measured by how 'OK' one feels once the ritual has been completed. Anything out of line that feels 'wrong' can cause extremely high levels of anxiety and frustration and an overwhelming need to repeat the process to get it 'right'. Only when I was satisfied that all was well (that is, my anxiety was alleviated), was I able to turn off the light and go to sleep, flicking the switch two or four times, as this was another of my OCD rituals – the need for even numbers.

As the years moved on, my nightly rituals progressed and I became more and more creative in what needed to be attended to before I was able to retire. At one point in my life, I had to start my bedtime process at least a half-hour before I could get into bed as this was how long it took for me to cover all bases. There were certain ways I needed to walk in and out of rooms, a particular way the objects in my bathroom needed to be ordered, the continuation of my toy arrangement on my pillow and a need to ensure that each of my dolls and teddy bears were 'fed' before bed.

I would move around my room touching the mouth of each and every doll to feed them. This was an incredibly long and arduous task as I had many dolls and, to make matters worse, my choice of drink was orange squash, which stained the fur and made the surfaces of my room sticky! I absolutely detested carrying out these rituals, but felt totally out of control, as if I had no choice in the matter. I simply could not rest until everything was completed in exactly the right way.

If the process went 'wrong', I'd have to start all over again. It was torturous and quite simply, exhausting. The thing with OCD is that the sufferer feels that if the ritual is not carried out perfectly, something awful will happen and it will be because of them – they will be responsible. Someone you love will die, there'll be a car crash, someone will break in, etc. There is no end to these worst-case scenarios and they are forever changing, popping in unannounced at any given moment. Do this… or that will happen. It's unrelenting.

And as if all this weren't enough to drive a person to the brink of insanity, once I was in bed I'd have to sit up straight and say my prayers in a certain way and in a 'correct' order. The prayers got longer and longer and more specific and I would not be able to lie down and close my eyes until I'd said everything I needed to say, word for word, ensuring that every member of my family had been accounted for and each and every eventuality covered correctly. I felt an overarching sense of responsibility that any 'bad' outcome would be as a result of my negligence and therefore I would be left accountable.

When my mum tucked me in at night, I would need her to repeat certain words after me in a certain order before I could sleep and, if she didn't do it perfectly, I would keep the process going until it was done, driving her mad in the process. I'd shout to my sister in the next room to continue the same scenario although sometimes she wouldn't play ball and I would become highly anxious and desperate.

Away from the bedtime rituals, there were other ways the OCD would creep in and I'd find myself needing to ease my anxiety.

If I was writing something, I'd have to end a sentence on a 'good' word (forever changing) otherwise I'd see it as a negative omen. I'd force myself to keep writing until I felt pacified. I would often feel the need to go over a full stop or trace over an already written letter until it felt right.

Electronics and appliances were also the bane of my life. I would double- or triple-check anything that I may have used during the evening (lights, oven, washing machine, etc), even getting out of bed to re-check if I felt uneasy or if another intrusive thought – perhaps the threat of fire – would pop in. I'd even inspect appliances that I'd not used that day if the thought to check was compelling enough. OCD does not play fair.

The ways in which OCD showed up in my life are countless. I'd pick at my skin and scrutinise my face in a magnifying mirror, I'd count words in a sentence, read and repeat words backwards (quite a good party trick really, as I became pretty proficient at it!), walk in and out of rooms in a certain way, count my steps, eat only even numbers of crisps or sweets as a child, open and close cupboard doors… the list goes on.

It is difficult for me to give you a real sense of OCD, as one will need to experience it to properly understand the implications and knock-on effects. And let it be known that much of the time I was simply living my life, not consciously aware of or reacting to intrusive thinking, but obsessive thinking and behaviour formed the backdrop of my life. Chilling out or having a restful night in was potentially not the same for me as it was for others. Although, if one feels that jumping off the sofa every ten minutes to alleviate some anxiety, fear or compulsion that's surfaced is a form of relaxation, then hell, yeah – I was on holiday in the Bahamas!

The bottom line is, OCD is pretty debilitating to live with (not to mention exhausting and potentially embarrassing), with no end in sight. One can finally feel 'complete' with a ritual, only to have the anxiety creep in a short time afterwards and therefore a need to repeat the whole process once again. It's a vicious cycle – there really is no end. The feeling of anxiety will always resurface, followed immediately with a need to eradicate it.

Using OCD to manage an internal experience will never halt or put an end to the 'problem'. It would be years before I came to understand that managing any internal experience by carrying out external behaviours is not the answer, for we are looking to deal with the cause, not the symptom… but that's for later on.

Food/Body Image

Food would also play a huge role in my bid to pacify my inner turmoil. Now, every human being needs to eat, but there's a big difference between eating to feed hunger and nourish ourselves vs an attempt to fill an internal void and suppress less-than-preferred emotions. As with everything, we have healthy and unhealthy relationships (in all areas of our lives) and my relationship with food was anything but healthy.

I had a preoccupation with my stomach, as I recall, from around the time I entered senior school at 11 years old. I'd had two cysts growing on my ovaries from a very young age, which gave me terrible stomach-aches and severe bloating, which I felt incredibly uncomfortable with, both internally and externally. These cysts weighed in at seven pounds and made it difficult for me to button up my jeans or sit comfortably and, once again, I felt awful in my body. Once they were removed, my stomach went from resembling a blown-up balloon to being concaved. Even now, I can remember how much I loved this feeling of being 'skinny'. I was obsessed with having a flat stomach and, for me, this was the optimum.

But, I would not be allowed to rest in this post-operative glow for long, for I have a slightly rounded stomach naturally and it was only a matter of time before it took on its inherent shape. Our bodies and minds are always looking to move back into balance and return to their natural form.

More importantly, for me, I felt this just wasn't 'right'. I would compare myself to friends with washboard stomachs and find myself lacking. I saw this as yet another confirmation of my unattractiveness and I felt disgusting. I started monitoring my food intake, calorie counting and eradicating any fat (good or bad) from my diet and continually feeling and checking my stomach. I would feel wretched if there was a hint of bloating and I would want the food (and emotion) out of my body.

I can remember attending a New Year's Eve ball with my friends and planning on wearing a tight-fitting, red velvet dress (no judgement, please!) and I would practice sit-ups daily on the build-up to the big night. This preoccupation with my stomach was to be a battle for me for many, many years. I was so uncomfortable in my body and since we hold so much of our emotion in this area (with me suppressing so much of who I was and swallowing down the words I wished to speak), it was no wonder I was experiencing such an intense level of discomfort here.

As an aside, you may be interested to know that the

gut is now seen as the second brain of the body – it is here that our thoughts and emotions are stored. Our digestive system doesn't just deal with the digestion of food, but it actually mirrors how we 'digest life'. If one has a problem 'chewing on life' (as was the case with me inside of a warped view of myself and my world), this resistance or difficulty in going-with-the-flow in our attempts to control, will be mirrored in the flow of our digestive system/gut.

In my case, I was completely out of my natural flow and this unhealthy relationship with life and the feelings of being stuck, showed up in my inability to digest and release – I was holding on to so much and I therefore felt 'bunged up' and constipated *('unable to act in a relaxed and natural way because of self-consciousness or mental restraint')* both in the physical sense but also emotionally. I couldn't (I didn't know how to) let go. I was unhappy and uncomfortable with both my internal and external experiences and so the battle ensued.

This preoccupation of needing everything 'out' took me out of my life. I would take laxatives, smoke cigarettes and drink coffee – whatever it took to clear out. If I hadn't been able to go to the toilet 'enough' or I still felt 'full' or bloated, I would struggle with this, feeling disgusting and unable to leave my home. The anxiety that I would not be able to release fully was extreme.

The severity of this process waxed and waned over the years, although it gathered momentum and was with me for as long as I can remember. Indeed, I think back to when I did not feel like a prisoner held hostage to this preoccupation and I cannot wrap my head around how I actually lived and existed without the worry of going to the toilet!

This is the thing with addictive processes; sometimes one cannot recall when they started or even how a particular addictive pattern came to pass (excuse the pun). When I consider how this obsession materialised and manifested and the degree to which it blighted my life, I am baffled and flabbergasted that I lived this way for so long. I most definitely did not sit down with my notepad and pen in an attempt to brainstorm 'the most effective ways to relieve bodily discomfort and suppressed emotion' and come up with this little gem of a process as the best conclusion!

It doesn't matter how much we attempt to control our lives with outward behaviours, the healing process is an inside-out job and no amount of external control is going to solve the problem. So a battle it was and with this particular fight, I would always end up losing.

Addictions worsen with the passing of time and increase in severity, and in my case this desire to clear out took over. Indeed, it became a felt bodily need. I'd been training my body to release with coffee, cigarettes and suppositories for years and it was visceral. In fact, each and every morning, this ritual was built into the set-up of my day, it simply took priority and under no circumstances would I plan my daily activities to run into my evening plans without an (ever increasing) pitstop home. If I am to be totally honest and transparent, at this time of writing, I can still struggle with this – we are all a 'work in progress' and I would be remiss if I allowed you to think I'd reached a place of total freedom from any addictive thinking or tendency. It's simply not the case.

The name of the game is progress, not perfection – it's not always about the destination. One's journey and level of 'success' can be measured by where you've been and how far you've come. Self-judgement can be detrimental to our sense of wellbeing and can truly hold us back. Comparison is a dangerous game. This obsession gave me an element of (short-term) relief and was just another way I had learnt to hide (behind an addiction) and avoid any internal introspection. I wasn't quite ready to be present with myself and look inside, which is the only way to true freedom.

This process had me on my knees hundreds of times over the years and I was so ashamed of it that it kept me prisoner and isolated – at least, I allowed it to. I can imagine someone with bulimia will strongly identify with this, for the only real difference between us is they vomit and I shit! It had been me who had created this in the first instance and now I felt like it had me by the throat.

This ritual and obsession of 'needing everything out' took precedence and became so integral to my existence that it took centre stage and was the single most important thing in my day – my wellbeing was dependent on it. And with any addictive cycle, the relief is short-lived. No sooner had I cleared out (and by the way, this stopped working as time went on and the process actually caused me to feel worse), when morning rolled around again. I'd eat meals, feel full and bloated and I'd need to start the whole thing over again. As I've mentioned, I don't know when I first felt the need to control something as natural as the expulsion of waste from my body (for the body intelligence has this in the bag!), but control it I did, or at least, I tried.

However, it is what it is and we do the best we can with the thinking we have in any given moment and, as human beings, if we have a need, we will find creative ways of meeting that need. In my case, with such a strong internal sense of self-disgust, I truly could not bear to be in my body and I couldn't cope with my feelings – I wanted everything 'out' and this became my coping mechanism.

This process I found myself inside of makes sense to me now. Quite simply, I needed to feel empty of the crap – literally and emotionally – and where the emotion is concerned, much of it wasn't even mine; I'd taken on everything around me. If you think about it, the coping strategies we come up with as human beings are pretty incredible, as is just how much we can contain and withstand. We'll do anything to ease our suffering in order to feel better and, back then, forcing my body to release provided a sense of relief (if it worked out 'well') and so it seemed like a good idea. In a way, it worked.

Just like someone with bulimia will binge, I also

comfort ate in a bid to stuff down emotion and feel 'better'. When I had no evening plans, I'd consider dinner options for most of my waking day and couldn't wait to be in my pyjamas by myself in front of the TV and eat. If I did venture out on an evening (and found myself uninspired or bored), I'd be thinking about what I'd eat on my return and would regularly be found leaving social events early to be with food. Of course, I would not make this public knowledge, always coming up with a viable excuse as to why I had to escape.

On these nights, I would hole myself up in a room with my dinner, a huge bag of popcorn and red wine, over-eat and feel sick and bloated again – cue cycle! On occasion, I would avoid buying too much food in an attempt to stop the binging, but it wouldn't matter. No sooner had I finished dinner, I would feel the all-too-familiar sweet craving and I would jump in the car in my pyjamas and drive to the local high street to stock up.

I would need to physically put myself to bed in order to stop the consumption of food. I do wonder why I didn't make myself sick, choosing instead to release in this other way, but I guess it just wasn't my thing. I can only assume that with my preoccupation with my skin, I didn't want a red face and blotches from vomiting. A lesser of two evils maybe, but tortuous nonetheless.

It was obvious I was comfort eating to avoid my feelings, but I was also eating to fill a 'void'. I remember this feeling of 'the void' being apparent from an incredibly young age. Even as a small child, I recall being in the bath and thinking, 'I need something – what is it?' The best way I can describe it is as a feeling of emptiness. Even then, I was looking for something to 'fill up with' and 'take the edge off', searching to make the feeling go away and feel better.

As a very young child, I remember being unable to pinpoint what the 'need' was for. Was it food? Was I thirsty? I needed *something*, but nothing I thought of felt right. I was never quite sure what I was longing for; I couldn't identify it. At this time, I may have grabbed a candy bar or a packet of crisps. Innocent enough I guess, but as time moved on, these 'quick fixes' wouldn't quite cut it, the need would gather momentum and would progress to a point where I was reaching for the narcotic instead – a little more serious, I'm sure you'll agree.

Drugs/Alcohol

I had dabbled with marijuana over the years, but it was not my drug of choice. I was prone to paranoid thinking and weed took my paranoia to a level that was truly debilitating and frightening. When I smoked a joint (or took even a couple of puffs) my self-consciousness was off the charts. I was scared to speak, oftentimes stumbling over my words, which felt too loud and clumsy as they hung embarrassingly in the air, inviting possible ridicule and humiliation. I wouldn't make eye contact for fear of being noticed in my intense anxiety. I felt frozen in a group. There were countless times I left social gatherings early after the paranoia escalated and rendered me incapable of being in company for a moment longer.

Alcohol had always been present in my social circles from a very early age. My friends and I would buy cheap, white wine and cider on weekends from as young as 14 or 15 years old, possibly younger. There would be many evenings in at friends' houses when parents were away or out for the evening and therefore plenty of alcohol cabinets to take advantage of.

I had always been extreme in my behaviour and I would drink until I made myself ill (although it didn't take much), spending many a night lying on bathroom floors, as the world spun uncontrollably, rising only to vomit into the toilet bowl – if I was lucky enough to aim straight in my inability to focus. I would feel desperate for the feeling to pass; convinced I was going to die. I was unable to unlock the door of the bathroom when someone knocked to come in, such was my drunken stupor and inability to move.

As the years progressed, so did the drugs. I dabbled with ecstasy, (magic) mushrooms, LSD and speed (amphetamine), with cocaine being the most regular and familiar addition to any night out or even, night in. I didn't need an excuse to take this drug; there really wasn't a social event that was off-limits.

It started out as a bit of 'fun'. There'd be ecstasy at raves, taking me from my reality into a dimension that was euphoric. I felt love for everyone, colours were vivid, music pulsed in my veins – I was flying and truly 'out of my head', experiencing feelings that are hard to describe. Life felt incredible.

There was also the little detail of hallucinations (on one occasion I was convinced I was in the middle of a game of backgammon whilst I was, in actual fact, in an underground rave!) and the inability to remember what I had said only moments earlier. There were countless occasions where I would be deep in conversation with someone, only to repeat after each sentence, "What are we talking about?" I had no memory recall from only seconds ago. Drugs obviously play havoc with the mind and cognitive functioning.

Important to note that I wasn't taking massive amounts of any drug, but I have an incredibly sensitive physiology, so the effects of any mind- or mood-altering substance are extreme for me. I can feel the effects of alcohol after only a sip and I would sometimes be one of the last people standing on a night out, so you can imagine the mess I'd be in.

When I wasn't enjoying the 'high' and becoming one with the music, I would be staggering around clubs, losing all sense of location, continually checking I had all my belongings with me, repeating my words on a loop and generally existing in a dazed and disorientated state.

All drugs could cause me acute self-consciousness, but with speed especially, I could find myself frozen on the dance floor, unable to co-ordinate my movements with the music, my skin vibrating and crawling, convinced that everyone in the club was staring at me, pointing, whispering and laughing – a life experience one could really do without.

Psychedelics and hallucinogens, like mushrooms and LSD (strangely enough, I only tried the latter on one occasion) were reserved for places that were less congested, where there was a degree of 'safety'. Psychedelics take you completely out of your reality and it's inadvisable to be in a heaving club when you're experiencing other dimensions and convinced that your boyfriend has turned into a dragon (true story!)

Unlike the synthetic drugs that brought me to my knees when the high wore off, I loved the experience of magic mushrooms/psilocybin. The feeling of being in an alternate universe and dimension was cosmic. I felt wrapped in cotton wool; everything was alive and moving with its own heartbeat and rhythmic pulse (inanimate objects included) and life was an awesome adventure – exciting, fascinating, expansive and all-encompassing. I was One with everything. And the best news for me, there was no comedown as the effects wore off; I simply came back down to earth whereas, when the synthetic drugs loosened their grip, I had a one-way ticket to hell.

The Heartbreak

In the latter stages of my teens, when I was around 17, I had a heartbreak that would subsequently have me enter into an altogether more extreme and dangerous relationship with narcotics. As I mentioned, drug taking had started out as 'fun', an addition to a night out, but with an unexpected and traumatic turn of events, my experience of drug taking did a one-eighty – I slid rapidly into a downward spiral and it turned dark.

As I have alluded to, I had always been looking outside of myself and finding myself lacking and this continued into my friendships – seeing girlfriends as being better than me, prettier than me, living in 'better' homes with 'cooler' siblings, more popular, etc. I would continually feel as if life was against me and I would find myself longing for the things others had, whether this be self-confidence, their relationships (with the boys I wished would notice me), the friendships they had, the clothes they wore or their level of attractiveness, etc.

These feelings of unworthiness, unattractiveness, self-loathing and self-disgust were sending a strong message to the Universe and, as we attract in from where we're at (for we are vibrational/energetic beings – more on this later), it was no surprise that I was receiving exactly what I expected, namely evidence that I was 'less than' and 'not good enough'.

Due to my low levels of self-esteem, I entered into some pretty co-dependent relationships, a *'pattern of behaviour in which you find yourself dependent on approval from someone else for your self-worth and identity.'* Unless you've been inside of this dynamic, it is almost impossible to describe the depths we go to for external validation from those who cannot meet us and the fear we feel of losing what we think we 'need', whilst we continually skip over our truths, wants and needs – understandably making some rather questionable choices along the way. It's a total abdication of Self, and it deeply hurts.

I blame no external party for my cultivation of these types of relationships as I was fully in consent and have always made my own choices – even if those choices were unconscious or by default, for making no choice at all, is in fact a choice in itself. Unconscious or not, co-dependent relationships are horrifically painful.

I was lost and in an internally desperate and tangled state, blindly fumbling my way through life and because I was always scared that people would leave me, at times I was selective with the truth if I thought my words would be misunderstood or would have detrimental consequences. I came to know first-hand the meaning of 'what a tangled web we weave, when first we practice to deceive'. I will recount a little of my story here, but the finer details are unnecessary, for the story is not what's important. The 'drama' was simply a symptom of a cause and a catalyst for what I see as the inevitable – namely, my breakdown.

I was being eaten up inside by a situation that had occurred between myself and an ex-boyfriend of mine who, unbeknownst to me, had been dating my friend at the time of our liaison. When their relationship came to light, I felt like I'd been punched in the stomach and I realised that my dalliance would have catastrophic consequences if made public and so I chose to keep quiet. I was beside myself and that old adage of 'secrets keep you sick' was proven beyond a doubt.

I was knotted inside and at a loss as to what to do, desperate to right this perceived wrong and to undo what had gone before. And so, when I could hold the secret no more, I confided in a mutual friend of ours in a bid to share my burden and to gain some support or helpful advice. Possibly when it came to the crunch, knowing my truth and version of events, she could calm the waters and, if need be, act as a peacekeeper between my friend and I.

Being envious of my friendship, my trusted confidant skipped gleefully away from our meeting and sent a twisted version of my story hurtling down the phone line to the waiting ears of my friend, potentially even before she had left the driveway of my family home. She had betrayed my trust and intentionally distorted my words, but it didn't matter – her version of events was 'out there' and as she delivered news of my perceived crime, I was found guilty and my fate was sealed.

I remember the night I was confronted by my closest and dearest friend about this perceived betrayal. It was the same day I'd confided in our mutual friend. We had all gathered at a local pub, as we did weekly. My friend made a beeline for me and ushered me into the doorway of the pub. She was furious, raging inside and out and I was confused. As the penny dropped and my worst-case scenario played out, she spat some words in my direction (none of which were pleasant) and promptly left.

I was shell-shocked as my mind scrambled to make sense of what was happening; my brain felt like it would explode. There was no room for me to say anything, her level of disgust and anger was palpable and I knew she would not (could not) listen to or hear anything I wished to contribute.

I was left in a state of disbelief, in complete and utter shock – disbelief as my mind connected the dots and the betrayal sank in and shock at the deep knowing that the relationship with my best friend was over. Those few seconds alone in that pub doorway were some of the most horrifying and crippling moments I have ever experienced. I knew I had to re-enter the pub and I didn't know what was waiting for me on the other side of the door.

Shaking and numb, I eventually moved back into the body of the pub where our friendship group had gathered around my friend. In that moment it was clear to me that they had made their decision – they were sticking with her. I was not surprised. I had always felt in the shadows, so I knew I was not even in the running for favourite.

I moved over to a small group of people who were not directly connected to us, or the drama, and plastered a smile on my face whilst anxiety gnawed ferociously at my insides, my head and body vibrating and my ears buzzing. I pretended I could not feel the stares of those around me and the many pairs of eyes focused in my direction as my 'friend' stood in the middle of the group, relaying the events of moments ago – the moment that the world as I knew it had officially imploded.

I will never forget how I felt that night. My heart was in my mouth and my body shook. Adrenaline coursed through me on the back of acute fear and dread. I felt a level of anxiety I cannot put into words, and my heart broke. I had never, in all of my life, felt so desperately alone and so palpably scared at the thought of what was to come. I was bereft. That evening was pivotal in my life and would have far-reaching consequences. It would be a long time until I was able to trust again. A part of me died that night.

It hadn't been plain sailing up until this point anyway, but now I was also grieving the loss of my best friend and my friendship group. It felt like a divorce with people taking sides, and having been so grossly misrepresented I, unfortunately, was not the popular choice.

I was unable to sleep properly and spent my days

either numb or in feelings of deep grief, anxiety and acute paranoia, desperately pleading my innocence and beseeching those who would lend an ear to come to my aid. I was lost, alone and very scared.

Not only was I dealing with a broken heart, I also had to contend with the physical effects of this. It's hard to describe, but I'll give it a go. The thought of my loss would enter my mind (many times on a daily basis) and I would have to brace myself for the sensation that always followed – my heart would sink in my chest and my stomach would flip over. I'd close my eyes until this sick-inducing sensation would pass and I could breathe again. It would be years before this bodily reaction left me.

My mother didn't know what to do with me. I would downplay the situation, as I couldn't stand to see her upset on the back of my distress. As it was, I'd only shared a tiny portion of what had occurred to avoid having to relay the details and cause any further pain – mine or my mother's.

My life changed overnight. My circle of friends disappeared and I started socialising with another group of people. I had some good friends in this group too, but I hadn't voluntarily made this shift in my circumstances and so this wasn't my first choice. My loss overwhelmed me. I felt crushed that my old life, the places I frequented socially and my friends had gone in an instant, had been ripped away from me – more evidence of 'I'm not good enough/not worthy enough/I'm alone'.

I also recognised I'd done nothing wrong, not

intentionally anyway, and so I also deepened into the belief of 'I'm not good enough to make people stay, I'm bad – I always spoil things'. I learnt first-hand that nothing is forever and people leave, no matter how much you love them. I'd fallen so incredibly low and it would be a long time until I'd rise up again.

Looking back, I recognise that I didn't really acknowledge the trauma – not really. I talked about it, felt victimized as I suffered at what I believed to be the hands of injustice, but I most definitely did not seek help in my distress or understand the impact and repercussions this time of my life would have on me. I was navigating this time alone and I was not equipped to deal with my feelings and emotions. I had no reference point for them – this situation was an anomaly. It wasn't just friendship I lost, but also my trust in people and the limited sense of Self that I'd had. Everything had shifted and I hadn't seen it coming – my world had turned on its axis, flipped on its head in a heartbeat. I was in a continual state of shock.

I didn't realise how much this affected me. If someone I loved that much could leave me with no grounds for abandonment, then what hope was there? Life could not be trusted. People could not be trusted.

As a caveat, I used to wonder why I don't remember certain moments and memories of my friendships or early life. When friends reminisce, I know I was there, I have a (sometimes vague) recollection of events but I cannot connect to the feeling of it or see it clearly. I know the occurrence took place, I have the information, but it's purely cognitive.

I understand now that the memory of my teenage life/ life in my 20s is hazy because the trauma was so intense that I blocked much of it out, including the depth of love I had shared with my friend. The absence of it was simply too painful to feel, the loss was visceral. My mind shut out huge chunks in order for me to cope, distancing me from the feeling state.

It's a built-in protection mechanism. Our brain recognises that something is too painful to process and it gives us the gift of amnesia, whilst we develop coping strategies to ensure nothing like this ever happens again. It's wisdom, the mind/body intelligence.

But the coping mechanisms on the back of trauma do not allow one to live – not really. Everything becomes very small when you live in fear and constantly feel a need to protect and defend yourself. You're safe, but imprisoned. I couldn't connect with people. Not properly. I didn't allow you in, didn't know how to. If I didn't love you then I couldn't be hurt. It's textbook, but I've experienced it first-hand.

From my vantage point, I see how this time of my life shaped me. It underpinned everything. I built a wall around my heart and created 'rules' of engagement. I kept people at a distance and shut myself in. Panic, anxiety, paranoia, control, defence, fear and isolation became constant companions. Co-dependency took on a whole other level as my self-confidence took a nosedive. I had a constant need to escape and micromanaged all parts of myself and all areas of my life. When I think back on it, I'm not sure how I coped. I have, however, learnt that human beings are incredibly resilient – we never get more than we can handle, even when we're on our knees.

With that being said, let's continue.

Instead of gathering with my old friends on Saturday evenings whilst we dolled ourselves up for the swanky clubs of London full of A-listers and the social elite, I found myself with my new group of friends in underground clubs and raves, sometimes travelling up north to visit friends in university digs to be a part of the club culture there. And the one thing there was plenty of, was drugs. I was desperate to escape from the pain I felt inside. But, as is the case with all toxic behaviours, I was simply plastering over a wound which would reopen and continue to weep and bleed.

A night out 'raving' or clubbing would be reason enough for intense excitement. There'd be building anticipation as we thought about the upcoming event – what we'd wear, how we'd be travelling to the venue, which DJs would be playing that night, and the part that caused the most excitement and the adrenaline to rush – the drug order.

These nights would go on for hours, starting around 9.30pm, sometimes running until 6am – an opportunity to lose myself in another world for an eight-hour stretch, although we often wouldn't wait until our arrival at the venue before we partook of the drugs. When you're chomping at the bit to 'get out of your head', it's not the time you'll practise self-discipline and patience!

So, with everything sorted – tickets to the club purchased, drugs on board and the necessary transport arranged – we were ready for the off. I was being given (an albeit temporary) time out from the internal pain, noise and torment of my mind.

With drugs in my system and music that pulsated through my body, I could lose myself in a heaving crowd and temporarily forget how wretched I felt. Many of these nights were great fun, a real adventure and I loved the affinity, solidarity and oneness I felt with my fellow revellers. I was basking in the feeling of love brought on by the drugs and feeling elated with the intensifying rushes in my body as the DJs played their magic, teasing the crowd as they gradually increased the intensity of the music, steadily building up to a crescendo and when you finally thought you could take no more, the music would break and the crowd would go wild, united in feelings of ecstasy and euphoria.

And whilst under the influence of the narcotic, my brain would play tricks on me. As I mentioned, not only could I find myself slumped over a table in the midst of a heaving throng believing I was in the middle of a game of backgammon (clearly seeing the pieces laid out on the board and whispering to my friend, "It's your move,") but whilst I was dancing to the music, euphoric in my response to the vibrations, I believed that all was OK with my old friendship group.

Somewhere in my mind, I believed that we'd speak the following day and be united again. I would feel the connection with my friend and believe that it was still as strong as ever and perhaps, all that had gone before was actually not so horrific, not so devastating after all – I could pick up the pieces, salvage the friendship and patch it up. I believed in that same moment that she was feeling exactly the same way. Had I, in fact, simply imagined the fall-out? Perhaps it hadn't been so tragic after all? I was convinced whilst under the influence that all that existed between us was love – true and authentic connection and friendship. And whilst I danced in euphoria, I felt intense relief and excitement. I could finally breathe easy – it was all going to be OK.

The thing is, the effects of drugs last only for a limited amount of time and with any short-term fix, you're guaranteed only short-term relief. You're free for the exact time the 'high' lasts and with every high, there's a corresponding low – it's the law of nature. And that's exactly what I got, every time.

As the drugs wore off, my world would shrink back to size and my surroundings became distorted. The oneness and unity I felt with my new 'friends' in the club would turn into disgust and acute self-consciousness as I realised I didn't want them anywhere near me; who were these strangers who, just hours ago, felt like kindred spirits? I didn't know them; I didn't *want* to know them. They repulsed me.

With the music turned off and the lights turned high as closing time came to pass, my ears would ring and every noise echoed in the distance. I longed for invisibility and I longed to be home, safely tucked up, showered and clean in my bed. The anxiety would start to build and rise with the desperation to escape the 'safety' of the club, now feeling like purgatory.

Looking anyone in the eye became impossible as the stark reality of my surroundings came into view – the dingy club, the sticky floor, the smeared make-up-stained faces, the awareness dawning that I'm still in my clubbing garb and the morning has arrived and, worst of all, the dread of what is to come looming largely overhead, slowly creeping around me as it finally overwhelms and envelopes me. There is nowhere to go. I am about to visit hell and I am desperate. Desperate to be alone. Desperate to be held. Desperate to be known. Desperate to die. Desperate to be loved.

Comedowns from drugs were always horrific for me. This is not the case for everyone, but I spiralled into despair. Whether it was due to my physiology, my shaky relationship with my Self, my tendency towards paranoia and loneliness, fear of life or whatever other possibility was up for grabs, my experience was bleak.

With the loss of my best friend, the 'usual' loneliness,

isolation and heartbreak was magnified to such a degree I am not sure how I withstood it. The familiar feelings would re-visit me as I stood on the beer-soaked floor of the club and sat in the back seat of the car on the way home.

The brain that had, only a short while ago, led me to believe that my world was a happy place to reside in and I had misjudged the severity of the situation, would cruelly lift the veil of illusion and I'd remember – my world was in tatters. My friends had gone. I had been judged and I'd been found guilty. I was alone. The dream was in fact a waking nightmare and as the feelings of deep grief wound around my heart and constricted in my chest, I wanted to die. There is no way to make this pretty – I did not want to live any longer and I prayed for oblivion, I prayed for death.

The pain would intensify as I thought about the night my 'old' friends would have enjoyed. I imagined them huddled together in the car, stopping for bagels on the way home from town, animated and excitable as they swapped stories with each other, connected in their memories of the night, their shared history and their friendship.

They'd be tucked up in bed by now, sleeping soundly whilst I had just started my descent into hell. The journey home from the club in the early hours of the morning felt endless to me, it was torture. I couldn't look at or speak to anyone in the car – my words would hang in the air, too large and loud for the space. And as my reality and pain took over, it was stark and shocking all over again and I was desperate to be at home.

Thing is, I would receive no respite from the pain there either, but at least I could have a hot shower and be in my bed. Sleep would elude me. I would not be given the oblivion I longed for. The effects of the drugs had not left my system (and wouldn't leave me for hours/days) and my mind would torture me, taunting me again and again as it played the same record on repeat. I could do nothing, but rock endlessly in the foetal position. I was bereft and empty.

When I was finally given respite and the gift of sleep, on awakening I would be given a nanosecond of blissful ignorance before my brain moved into gear and I was hit with the truck of my reality once again. My heart would hammer in my chest as I was thrown into panic and anxiety. My body and mind ached; my mouth held the metal taste of the drugs and a residue lay on my skin.

The paranoia the following day was indescribable. My brain would torment me in every second of every minute of my waking state. I would churn over everything I'd said or done, finding endless reasons to spiral into uncertainty, anxiety and fear. I would call the people I'd been out with the night before, checking all was OK, making sure I'd done nothing 'wrong', looking for reassurance for something I may have said that could have been 'inappropriate' or offensive. I was in a state of constant and heightened anxiety, always anticipating abandonment and rejection – the pounding in my head and the hammering of my heart a constant drumbeat in the background of my life.

Not only did I have to contend with this, but whilst I was attempting to recover and piece myself back together (at least, to the version of myself that I was familiar with away from the influence of drugs), I would think about my old friends being gathered around the table of some cosy brunch or lunch establishment and I would be wrenched right back into pain – cue palpable ache of grief, sinking heart and flipping stomach. Where were my friends? Where was my support? Who knew me? Who cared? Who was even thinking about me? The phone didn't ring. I had nowhere to go and in my shattered state I couldn't leave the house even if I did. This was loneliness dazzling in all its glory.

It wasn't just paranoia that I had to deal with, there was also sleep deprivation, nose bleeds, headaches and a brain that had adopted the role of torturer, relishing and feeding off my anguish. Recall of the night caused my whole body to recoil as I closed my eyes in denial, attempting to block it out. I had no rest from this cycle. I was either thinking about taking drugs, taking the drugs, or coming down off the drugs and, as I have documented, this came with a whole host of emotional and physical repercussions.

When you're in the cycle of addiction, you're gripped by it, your world changes and it becomes dark. Addiction is pretty much like childbirth – you have selective memory syndrome, forgetting the severity of the pain from the experience and no sooner has the nightmare abated and you've moved into some sense of 'normal', than you're thinking about the next opportunity to do it all over again. This is euphoric recall – the brain will remember past experiences in a positive light whilst eradicating the negative and painful experiences.

It's important to note that I wasn't taking huge amounts of drugs and it most definitely wasn't an everyday occurrence, but my physiology is such that it took only a small amount (much less than my counterparts) to send me 'over the edge' and my recovery took much longer than everybody else's. The effects of a night out could last a full two or three days for me. I'd always been a deep thinker and with my tendency toward negative self-talk, it is unsurprising that my mind took me to some pretty dark places. A sip of alcohol could compromise and intoxicate my body and mind, so you can imagine how messed up I could be after a night of using narcotics.

Drugs became not only something I did on a night out, but my 'using' at times became solitary and isolating. With cocaine, I found it impossible to sit still and if I found myself alone and 'high' I would leave the flat and just walk. Anywhere. I needed to keep moving. There were occasions where I would wander into drinking establishments and try to make connections with whoever was there – anything to avoid being alone. I was out of my mind and desperate for connection. These were possibly some of my loneliest moments and lowest ebbs.

I never wanted the night to end, wanted to keep

riding the high. I couldn't bear the thought of being home alone and in my panic and desperation, I've been known to jump out of taxis taking me home, leaving my friends inside, as I made a desperate dash back into the club we had exited only a short while ago. Once again, I was alone and scouring the venue for people to connect with. It was dangerous and pitiful. Nobody in my life knew what was going on or just how lost and alone I felt. I would do anything to delay my demise and inevitable decline into hell.

I recall a time in my life when I had travelled to Israel with a couple of girls. We had been excited about our time away, planning to spend time on kibbutz and immerse ourselves in Israeli culture and the kibbutz experience. The need to escape and run away was still with me and so, true to form, once we had joined the kibbutz, it was only a short amount of time before I upped and left and went to meet another friend in another part of the country.

I joined this friend on her kibbutz with a group she was travelling with and when their time ended in this current location, they left and I stayed. I have no idea how this came about – how the kibbutz allowed me to stay on without the group and how a travelling experience with friends had ended with me travelling alone, but that was the pattern I had found myself inside of and it had showed up once again.

I made friends with some of the kibbutzniks and joined them on a night out at a rave in the mountains. I had only known them for a short while and could not speak their language, but when you're in an addictive cycle, it's amazing how you'll find people and situations that allow you to continue the pattern. And these individuals had the same agenda as me.

We arrived at the secret venue that was, being in the mountains, in the middle of nowhere and we danced the night away, strongly bonded in our euphoria whilst the drugs were working. But, as was always the case, the drugs would wear off. When the music stopped and we received our cue to leave, we continued the night/morning at the home of someone in our party and I found myself in the all-too-familiar comedown hell.

In this instance though, I was in the garden of a house in the middle of a country I was not familiar with, surrounded by people who I did not know and did not speak my language and my pain, desperation and loneliness was exacerbated. Again, I longed to be 'home', but I had no way of travelling back to the kibbutz, no clue where it was or even how to contact a taxi service.

The summer in Israel is unrelenting and even at this time of the morning, it was sweltering and the heat only added to my torture. The familiar pain and feelings were with me again. As I say, I couldn't speak their mother tongue and I am sure I took the brunt of a few jokes – a random, mute English girl in a group of bonded friends, unable to speak and acutely self-conscious.

I remember feigning intense interest in some flowers

in the garden in an attempt to detract attention from myself and when I had exhausted this avenue (of flower whisperer!) I asked if I could lie down in a room inside the house in my desperation to be alone. I needed to at least attempt to fall into unconsciousness in a bid to have this hell subside.

As I knew would be the case, sleep eluded me, but at least I was alone, away from the watchful eyes and the sound of a language I could make no sense of. Eventually I was rescued from this particular hellish experience when my new friend had had enough and was ready to leave, but the memory has lingered. My time on this trip was truly awful – the only words that sum it up are 'profound loneliness' and this only lightly skims the surface.

Although I am painting a very dark picture of my life, it wasn't all doom and gloom. Over the years I was still working, I had friends, a loving family, a social life, some lovely holidays abroad and I had some great times, but behind all of this, running in the background of my life, was a deep suffering and grief.

My closest friends had no idea of the depth of my pain and my parents were oblivious. They knew I experienced a lot of anger, had a tendency towards feeling low and despondent and could be 'difficult' and that I could not stay in jobs, had an inability to finish anything and that I worried relentlessly about friendships. But to the extent of the 'problem', they were completely unaware – maybe they thought this was just 'me'. The pain, the struggle, the feelings of depression, the loss of Self and the desperation I felt to be whole, to experience love and to live in joy, reached a point of 'unmanageability'. My situation had become untenable and I was headed for a breakdown.

Running Towards

Before I give you the details of the night I finally fell to my knees and surrendered, it is incredibly important that you understand something. This very dark time of my life is also known as 'a dark night of the soul'. Within certain psychology circles it is termed as a Crisis of Meaning or Spiritual Emergency – one simply cannot continue in the way they have been living (so far away from their truth and essence) and any avoidance tactics functioning as diversions from internal introspection become redundant, they simply stop working. The world turns black and one can be found on their knees, bereft, at the end of the road.

Something has been vying for our attention for a long, long time and we have ignored its call, so the knocking becomes a little louder, until it cannot be ignored any longer. It knocks until we open the door and face it head on. Only then, the healing can begin. This is the break(ing) down that precedes an individual's 'waking up'.

This waking up allows us to finally become alive to the Truth of who we are underneath the distortion and addictive patterns of thought and behaviour. We can start to see who lives under the mask. We see through the illusion of our stories, beyond the small-self identity/ personality and realise what's possible.

For the personality is something we have created, not something we are. Over the years, I have had a very real sense and experience of this personality construct being separate from me. I have seen that who I believe myself to be is simply a made-up story. More on this later.

As I have mentioned, I have always been aware that there's more, so much more than we can ever imagine. I noticed from an early age that the things I was interested in didn't seem to be the norm. I had always been interested in the 'bigger' life questions. Who am I? Where am I? How did we get here? What's beyond the known – what lies beyond this 3-D reality? I poured over books on different subjects (still do!) – aliens, UFOs and life on other planets fascinated me, as did life after death, quantum physics, the potential of who we are as human beings, other dimensions, the angelic realm, etc. In fact, all of which seemed to be labelled 'out there', 'woo woo', 'spiritual' and a bit weird, was where I felt most alive.

The times when this part of me showed up in the world seemed to be the exception rather than the rule. No one around me lived or thought this way and those who did share my interests seemed to be out of reach, they were certainly not part of my community. My views, opinions and beliefs have always been seen as a little 'out there' (even ridiculed) and I wore this label of being 'weird'/eccentric for as long as I can remember.

Up until this point, the majority of conversations around me had consisted of small talk, gossip and banality – personal drama was rife. When I was out socially, most of what was happening just didn't interest me and I had to feign interest. I was bored, unfulfilled and regularly felt that all-too-familiar compulsion to run away.

In my daily life, I showed up as Emma functioning under her labels, seemingly fixed ideas of herself and adhering to protocol. Not only was I fitting in with an external reality that felt uncomfortable and alien to me, but I was also denying my Truth, my internal reality.

All of this 'fitting in' was draining my energy and depleting me. It's exhausting to continually wear a mask – inauthenticity is hard work. I felt like an outsider and a fraud. I 'played' this way for years until it became totally insufferable for me. I simply could not withstand it. The distortion of myself was intolerable and I simply found it too tiring to be in company; it was easier for me to be on my own.

The things that made me feel most alive were reserved for the times I spent alone. The 'real me' was hidden behind a mask and a closed door. I wasn't nourishing myself in the 'best' way and therefore it's no wonder I was feeding myself in other ways.

Within my drug taking, I had some truly beautiful and spiritually connecting experiences. At the 'peak' it felt euphoric – I was flying. I felt fully alive, the trees/

nature were breathtaking; my potential felt limitless and possibilities endless. I felt a freedom that I did not feel in my 'normal' existence. The 'high' not only took me out of my reality but took me into an alternate reality that felt more real to me, a place that allowed me to touch and live in a space of pure potential and the joy I was longing for.

So, when I reflect back on my journey through addiction, it is incredibly important to understand that I was not just running away from something, as much as I was running towards something else. Yes, I felt a strong desire to escape from my 'reality', but it was much more than that. This running 'away' was also a bid for deeper meaning, to make contact with the part of me that lay under the surface – the 'Real Me' – my true essence. I wanted to *feel something*. I wanted to feel more *alive* and to go to the place where I sensed Truth lived. I didn't know it then, but I was actually searching for my Self, for Love – longing for freedom.

There were a few people who were open to the types of (deeper) conversations I was interested in, but they were few and far between. I do see that I was given an outlet for this part of me over the years with some of the connections I forged. I seemed to attract some of the people who could 'meet' me, but it was fear that kept me from allowing this part of me to shine through and be fully visible in the world – fear of judgement, fear of loss and fear of being abandoned.

We all want to be accepted and be part of a tribe, it's

an intrinsic human need and desire and because I felt so different from those around me and in a minority, I guess I felt that I would be at a loss (people would leave) if I showed up in my authenticity, venturing into the unknown, living outside of the box and going against the grain. It was totally outside of my experience and understanding – would I be OK if I coloured outside of the 'lines'?

I thought I'd lose the things I cared about and in a way it's true, things will fall away when we change. People in our lives may depart when we show up differently and we no longer have a meeting ground or the same things in common. It's entirely possible those people will stay and the dynamic itself will evolve, who knows? But when we change our tune, the dance itself needs to adapt to the music and some people in your life will keep on with the tango whilst you gyrate to a totally different beat!

But here's the thing, nature abhors a vacuum and when people/things move out of your life, space becomes available for new people and things to flow in, which are resonant with the 'new' you. Life cannot pour into a full cup, we need space in our container to receive.

Around this time and in a bid to help me, my mother made an appointment with my local GP. I hadn't been open and honest with her so there was no way of her knowing the real underlying cause to my 'depression'. In my desperation and bid to move out of this debilitating cycle, I agreed to see this doctor. I remember being quite open with him with regard to my drug use. I remember his blank stare and shocked demeanour as he scrambled to find the right words as I bared my soul. I remember how loud and telling his silence was and, at the risk of being judged, I pulled back on the truth, making light of it. Although he was altruistic and well-meaning in his bid to help, he was ill-equipped to assist and I felt little comfort from our time together.

I also agreed to counselling at this time and, again, as well meaning as the therapist was, she was also unqualified in this area and therefore unable to help. And because I was scheduling appointments whilst still using drugs at the weekends, I rarely showed up. I'd wanted to, really I did, but such was the addictive cycle that I had no way of abstaining from drug use the night previous to the session and, due to my debilitating state and the exhaustion I experienced the following morning, I was simply unable to pull myself out from under the duvet to make my way there. I paid for many sessions that went unattended.

In fact, there were many appointments – birthdays and social occasions (not to mention workdays) – that I didn't show up for. I would feel so angry with myself on these occasions as I made yet another excuse as to why I would be absent. I wanted desperately to be in company, but it wasn't an option – I was too sleep deprived, shaky, paranoid and anxious. And once again, I felt I was missing out on what it was that I desperately longed for – love and connection.

It was beyond frustrating. I wanted to stop, but

felt powerless to do so and so I kept on repeating the same scenario time and time again, thus reinforcing the addictive cycle and deepening my sense of self-loathing. To the outsider, what was so difficult? If you don't like what you're doing, just stop doing it. Not so easy when one is in the grip of this process. With all the will in the world and with the best of intentions, you will fall short.

Throughout all of my dark times, I had always read, choosing books (although I know they chose me) that spoke of the truth I was longing for, a truth that was, thus far, beyond my lived experience. There was a deeper part of me that was always nudging me on my path, towards the right teachers, friends, events, jobs, meetings, etc. I see that now.

I remember one of the first books that impacted me the most and started me off on this journey of self-discovery was *The Celestine Prophecy*, which speaks of the 'bigger picture' of life. It was a fascinating read for me and made so much sense, joining more of the dots and affirming to me, yet again, that there was more to life than what I'd thus far seen, lived and been led to believe. Although I have a foggy memory with regard to much of what has gone before, I can always remember where I was when I was reading my books – they were glimmers of light that punctuated the dark. Books were/are always with me. They have been my lifeline.

And so, although much of the time I felt like I was dying inside, my books provided me with a connection to the divine/my essence/the Truth of who I truly am, who we all are. Even though it became dark for me, I knew there was beauty. I had hope. I had a sense of my potential. I knew there was a grander version of myself just waiting to be given full permission (by me) to be visible in the world. I was being called to release and let go of the old story of who I was (the small self), the story that I was reinforcing on a daily basis, both in behaviour and in thought. I was being invited to relinquish the outdated false narrative and paradigm and allow this part of me to die whilst I birthed the 'real' far greater and grander version of Me and embrace a new story. I was being called to live the Truth of who I truly am.

It was in one of my darker moments, that a book came into my life called *Hope for the Flowers* by Trina Paulus. It's a simple little book, beautifully written, with large writing and lots of pictures and is fundamentally about becoming your true Self. Once again, I remember exactly where I was when I was reading it – lying in bed in a flat I was renting just before sleep... tears rolling down my face as I felt the truth of the words. I knew this book had been given to me at a time when I most needed it, with a message of what is possible and a promise that it would come to pass... for me, someday, sometime. *Hope for the Flowers* touched me deeply and held me at a time when I was experiencing acute pain, giving me exactly that... hope.

The Breakdown

So here I was, depleted inside, feeling lost and alone. I was living in a flat in Hendon, London, at the time and, although I was alive and breathing, I was actually barely functioning and in a lot of pain. I was going through the motions of daily life but the lights had gone out. I found joy in nothing. The only two things that held any appeal were sleep and drugs. I was still speaking to friends, seeing my family, holding down a job (just) and socialising, but I was on autopilot and nothing made any sense any more (had it ever?). I could feel no joy or excitement and the veil of darkness was immovable. If someone had offered me a ticket to Barbados or to the destination of my choice, all expenses paid, not even that would have sparked any desire within me.

In my state of destitution, I could see no point in anything. Nothing held any meaning. Previous to me experiencing this, I would not have known this reality and sense of existence was possible, it was beyond my understanding. This was an unimaginably dark night of the soul that one cannot explain. I felt like 'I', as I had known myself to be, had died, although I was still living and breathing as a 'non-person'. The rug had been pulled out from underneath me and I could see no way out, no light at the end of the tunnel.

There was a night out with friends in March 2006. We were gathering in a pub in London before moving onto a club. Things had gotten so bad for me at this point that I was desperately trying to stop the addictive cycle. I could not take one more night of suicidal thinking and rocking myself to sleep in the foetal position. I had, therefore, made a pact with myself that I would not partake in any drug taking.

To ensure this, I decided to remove all temptation and became discerning about the company I kept. On this particular night, the friends I was seeing were 'straight', outside of the drug taking circle. They drank socially but narcotics were (apart from the rare occasion) not part of their picture. I was attempting to control my external environment and circumstances in a bid to eradicate the pattern. I really believed (hoped beyond hope) that if I kept all temptation away from me, I would no longer be sucked down the rabbit hole. As I have stressed, this method is never going to prove fruitful. By the time one is involved in the 'symptom', it's already too late. Freedom lies inside, we must target the root cause, for there lies the cure – external methods of eradication are futile.

So, with no temptation around me, I felt I was 'safe'. I arrived at the pub, ordered a drink and no sooner had the alcohol taken effect (one or two sips as I have alluded to) than I was on the phone to the drug dealer. That's the thing with addiction, you can give abstinence your best shot with the greatest of intentions whilst sober, but the second you introduce a mind-altering substance (alcohol being one of them), you've had it. Rationale goes out the window and you have a one-track mind with the only thought being, fuck it.

With the definition of insanity being 'doing the same thing over and over again and expecting different results', this night was only going to go one way. The drugs arrived, I did my thing (secretly – I had become expert at masking my behaviour) and we moved onto the club. My friends, who were now all pretty drunk, were oblivious to my regular visits to the toilets and my drug-fuelled state of mind. I loved the anonymity, the feeling of being wrapped in cotton wool in my own secret world.

Closing time rolled around all too quickly for me and the old familiar panic started to build – I could not go home now, I could not be alone. My friends queued for their jackets and ordered taxis whilst my mind scrambled to find a solution to the problem, namely, the impending journey home, back to hell. As 'luck' would have it, a friend of mine was also in the party mood and wanted to continue the night at a rave in London. Relief washed over me. We jumped into her car (she was, unbelievably, stone-cold sober – baffling to me) and off we went.

This night was pivotal. I have thought about the

occurrences of those next few hours of my life many times over the years and truly, I now know it was all happening perfectly to bring me to the exact point I needed to get to in order to change my life – namely, on my knees, 'broken' and surrendered.

I had a little cocaine left and made my way to the toilets. I was a mess, staggering, eyes unable to focus properly, rolling in their sockets in a state of confusion. I remember wearing a new necklace with green gems. I must have caught it on my way into the ladies in my desperation to be behind the closed cubicle door and the stones went scattering every which way across the floor. And there I was, crawling around on a dirty floor trying to retrieve every one of them in a disoriented state. In a way, it represented where I now found myself in life, namely on my knees in the dirt, scrambling to find the broken parts of myself in a bid to piece them back together again and restore them back into something precious and beautiful.

I finally entered the cubicle, put the lid of the toilet seat down and tipped the remainder of the drugs onto the loo seat. The bad news for me was this – in a bid to control drug use, this particular club had smeared a Vaseline-type substance over every surface and the powder simply dissolved into the slime.

I was in disbelief for a moment, my mind not quite registering what had happened, unwilling to accept it. I was panic-stricken and now in a desperate state. My 'high' was wearing off and I had nothing to take the edge off.

Time was ticking. It was now early morning and I knew my friend would want to leave soon and I would be in my familiar hell. I couldn't bear it. I simply could not withstand it. The word desperate does not come close to the intensity of my experience – the fear of the inevitable was palpable. I wouldn't allow it – at least not yet. I would do anything I could to stave off the interminable suffering.

I teetered and stumbled around the club attempting to identify the resident dealer. At this point, drug preference wasn't an option as time was of the essence – I was in the market for anything. I was asking for ecstasy, which in itself was strange, as I hadn't taken it for years. I guess I thought it would be easier to find than cocaine and I needed *something* to take me back into oblivion.

As the minutes continued to tick by, I could find nothing. I stood on a raised platform to the side of the dance floor and surveyed the area. There, in the middle of the heaving throng, I homed in on a guy taking some kind of substance from his open hand and I remember in that moment trying to catch his attention, desperate for him to make eye contact, willing him to look at me, even for just a moment. Just enough time for me to clearly communicate with him via my thoughts: 'I don't care what you've got, I want some.'

Just then, my friend came and said she wanted to leave. My mind scrambled to try and find a viable reason to stay, but I came up with nothing. I was beaten, inside and out. It was daylight outside and the birds were singing, a noise that I came to detest in my drug-using days, for it signalled the end of the night and the beginning of hell. I had sobered up, could taste cigarettes in my mouth, felt the grimy residue of the drugs on my skin and I wanted to die.

I felt horrendous. So utterly alone, profoundly empty and full of fear. I could see no light at the end of this tunnel. And perhaps the worst of it all was the thought that kept niggling at me, kept pulling at me from the back of my mind – I knew, in no uncertain terms, that had that guy on the dance floor made eye contact with me, I would have left my friend and stayed with him. He had what I wanted and I would've done anything to have it, potentially even risked my life. Over everything else, drugs had won.

The knowledge that I potentially would have (in my drug-addled state) gone to the home of a stranger to chase a high was stark and shocking to me. I was in a state of total disbelief. This, above everything else, scared me the most. I no longer knew myself. I couldn't trust myself. How had I ended up here?

My friend dropped me home and I was bereft. I thought I'd felt the worst of the pain in my life, but I was mistaken, it had more to give. I searched for anything to numb myself – smoking cigarettes and drinking vodka straight from the bottle. It was the early hours of the morning at this point, springtime and bright light shone outside the window. It is truly difficult to explain in words the level of emptiness, exhaustion, anxiety, bewilderment, loneliness and grief I was feeling. I put myself to bed and hugged my legs tightly into my chest. Once again, I rocked. And just like every time before, I was not going to be given the luxury of unconsciousness. Sleep would elude me and deny me that pleasure, leaving me awake to withstand more of the torture of my mind.

I had hit rock bottom. The game was up. After 11 or so years of this, I could continue no longer. I couldn't live this way anymore. When it felt like a reasonable hour to make contact with the outside world, I called a friend who had been with me the night before and with my heart hammering in my chest, I uttered the words that had needed to be spoken for a very long time. "I need help, I'm in a state; I have a drug problem." This is the first time I had said this out loud and, as no one around me knew the extent of my drug use or my internal struggles, it made sense that my friend tried to convince me otherwise as she assured me that I'd just had a bad night. But I was adamant, "No, that's not it, it's more than that. I need help."

To this day I am grateful for her support. Within half an hour she was with me. She took me to my sister who called my mum and made the difficult phone call telling her I needed help. I am not sure if we mentioned the drugs at this point, blaming my 'problems' on depression. And if drug use *did* enter the conversation (for I have a vague recollection of an intimation towards it), it was never mentioned again. I find this level of denial fascinating, but with compassion in my heart, I can understand it.

I went to stay with my parents, made a couple of phone calls to people who I knew were in recovery from drugs and therefore members of the 12-Step Fellowship Programme of NA (Narcotics Anonymous) and within 24 hours, I had been admitted into rehab for a month's stay. That day, back in March 2006, marked the first day of my recovery and my journey back home, to my Self.

PART II

Relationship to Self

Recovery

My sojourn into rehab was authorised by a 'top' psychiatrist who had assessed me and concluded that I was indeed a fully-fledged addict with the 'disease of addiction'. To him, this was a done deal and not up for discussion. Even with a diagnosis from a supposedly knowledgeable and highly regarded individual and specialist in the field, I was adamant that this wasn't the case. If anything, I felt I was in actual fact, experiencing depression and this was the reason I had used drugs. He seemed to believe it was the drugs that were causing the depression and I had misconstrued and misunderstood the process.

The psychiatrist promptly enrolled me on to the addiction programme whilst strongly suggesting I take a course of antidepressants. It is incredibly important to note that even at this stage, I knew that I didn't need the pills. I knew on a very deep level that there was nothing intrinsically 'wrong' with me and I sure as hell wasn't about to ingest more drugs that would alter my brain chemistry, dull my senses and mess with my emotions and physiology.

I knew that my behaviours were my coping mechanisms, the way I had dealt with the 'problem' of being me and the profound emptiness and spiritual void I felt inside. It wasn't me (my Self) that was broken, for this is impossible. I knew something was wrong, but I knew with certainty that I was not broken or defective in any way. I was 'simply' existing within a warped idea of myself, swallowing down my words, fitting into a shape that was not me and living a life that was nowhere near my potential – at least, it was certainly not resembling anything close to that which I knew to be possible.

It seems the prescriptions issued by both 'life' and the doctor were a long way off from that which was to promote my optimal health. Pills were not an option. I desired to feel fully alive, not to exist in an altered state of consciousness and I was willing to do whatever it took to find the freedom I so deeply longed for. I didn't yet know where this commitment to my freedom would lead me.

In hindsight, there were 'issues' with this rehab (and indeed, with many of these institutions and the 'recovery process' as a whole) and, in the years that have followed, I have viewed my time in that particular establishment through a very different lens from that which I peered through as an inpatient. At the same time, credit is due, for I acknowledge this period was a very necessary part of my process and journey. For all the perceived 'faults' of an institution such as this one, I am incredibly grateful for my time there, for if it weren't for this chapter, I wouldn't be here.

For the 28 days I attended the addiction programme, I was immersed in therapy sessions, group sharing and Narcotics Anonymous meetings and I became familiar with, and was integrated into, the 12-Step Programme of NA. I was, of course, also abstinent from drugs and alcohol and therefore the fog that had accumulated was given the space it needed to clear a little.

Within group work I found so much identification with others who had walked a path of addiction and, for the first time, I found myself in company with those whose pain felt as deep as mine, as they too struggled to keep their heads above water and to cope with life.

This was a healing balm for me, as after many years of struggling and journeying alone, I finally felt understood by the therapists and my peers. My behaviours and the chaos in my life started to make sense. This was a huge relief for me as I no longer felt like the 'odd one out'. I shared the secret that was keeping me sick, isolated and alone – I was no longer 'separate'. I had been given a 'Get Out of Jail Free' card. This was the beginning of a new level of relationship with and understanding of myself, as I came to view myself through eyes of compassion rather than peering through the lens of blame and self-loathing.

With this compassion and self-forgiveness, space was made for clearer vision and healing. So much of my energy had been consumed in fear-based thinking, keeping up pretences and futile efforts to control my external world.

Now I could pour my energy into a different direction. Manipulation, defending myself, micro-managing my behaviours and hiding my 'truth' from the eyes of others had been the daily norm for me and I'd had enough.

This very early abstinence and recovery period was also one of the most frightening and uncomfortable times in my life. The future that lay before me became stark in appearance as the truth dawned on me that with this new life came abstinence from all mind-altering substances and there would no longer be anything to 'take the edge off'. This wasn't just a respite from my daily life; this was an integration period for a new way of living. It became clear that everything in my life needed to change – my routines, my friends, my social interactions and my work. It was all up for re-negotiation as I considered living a life free from substances, stone-cold sober, with no coping mechanisms, no denial and no avoidance strategies. I was to face my self head on, naked and vulnerable. I had a renewed sense of responsibility which meant the outward finger of blame was redundant – there was no longer anyone to point the finger at as it turned swiftly onto me.

I had to face life on life's terms as I embarked on the real journey of self-healing and a new reality, a reality where I was present and aware, making and owning my own choices. I was able to take a long, hard and honest look at my behaviour and the addictive processes that I had been inside of. I came to view my life through new eyes, with clearer vision and see all that had thus far been invisible to me, hidden under a cloak of denial as I had blindly followed my urges and habitual patterns. I understood much more about my behaviours and it was at this time that I started to take responsibility and surrendered a little in a bid to change my life. In all honesty, I think it was the first time I had actually looked at myself moving through this addictive pattern, named it as such, recognised it was not the whole of me and saw the bigger picture in all its glory.

The drug taking, co-dependency, alcohol, OCD and food issues had been so much a part of me, had made up so much of who I believed myself to be, my identity, that I had truly never viewed them as separate from me. There hadn't been the space to even consider there was something occurring 'outside of myself', with me being so immersed in the process. I certainly didn't see clearly that with every ingestion of narcotic, sip of alcohol, participation in OCD and co-dependent behaviours, I had been making a choice. The 'gap' between the thinking and the action (drug taking, ritual, etc) had not been noticeable to me – I had acted robotically, in blind compliance.

I'd been under the influence not only of mind-altering chemicals, but also of incredibly familiar and compelling thought patterns that were followed by a strong urge and my immediate action on the back of it. I was totally subservient to the processes. When a drug-taking thought entered my mind, there was very little consideration, no serious contemplation or weighing up of consequences and no idea that I had a choice. On some level, I had accepted that this was part of my life and part of who I was as an individual. The cycle had made sense to me – I felt crap inside, so I changed it.

Up until this point, I hadn't had a clue how to be 'different', no idea how I was to live differently. I was so weighed down by a cloak of pain that I had held close to me for many years, unwilling to let it go. This pain was my excuse to 'use' and 'act out' – with that finger of blame pointed forever outwards. I had never understood this cloak to be something separate from me; indeed, it had been like a second skin. Eventually I came to see that I could simply take it off. At some point, with this new perspective, I made a decision to let go.

There I was in rehab, abstinent from drugs and alcohol, coming to understand my co-dependent behaviours and all that had led me into the destructive cycle of addiction. I spent my time sharing my feelings in peer groups, learning honesty where previously there had been lies, becoming visible where once I had hidden and moved away from victimhood to find the courage to step into my power and take a stand for myself and my life. I was moving away from the shame that had hovered over, within and around me, invisible and toxic. I attended psychodrama sessions, which were incredibly powerful, allowing emotions that had been swallowed down, repressed and locked away to finally surface and have the space they needed to be expressed, moved through and set free. This truly was the start of my healing.

Unbeknownst to me, in this healing process of shedding the old identity, a new problem was being created – a problem that was potentially as damaging as the addictive process itself, which I would end up living inside of for a substantial amount of time after my exit from rehab. In relinquishing the past 'me', I was about to take on an alternative identity that was not without its own problems and challenges, an identity that would act as another invisible prison. The 'me' that I had been was being replaced with another version of myself and another label that I would carry with me for the next ten years of my 'recovery'.

To be involved in an addiction programme, one needs to be an addict. At this time (and potentially also by the time you read this) it was believed that an addict was not someone who had simply been inside of a cycle of addictive patterns of behaviour that had operated as a coping strategy due to past pain and trauma. But in fact, addicts were seen to be fundamentally flawed and defective human beings. I was told that addiction was in fact a disease, something one was born with and I was one of the unfortunates.

I was informed that I was one of the poor souls who had come into this life with a shortcoming and the best I could hope for was a life of abstinence (from substances, co-dependency, food, etc) whilst attending regular 12-Step meetings and maintaining a sponsor (one who acts as a mentor, guiding another through the 12-Step Programme of Narcotics/Alcoholics Anonymous). I would have to be on my guard from this day forward, on high alert from the addict within me that could rear up at any moment and lead me down a watery path, sending me descending down the spiral of addiction once again.

I came to believe that, unless I kept a thorough check on myself at all times, keeping the addict within me at bay and living a life very close to 'the fellowship' (of Alcoholics/Narcotics Anonymous, etc), this monster addict inside of me would rage and rise up, leaving carnage in its wake, ultimately leading me to jail, institutions or death. Not the most uplifting of future outcomes, I'm sure you'll agree.

So, as I was learning to find inner peace and create a life free from addiction, I was unconsciously hemming myself in once again. I came to view myself as a defective human being, operating under the label of 'addict' and coming to understand that I was unable to live and enjoy life as others do. I learnt to refer to 'normal' people as 'civilians' (very common in the meeting rooms of NA), as if I were an altogether different breed of human, unable to be understood by the 'normal' human race. The only real hope of true understanding and identification could be found solely with other addicts. I came to believe that my life would be 'small' – as I strived to keep myself safe, my energy once again invested in control, although in an entirely new direction.

More than anything, I came to believe that my life

would become really rather boring! What on earth would I be participating in day-to-day? How on earth would I socialise without the option of even an alcoholic drink? How would I date? How would I have sex (or even – banish the thought – dance) without a drink or drug inside of me? For as long as I could remember, the Emma that had moved through the world had been a chaotic, distorted version of what was possible, her truth hidden behind a smile, a closed door or anger, living for the highs, suffering the lows and, therefore, to imagine myself showing up simply as Me, naked and bare without a crutch, was totally beyond my comprehension. It was a frightening consideration.

Through the rehabilitation process, I was left convinced that *I* was the problem. I was sold on the idea of addiction as a disease – how could I not be? All the evidence seemed to tally up, stark in its nature. My inability to simply enjoy a night out without leaving a stream of carnage in my wake, the large amounts of money spent on supporting the addictive process (drugs, alcohol, taxis, etc) and coming to see my eating habits (both under and over) as compulsive, obsessive and 'abnormal' and conceding through seemingly conclusive evidence that the relationships in my life were co-dependent, functioning simply as plasters over a gaping wound. With this résumé behind me, it seemed clear to me that I was at the mercy of compulsive and obsessive urges beyond my control and, therefore, addiction as a disease (with me simply being an unconscious pawn in its game) made perfect sense. With this amount of 'proof', how was I to argue to the contrary?

This lens of addiction had been hammered into me so proficiently that this label became a strong identity and I held on tightly, living under a veil of fear that had me believe that if I took my eye off the ball for long enough, I'd be a goner. I was told I was unable to put anything into my system that changed the way I feel, that as an addict I suffered an allergic reaction to substances – 'one is too many and 1,000 never enough' when pointing to an addict's inability to control their drinking (just one of the many AA and NA slogans). The game was up for me. I'd never again be able to enjoy a glass of wine with dinner or a cocktail on the beach, convinced that this would be my demise and, ultimately, my descent into hell.

I left rehab grateful for my newfound abstinence and clarity. I was thankful for the care and concern of the practitioners but, at the same time, I felt scared. Once again, just like it had been previously, everything was to be controlled, micromanaged and observed through a microscope, albeit in a 'healthier' (or so I thought) way. I was to attend 90 meetings in 90 days, (at least three per week thereafter for the rest of my days on Earth), take on a sponsor (and eventually, sponsees) and work through the 12-Step Programme of NA.

Now, I am an intelligent woman who does not fall prey easily to others' worldviews, but at this time I was scared and vulnerable and this diagnosis of addiction was (and possibly still is) compelling and appears to be totally legitimate given the 'evidence'. There is a description and profile of what an addict looks like, a list of behaviours and traits that, of course, when I was in the grip of addiction, closely resembled me – an inability to stop 'using', compulsive behaviour, non-conformity, denial, low self-esteem, lack of intimacy, etc. When presented with this list (and many other character traits or defects) I could not dispute the similarity and, therefore, I was in agreement as I concluded that yes, this *was* me.

It stands to reason that a person moving through addictive tendencies will indeed fit the profile and description of what an addict looks like. Of course they do. But this is a list of behaviours, external to a human being; this has nothing to do with the human being it-Self. It's comforting to have a problem (addiction) and be given a solution (addict) – it fits neatly into a little box. It's just not going to be so Self-serving to move through life with a fundamental belief that you are defective and somewhat broken.

So, yes, addiction exists as a behavioural pattern adopted by a human being where there is an inability to cope with pain or trauma, when oblivion looks more appealing than being conscious and awake. Yes, addiction cycles exist *outside* of a human being, but this is not *who* a person is, it is simply a way a person is *behaving*. There is a fundamental flaw in the teachings – nobody is born with the disease of addiction, this simply does not exist.

To brand an individual as an 'addict' from the get-go is a misunderstanding of gross proportions and is an incredibly debilitating and dangerous diagnosis, potentially causing more problems than the addiction itself. Abstinence was and is important and I needed to be free from drugs and alcohol to become fully conscious of what was taking place in my life, but the labelling was deeply unhelpful and problematic.

Operating within the constraints of this label, I existed with a perpetual undercurrent of fear running in the background of my life, although, for the most part, it ran under the radar of my conscious everyday thinking. Its effect was powerful nonetheless, leaving me scared to let go and take my eye off the ball for fear that the addict within, always ready to move into action, caught me unawares and pounced.

I defended the diagnosis to others ('civilians', we were told, cannot hope to understand the addict personality) and therefore, once again, I was left feeling like an 'outsider', only to be truly understood and accepted within the fellowship of NA. I held on for dear life. So, the level of freedom I had gained was tainted, albeit less obviously debilitating and dangerous as it surreptitiously lurked out of sight. This is not freedom – this is a sober prison.

'Recovery' outside of rehab was not plain sailing. I still had the issue of me to deal with. My brain was so busy and moving so fast, filled with so much negative self-talk and distorted thinking that I simply could not hear my own wisdom. Having been so long ignored, my internal navigation system was way off radar, meaning good decision making was a virtual impossibility. I had no idea in which direction the compass was pointing and I most certainly could not determine the route. It was an incredibly confusing time for me.

So, at this stage of my 'recovery', the strict rules and adherence of the 12-Step Programme, providing a guide for living and a moral code of conduct, was a good support system. It kept me on the straight and narrow and, most importantly, abstinent, as I made my way through alien territory in a strange and scary world.

All the control issues were still there – the need to clear-out, my relationship with food, the relationships in my life in all areas, my social positioning, my mindset – all my limiting beliefs and familiar unhelpful thinking, etc. It had been a lifetime of conditioning and control and now I needed to learn how to live differently and re-member, literally put myself back together again. Who was I before I'd forgotten? Before I'd hidden behind a mask? Only now, I had nowhere to hide and nowhere to escape to. The veil of denial had been removed. I had to face myself head on, naked and vulnerable. I'd need to find a new way to 'cope'.

Into-Me-You-See

Before I move on to my experience of life in sobriety, there is something of importance that needs to be highlighted.

Throughout my time in the addiction programme, something became apparent to me that was a huge (if not potentially the sole) contributing factor to my 'using'. Apart from all the previously discussed suspects that lay at the root of the addiction cycle, there was one fundamental issue that had contributed to the feelings of isolation and loneliness, an issue that may well have precipitated the intense desire for escapism in the first instance, underpinning the cycle and spiral of addiction – my wholehearted need and desire for Love and acceptance.

Intimacy is discussed at length in many therapeutic and healing circles as a fundamental need for all human beings. We all have a need to be seen, loved and accepted, but *truly* seen, at our level of essence, at our core – the 'us' that exists before we deem ourselves unacceptable and construct a personality that moves with us through our day-to-day lives. We need to know that who we intrinsically are, is *enough*.

Intimacy is not solely the act of sexual intercourse, but is in fact the meeting of two human beings on a soul level. Intimacy is 'into-me-you-see' – seeing inside of another. This is a connection between two people that precedes and penetrates the personality construct. It is a connection at the level of heart and soul; a connection that is borne from our transparency, where we welcome and allow another human being inside of our hearts, to truly meet us and come to know us at the level of our *being*. This type of connection gives us permission to be fully our Selves. Regardless of what we do or how we behave, we know we are enough and we know we are loved.

Intimacy is modelled to us; it is a learned way of being. We will have no language for this type of connection if we have not been taught this from childhood. If heartfelt connection has not been our way of life, we will have no benchmark. If we have not come to believe that who we are is perfect and we are loved, regardless of any perceived flaws, capabilities (or lack thereof), appearance or skill set, we will severely struggle in this area. Our need to be loved and accepted is critical.

As babies, we are constantly looking to make sense of our surroundings, coming to learn who we are from the outside in. We find ourselves in the eyes of another, through eyes of love. Primarily our messengers will be our parents and caregivers and then, as we grow, our peers, teachers, societal structures and many other outside influences and 'authorities'. If we receive messages that carry a charge of judgement or displeasure (verbal or otherwise), we will make meaning of these messages and find ourselves lacking. If messages of affirmation are absent, or our feelings are being ignored, unnoticed or judged, we will find other ways to meet our need for acceptance – bending our shape in order to please others, denying our feelings or behaving in ways that are unnatural and alien to us which elicit a positive response – i.e. 'there's a good girl/boy'.

As I said earlier, we will be-come what we need to be in order to be accepted within the family, peer group, tribe, etc. We need positive mirroring. Not only is there a need for authentic, heartfelt connection, to be loved and accepted for who we are, but so too is there a need to be a 'part of'. We are tribal beings. We long to be part of community in whatever form that takes.

So strong, compelling and in-built in us is this need, that we will Self-abdicate in order to meet this yearning. As adults, we are more than able to make choices that best serve us, discern between that which is beneficial for us and that which is detrimental to our wellbeing; we are able to survive outside of a system, community or peer group, but as children this is simply not possible. At this tender age, we have not yet created the capacity to make decisions from a solid foundation and a known sense of Self – we are not yet Self-aware. Connection and acceptance are our lifeblood.

As I have documented, there was so much love around

me, but positive mirroring – not so much. I came to an early conclusion that I was flawed. I came to believe that I needed to be something other than my Self in order to be accepted and loved. I am not an isolated case. It breaks my heart to consider how many millions of children suffer and struggle in this way.

Self-esteem is borne from positive mirroring. If we do not have this, we do not have the necessary tools needed to create a life of joy. For without a healthy level of Self-esteem and a hearty dose of Self-love, we are open and more susceptible to 'problems'. We cannot conclude that we are good enough and lovable if we have not been taught this. If we have received messages that we are flawed, we cannot deduce that we are otherwise. At a young and impressionable age, we do not have the ability to discern that the messages we have received may have been 'wrong', that perhaps we had been misinformed, that in fact what we think to be true could be revised and re-negotiated. We take feedback as truth.

For the most part, this issue with 'upbringing' is borne from innocence, with no malicious or ill intent; we do the best we can from our level of consciousness and this applies to society also. For society as a whole is also our teacher. There are many fixed ideas of what is best for our young, what is right and what is wrong and society is constantly striving to fit us all into neatly packaged and clearly defined boxes. We are all striving to 'fit in' – within systems, society, protocol, etc, but this 'right' way is a misunderstanding of vast proportions and has very obvious and detrimental consequences.

As adults, we do our 'best', work hard to care for the young (oftentimes abdicating and skipping over our own needs and aspirations to be in [perceived] service to another), only to scratch our heads in bewilderment as we watch the one we love plummet into an addictive cycle and find ourselves feeling powerless as our loved one is labelled with (a) mental illness, a depression diagnosis or the like.

In being unable to 'meet' a child emotionally and in disregarding what is best for them (instead, adhering to that which is prescribed as 'right'), we create a void within that being that will ultimately lead to dis-ease, illness and a need to fill up... with something. Cue addiction.

I remember a time when I realised an adult in my life had been wrong. There was a moment when I had been told something (although I do not have memory of the exact communication) and I knew fundamentally that the opinion or information I had been given from this trusted adult was incorrect and it confused me. This was an adult, someone I looked up to, a source of wisdom and information, font of all knowledge and what they had uttered was absolute rubbish and they'd delivered the information with conviction! I was astounded.

I was a young child and I found this moment shocking. It rocked my world as I swiftly came to realise that adults did not know everything. It was kind of scary, to be honest.

What now? Who's right? What is the Truth? Where/who do I turn to for the full picture? It was probably something 'small' that caused this insight, maybe an opinion that I knew to be incorrect or which felt unjust, but still, as a child, it was an eye-opener for me and very disorientating.

At this juncture, I would not have linked this insight to the messages I'd received with regard to my identity; namely, if adults can get things wrong, perhaps the information I had received with regard to who I am as a person has not always been the truth. The two areas seemed to be mutually exclusive. For the time being, this insight applied to information 'out there'. I would eventually recognise that my perceived flaws and defects were exactly that, someone's personal perception of me and not who I was.

At some point in my life, when the positive mirroring was absent, I decided that it was a wise choice to hide (my Self), to close down and go inward instead of showing up fully to be met with (a level of) disapproval – it was just too painful. I wasn't behaving appropriately; I was too naughty, aggressive, angry, passionate, not 'clever' enough, too sensitive, etc. I spent an inordinate amount of my life feeling grossly misunderstood. I was angry because I was hurting and I misbehaved on the back of this hurt. I see now that my passion was to be celebrated, not pacified. On some level, I came to the conclusion that it was easier to close my heart than to risk having it hurt each time I showed up as my Self to be told I was 'wrong'/not good enough.

It stands to reason that people who have themselves existed within a prescribed society, been judged and deemed to be lacking, will have no benchmark of how to hold another in unconditional love. They too would have closed their own hearts in order to protect themselves and will, therefore, be unable to meet another where it is (was) most important – they will not (for the most part) have the eyes to see us or the ears to hear us.

We are all repeating patterns of the past, of our lineage, and we will continue to do so until someone along the way changes and re-defines the status quo, thus bringing about a new paradigm and reality and birthing healthier individuals and therefore, society.

So, that being said, whilst in rehab, the warped and distorted view I had of myself, together with a deep longing for love and acceptance, which had been masked under years of addictive tendencies and behaviours, was made visible to me.

I attended a psychodrama session (where peers would be the 'actors' in a situation in my life story with me taking the part of me!) in which I fell to pieces. The details of the specific scenario are not what is important; what *is* important is that I was given the space I'd needed to speak the words that I had longed to give voice to but, feeling unable to, had swallowed down and, in this moment, I fell apart. This was the first time I had allowed my pain to be visible to myself and to others.

Up until this point I had turned a blind eye, as I was somewhat unaware of the depth of these emotions and was, on some level, afraid of lifting the lid on them. It was the first time I had truly acknowledged the pain and loss of not having had deep and intimate relationships in my life and the pain of not being truly seen and unconditionally loved... as my Self.

The second time I came to see this 'void' (also whilst in rehab) was on receiving a phone call from a friend of mine. I hadn't been allowed contact with the outside world for two weeks and on this specific day I returned to my room to find a message flashing on the telephone. My friend conveyed that she missed me, loved me and hoped I was OK.

I remember how uncomfortable I'd felt on hearing her voice and her words on the answering machine and the intense desire I'd had to swiftly eradicate and delete the message. I was surprised and taken aback with my reaction. I wanted to understand why I'd recoiled from these loving words. My response made no logical sense to me. What was this discomfort? Why did I find it so hard to receive a message of love? I sat with it for a while and considered that perhaps I thought I somehow didn't deserve it, that I wouldn't be able to maintain it. It was only a matter of time until I'd screw it up (the friendship), feeling as I did, unlovable and, therefore, unworthy of love. I didn't trust it to stay.

After a while, it occurred to me that I didn't know how

to let love in – it created a sense of panic in my body. Yes, I'd bandied around the words 'I love you' a million times over the course of my life, but they were just platitudes. And yes, I had friendships, but I don't know how much of Me was actually present and how much of it had been role-playing. For the most part I felt like I existed behind a glass wall.

Whilst I was in rehab, naked, alone and vulnerable, space had been made for the voice and words of my friend to penetrate my armour and I simply didn't know what to do with it. It was the first time I had been aware of my reaction and noticed my responses – that which had previously been unconscious to me was becoming visible. I became interested and curious and, more than anything, I recognised that the absence of love and heart connection was causing me acute pain.

Relationships

So, with this in mind, I started to question and consider my past relationships, which now made more sense to me. How was I to create relationships with friends/boyfriends/ family members that were healthy and based on true intimacy if I'd never had this modelled to me and I'd been viewing myself through a lens of self-disgust? I had no reference point and no idea how to practise vulnerability and transparency, especially when I thought that I was so awful. I'd had no experience of what it meant to be fully visible and build from a strong and mutually loving and giving foundation; I couldn't fathom what this felt like or even that it was possible.

I simply did not have the ability to forge strong emotional connections, at least, not ones that were healthy and borne of mutual love and appreciation. Up until this point, dangerous and damaging had been the order of the day. There was no way I could have shown up as a mature adult, offering another a safe space to be themselves (I wouldn't have had the notion to choose it), when all I was interested in was selfish gain – what I wanted, what you could give me, what looked 'best' for me, what (at the wrong level) served me.

It wasn't only emotional intelligence that I grappled with; external displays of affection were just as tricky for me. I had not learnt how to allow or invite another into my space and hold them in an embrace – even for a very short period. I felt awkward and embarrassed. Something as simple as a hug could cause significant amounts of anxiety within me, I felt rigid and I clammed up.

I used to think about the greeting of a person way before I met them. One kiss or two? On the cheek or in the air? Would we bump heads or noses? Was I going to be left hanging with my cheek in the air? Or perhaps the situation called for the dreaded hug? How long should I hold it for? Would I be holding the hug for too long, looking desperate and needy or would I pull away too quickly, leaving the 'hug-ee' feeling awkward and embarrassed? It was overwhelming. I knew it was socially expected so I'd have to find a way to wing it.

I couldn't *feel* or enjoy a hug – I *did* a hug. I was thinking through something that should have come naturally to me. How can a person think through a hug?! It's a natural response to greeting someone you have affection for… or not, as the case may be.

I was so up in my head, so cut off from bodily instinct, that any in-the-moment appropriate responses and automatic loving gestures had to bypass my thinking and rational mind. I was so severed from my body-mind that the only thing I relied on for guidance was my brain. I truly had no idea there was an alternative source of guidance and intelligence – an instinctual, heart-based response to life. I was always thinking instead of feeling my way through life.

With my history of using OCD or drugs to numb out the pain and escape my reality, I was always going to attract a romantic partner at the same level of (low) Self-awareness, someone who was also living a lie and disconnected from them Selves. We attract in from where we're at and, therefore, a 'healthy' individual just wasn't going to cross my path in my state of dis-ease and, even if he did, I wouldn't have had the eyes to recognise him and would potentially have found this type of connection boring.

Therefore, my relationships with boyfriends were simply disastrous. We were kids acting out our pain. We were cell mates, not soul mates. Whether silently or aloud, both of us were kicking, screaming and battling with our suppressed emotions and repressed needs and sometimes this showed up as rage and aggression in our desperation to be met and to experience true and authentic love, with an inability to do so.

Rather than fulfilling the role of a partner, an equal, someone with whom I could share life's journey with, any potential mate more closely resembled a hostage! It is said that we stunt our emotional growth at the age we start 'using' and I was 17 when I entered the spiral – so say no more. And for these reasons, with an inability to speak and display the language of love, a warped relationship with intimacy, a defended heart, a deep mistrust of people and a felt need to protect myself, I remained single for many years, outside of romantic relationships.

So, fair to say, there was much distortion in this area of my life and with my experience of relationships being heavily associated with drugs and alcohol (hedonistic, not tranquil; unhealthy rather than healthy), for the first few years of recovery, any thought of dating or sex without alcohol or drugs felt nonsensical to me. What was the point? What was 'fun' about being sober and totally present? Where was the pleasure in that? Weren't romantic relationships built on excitement, passion and lust? A relationship without drugs was beyond my known experience and it felt empty, boring and somewhat depressing. Oh, the irony, for it was the complete reverse – this type of deep presence and connection was the thing I longed for the most – it was the reason I was taking drugs in the first place!

I'd lived my life bouncing back and forth between extremes – high drama, intense rage, feelings of grief and loneliness, drug highs and drug lows – anything to *feel* alive, anything to feel excitement and an element of danger. I was chaotic and restless, on the path of destruction, seeking oblivion from my reality and unconsciously I was always on the lookout for partners in crime – those who were committed to the same level of escapism and self-destruction. I craved and loathed this way of being in equal measure. I couldn't wrap my head around *just being*, in silent connection, that simply being (me) was enough, that in actual fact, that was where true pleasure and bliss were to be found.

Yes, I'd watched movies and fantasised about meeting The One. I'd had many perfect relationships play out successfully in my head, but I was anything but ready to cultivate the type of relationship that I knew in my heart to be possible and that I was deserving of. I just wasn't showing up in the 'right' way. I wasn't there... yet.

The discomfort I'd felt in receiving the message of love from my friend was such a huge insight to me and I thought about it regularly. It nagged at me. It was such a 'small' thing that had such a big impact. And when I looked back on the friendships lost along the way, I could see that I had never truly felt worthy of them. I didn't believe that anyone would really want to be friends with me if they saw inside and truly knew who I was. I certainly didn't believe they'd want to stay. I was always skating on thin ice, waiting to be left, not trusting myself to 'act' and behave appropriately. I'd always seemed to mess things up – at least that was my perception – and I worried that something I said or did would cause their departure. No connection felt 'safe' or strong enough.

I had an inability to deal with anything that felt painful. Any disagreement or disappointment (on the back of my not having behaved 'perfectly') or any experience of being left out, feeling unimportant, ignored or irrelevant, would cause me to feel immobilised inside and my head would pound with rising panic as I feared the worst or I'd fall into a depressive state. Or sometimes, if the stars were aligned, I'd get to experience both! I believed it would only be a matter of time until 'they' left… me.

Instead of talking things through and expressing my feelings in order to work things out and potentially strengthen the connection, I would simply sever it, cut ties and bolt. I'd rather 'get rid' of you before you 'got rid' of me. I didn't value myself, so how could you value me? I couldn't deal with having behaved in any way other than 'perfect' and I saw abandonment as inevitable, as at my core I felt rotten. I had the record of 'Emma, here you go again, you always spoil things', running through my mind. Who would want to be friends with the real me?

I felt alone in a crowd. I was physically present but emotionally and spiritually at a loss – I just didn't feel part of the group. I couldn't understand people who felt safe and secure in their friendships and part of a close-knit group of girlfriends, as I had always felt so alone, never trusting anyone. It wasn't the people around me that were lacking, they were all doing their best – I just wasn't showing up authentically. Holding myself back; too scared to be visible, showing up as a watered-down version of myself, carrying a sack load of fear and holding negative beliefs about myself.

It's not possible to feel anything but alone when you're

showing up wrapped in a cloak of armour, on guard and ready for attack. I had built a wall around me that kept people out, when all I really wanted was to let people in. And, of course, this protection mechanism makes sense if, at a fundamental level, I felt people were 'out to get me', but it equates to a fairly small life and existence. Having to monitor my every move, continually assessing my friendships and waiting for people to abandon me, was draining the life from me.

For this reason, although desperate for true connection, I would, for the most part, choose to be alone. It was too exhausting acting 'as if' and micromanaging myself whilst in company. Exhausting and debilitating, especially when not only was I scrutinising my every word and behaviour, but I was also anticipating rejection at the same time.

Learning how to be fully comfortable in my own skin, risking walking in this world with an open heart and being fully seen as my Self was a whole new process. I'd have to learn a new language. I had the theory in order, but living it would take some practice. It's scary to voice our truth when at a cellular level we feel fear, with our brain screaming at us, "Stop! Don't do it! Run for cover!"

I would hold back honesty with those in my life in case I wouldn't have responded in the 'right' or expected way. Maybe I'd make you angry if I spoke my truth rather than giving you what I thought you'd prefer to hear – a gentle stroke of the ego, perhaps. Would I incur your wrath or displeasure if I chose not to entertain a topic of conversation that disinterests me? Would I offend?

On many occasions, too numerous to mention, I told those little white lies to avoid social engagements and events that did not resonate with me for fear of judgement and pressure. "Oh, Emma, you're so weird, what's wrong with you? Just come, you may even have a good time. It's a numbers game, you never know who'll be there," and on… and on. An individual can only exist outside of their truth for so long – it's stressful and incredibly hard work.

In the early years of recovery, I found myself 'hiding' in another way. My life had changed dramatically and although I had some of the same friends, I was not the same person. The real me was moving to the forefront and becoming more visible as time moved on. I would hold back on sharing my passion for meditation, yoga, spiritual pastimes, etc for fear of judgement. I kept my worldview under wraps and the things I cared about in my heart were reserved for 'special' occasions, that is, where the forum was apt for disclosure. At this time, my preferred audience was limited.

It became increasingly evident to me that I was different to those around me and I hadn't yet found my place in life, hadn't yet found my Tribe. I was still scared that the 'real me' would prompt negative responses, humour, blank stares or a total lack of understanding and support. Again, another message that my shape is 'odd', 'weird' or a little 'peculiar'.

I wanted to feel joy; I wanted to be happy, fulfilled, spontaneous and light-hearted. I felt angry at life, resentful of my pain. Angry that I hadn't been allowed to be Me, untethered, fully expressed and accepted for who I am. Angry there had been so many rules, so much protocol. I grappled daily with a lack of self-confidence and an inability to sense my direction and navigate my way in life. I had absorbed and taken on so many insecurities, fears and warped ideas without my consent or even my knowledge. I was silently screaming. I felt the suppression of my true voice, my true Self. I sensed how this had been unconsciously passed down through generations and across society and now, it had reached me. It seemed it was my time to carry the baton… and the burden.

So, I moved through life holding my breath, holding on, scared to let go, to release my grip – scared to be visible, scared to trust. If I jumped, would the net appear? I was so tired of trying to prove myself. If I live authentically, would life have my back? If I show up fully, will you still love me? If I rattle your cage, will you stay? Do I actually want you to stay? Is our connection strong enough? What lies beyond the death of this friendship/connection? What will come in if I truly let go? If I let you inside, will you like what you find? Is the picture you have of me and the part that I've played the only thing that's keeping us here? Is there room for growth and evolution between us? Is there room for things to be 'different'? These were questions I pondered in the re-negotiation of my life whilst I longed to be fully visible in all my glory, free and unburdened. And loved. Loved, for simply and authentically being Me.

The struggle had been long and hard, but the real journey had only just begun. In some aspects, it was only going to get 'worse' and would be anything but plain sailing from this point onwards. The birthing process is never easy.

Oops!

A year and a half into recovery I had an experience that again shook my foundation. I'd been adhering to the 'programme' and following the suggestions laid down in the 12-Steps pretty much to a tee, when I was offered a position working as a personal assistant. The job was appealing to me, ticking many of my preferred boxes – location, industry, job spec, salary, etc. It looked like a fantastic opportunity and was alluring and exciting. Thing is, what I wanted and what was actually in my best interests were two entirely different things. The individual I would be working for was manic and chaotic but, as we know, this equated to excitement for me and once again, I ignored my gut instinct, turned a blind eye to the warning signs and jumped straight in. I was once again making choices from the wrong level.

I was sucked into chaos as I attempted to learn the ropes whilst grappling with a relentless schedule and continuously moving goalposts. I spent my time anticipating irrational demands and frequent mood swings and, once again, I was on high alert and my system was flooded with adrenaline. I was also on call 24/7 so there was no break from the insanity and it seeped into my personal life. All this, and the rapidly fluctuating highs and lows, took me right back into drama and my mind was a whirlwind. How easy it was to slip right back into the madness.

I was still fairly 'new' in recovery and being around an individual who was this unpredictable was too much for me. I wasn't yet strong enough and was ill-equipped to cope – still a baby in 'recovery' terms. Due to the working hours and the demands, I allowed my commitment to recovery to slide and, therefore, when on a date with a prospective suitor during this time, I slipped.

I turned up for the date running on adrenaline and therefore 'out of my mind', whilst my senses had once again taken their leave. When my date asked if I'd like a drink, I listened to the thinking that was addicted to drama and self-sabotage, the voice that convinced me that one drink would be OK, that I could handle it, that I'd be fine and, after hesitating for a nanosecond, I ordered a Bellini. I waited for hell to break loose and when it didn't, I promptly ordered another.

The date was a complete non-event, but the choice that I had made to partake in an alcoholic drink was an event in itself. I remember waking the next morning with the fear of G-d inside of me. I was terrified. How could I have spent a year and a half in sobriety, staying 'clean', getting 'well' and creating a 'better' life, to have it all taken from me in an instant? No planning, no sense of its coming – just like that, like a bolt out of the blue, the rug was pulled from under me.

I was in a state of shock. I hadn't spiralled into a cocaine-fuelled frenzy as I had been warned I would, but at the back of my mind I still did not elevate myself as a winner in this situation, defeating the odds and taking acclaim for slaying the dragon. For, really, I knew that all that lay between myself and disaster were two little pieces of information: 1) I was driving that evening and couldn't leave my car, and 2) I had no way of obtaining drugs.

Because, if I am honest, my immediate thought following the intake of the champagne had been the acquisition of narcotics. I always desired escape, wanted more – more drugs and forever higher highs, whatever it took to escape from Me. From the second that first sip of alcohol slipped into my bloodstream, my brain had performed calculations of record speed and I had deduced that securing narcotics was a non-starter. I'd deleted all the dealers' numbers and there was no one I could call, not now, not when everyone in my life knew I was abstinent. I recognised that I had averted disaster with only a millimetre to spare. It was crystal clear to me and it was shocking. I saw how fragile and thin the line was. The difference between sanity and insanity were two sides of the same coin.

I remember looking at my reflection the next morning and not recognising the face that stared back at me. Who was this person in the mirror? I thought I knew her, thought I trusted her; I thought she knew what she was doing. I didn't expect her to turn on me and bolt in another direction. How could I trust myself now? I couldn't trust my decisions. I had thought I was committed, unwavering and secure on the path, but it seems I was a live wire – a liability.

I remember sitting on my bed and clearly hearing the words, "Emma, you've lifted the lid," and I knew this to be a warning. My foundation was shaky once again. I was going to have to re-commit to The Programme, claim a white key ring (key rings are given to mark increments of clean time – white denotes surrender for those back from a relapse or at their first meeting) and start from the very beginning. It was somewhat soul-destroying, but it is what it is. I had succumbed and I'd need to start again. Another learning curve and at this juncture, more confirmation that the 'addict' is always lurking, ready to take me down in a moment's weakness. More evidence of the disease of addiction, or so I thought.

Despite this perceived setback, I picked myself up, dusted myself off and jumped right back into the old routine. I admitted 'defeat' to my Fellows (those in the 12-Step Fellowship), held my head up high and started again, from scratch. That year and a half in recovery was in the past, null and void and I was once again, just one day clean – just for today.

On the Up

Life started to 'open' up for me in recovery. I started to consider things that hadn't been in my awareness even a few weeks prior. I quit life as a PA and started to think about what it was that I truly wanted to be and do in the world.

Having not attended university and with a thirst for knowledge, it felt like the right time to immerse myself in something I loved, dive deep into something that my heart was calling for. This was a new arena for me. Instead of following the herd, I would live outside of the lines; I would listen to my internal calling and actually start making choices, rather than being blown about by the wind. I would allow myself to move towards a different destination from that which I had been heading towards. I would do whatever it took to follow the 'alternative' path and support this 'alternative' me. With a deep-seated interest in humanity and the psyche, psychology was an obvious and natural calling for me. It felt 'right'.

With this clearer head that I now carried on my shoulders, I started trawling the Internet for courses that felt right for me. There were thousands of options, so much information and I felt overwhelmed. Up until this point, I had been someone without the patience to fill out a simple form or even make sense of a utility bill or statement; all types of admin had previously been thrown in a box or relegated to the bin, I simply couldn't concentrate. Having to research on this level, read through an inordinate amount of information and consider options put me right back into fight or flight mode and I wanted to run.

Still, despite myself, I took a deep breath, made some phone calls, did a little reading, researched the qualifications I'd need to sign up to a particular course (with no A levels, many courses were off the table), looked into start dates, length of courses and did my due diligence.

What became glaringly obvious, was that most of these courses felt very scientific to me, far too mind-identified, logical and ordered, which was exactly what I was looking to avoid – been there, done that, got the stint in rehab! They simply didn't feel 'right' to me. I'd read the course content and feel nothing. I was looking for something 'softer' and 'deeper'.

So, I decided to refine my search and added the word 'spiritual' before psychology and, within moments, there it was. I came across a website that I knew immediately held the next stage of my development. The moment I clicked on the link and the website came into view I was overcome with emotion, intense excitement and my body tingled from head to toe. It came with an inner 'knowing' and certainty that is difficult to explain. I had found my next step.

I immediately went about the business of enquiring how I could become a part of the next training. It was a part of my journey that had my name written all over it! There were many incredible things about this opening into the next stage of my evolution/journey, not least being – whereas most of the colleges that offered psychology training were based in Central London, this particular institute was based right around the corner from me!

I had driven and walked past this building thousands of times before and on many of those occasions I'd been feeling lost, wandering and wondering, praying for direction and guidance, praying to be shown my next steps. And it was there all along, right in front of my face, right under my nose. This building had remained invisible to me. I'd not had the eyes to see. Until now. Until the time was right. I was astounded. I'd needed to be ready in order for life to show me this next part of my journey – the timing had to be right. As the saying goes, 'When the student is ready, the teacher appears'.

It had been necessary for me to be free from drugs and in a calmer, more grounded and open space. I was now able to come to this training in my 'right' mind, present and correct(ish!) This training required that I show up fully committed and willing to learn. I applied for the course, sent off my application and waited with bated breath to see if I had been accepted. And I was. I was delighted and excited. And so it began. I took on a part-time position as a receptionist in a hair salon and studied, right around the corner!

There is much to say about my time at this institute, but for now, it was a training I was crying out for – a Soul call. It was a spiritual-oriented discipline that spoke of the journey of the Soul, the Higher Self and a human being's search for meaning. The saying, 'Pain pushes until vision pulls' is certainly apt in this instance. I had needed to admit defeat and be on my knees before I would finally be willing to open my eyes and become aware of a vision that had always been lurking in the background, a purpose that felt compelling, important and 'alive' and follow the next, right steps. I felt as if I had arrived. If I had crafted an outline of the perfect training for me, sensed into what I would like to journey through and be a part of, it would have looked pretty much like this course offering.

I was overjoyed and, from the moment I started, I knew it was the perfect fit. I had found another body of people on a similar path, all looking to make sense of what had, up until now, been incredibly confusing. The course attendees had also been asking the questions I had contemplated my whole life – Who am I? Why am I here? What is my purpose? What is life all about? They too, had been carrying a heavy load. It was time to release the burden.

The three years I studied with the institute were enlightening, exciting and challenging, all at the same time. Like the 12-Step Programme, these teachings helped me to make sense of life and come to understand my journey thus far. This was my holy grail, the knowledge I'd been crying out for. I finally understood the struggle and came to see there was an alternative way of existing and living that would bring the pieces of the puzzle back together for me. I had always known there was more and this provided me with some of the answers.

There was much excavation that needed to take place in order for me to find the diamond, the shiny Self that lived within me. And time and time again, I was brought to my edges whilst being called to move through and past them, into a new and more expansive understanding and way of being in the world. This was the kind of growth I knew was possible and with a strong desire to serve humanity and a mission that was calling to me (which was still somewhat outside of my eye line) this discipline provided me with tools to serve myself and others in order to ease the struggle. This therapeutic approach allowed an individual to move away from distortion into a place of clarity and possibility, thus allowing them to move towards be-coming who they truly are.

As an add-on, it's important to again make reference to my entry onto this course. There is an inner knowing, a wisdom that's always there, guiding us and directing the course of our lives, although we're usually too busy in our minds to hear the quiet whisper. And when we do hear, when we are able to listen and discern and we stumble across (by divine providence) the next right thing for us, we just know. Like a tuning fork, it resonates and we know we have found our *Yes*.

Seeing the website for this psychology training had felt 'right'. It was a knowing that went way beyond the conscious mind. My body responded with what I now call my 'truth signal' – I felt a rush from head to toe and my skin was covered in goose bumps. I felt excited and joyful. We need to listen and get quiet enough to hear. The things that are good for us are usually in plain sight, but we need the eyes to see them.

Although my studies were opening up a huge stage for me, an arena that had been invisible to me prior to my learning, there was still much disparity and conflict between the me that attended college and the me that navigated the 'real' world. And they really were two different worlds. At college I could and would be my Self (as much as I was able to) and outside of this space and format, I would slip right back into the version of myself that had always been my 'norm'. It was painful and difficult. I hadn't yet got to the stage where I was confident enough to be open and transparent with what I was learning and who I was becoming and speak my truth. People 'outside' just didn't seem to understand and they weren't particularly interested. I still hadn't surrounded myself with many like-minded individuals and, therefore, there was still a great divide and I really felt the 'gap'.

I'd absorb the teachings, hang out with my college

friends (although still not feeling the connection I longed for) and go home to my flat and feel… well, flat! I'd long to be in the company of friends, but knew the conversation/ environment would not nourish me and I couldn't bear to entertain it. I knew if I ventured out, I'd present a version of myself that was not the real me and the longing I craved for would elude me. The whole exercise would defeat the purpose – longing for connection, being in company = feeling lonely. And so the cycle continued.

I'd stay home, feel disconnected and alone and yet it was comforting in its familiarity, uncomfortably comfortable. It was the 'known' and at least I would not have to bend my shape. I could be me. Alone, but me. And for now, I'd take that. It was the better option as far as I was concerned although my heart ached at times and I still felt 'left out'.

There was also a lot of self-judgement as I regularly questioned my choice to be at home on Saturday nights. Was something wrong with me? Why didn't I want to frequent the latest trendy hang-out with some of my friends? Why did I feel almost allergic to the over-stimulation of these establishments? Why didn't I want to be seated at a dinner table past 9pm like 'everybody' else – virtually my bedtime?! Why did I find it so difficult to be involved in small talk when it was the 'norm' for others? Why didn't I find what they found interesting, interesting?! Why was I always searching and others were content with the status quo? Was it them or was it I who was 'weird'?

Was there something I wasn't seeing?

These and many other questions spun around my mind and I had to keep trusting that I was moving in the right direction, even though the path was hazy and I still felt so disconnected and alone. And lonely it was. Please understand that, really, there was no one in my world that I had allowed to truly see and know me – how could I? *I* didn't truly see and know my Self. I was still hiding.

And this is why it's so important to find your tribe, because there are millions of people who were having different conversations and doing different things – many people who were more like me. I had honed in on and was comparing myself to those who did not speak my language, who operated differently from me and so, no wonder I felt like the odd one out and found myself lacking. And I have learnt that if you're looking for your tribe, the people who 'get' you, they need to know where you are, so you'd better start showing up. You'd better raise your head above the parapet, give them a wave, flash them a smile and beckon them forward.

There is no judgement here, no one way is right or wrong, it's just that we are all different breeds of human – same world, different worlds. When you change, your relationships and connections will change – not everyone is made to stay forever. People come into our lives for a reason, a season or a lifetime. We all have different preferences and passions that ignite our soul. One shape does not fit all.

Life continued to move on. I studied, worked part-time, attended NA, CA and AA meetings and generally tried to find my place in life. The aim has always been to find inner peace and to live a joyful existence, to uncover my natural state – that which existed before my shape was distorted. In my teenage years/20s, I attempted to obtain the peace and joy of the early years through drugs and alcohol and now, in sobriety, I pursued this allusive peace and joy through my studies, my books, a code of living through the 12-Step Programme, therapy and meetings.

There were many great moments in my life. I travelled to far-flung places in the world, I read many incredible books, I felt a huge amount of identification with others, I forged friendships (and lost some), found 'home' in my studies and continued walking a path that felt true to me. Still, in the background, there was a somewhat negative stream of thought running through my mind. The movie I was watching was not my first choice of viewing, but I felt powerless to change the channel.

Control was still very much evident in my life. I was scared to let go, go with the flow, jump and let the net appear and allow life to hold me. I didn't know how to trust. My life was 'scheduled' and 'small'. I was adhering to an internal dialogue and timetable with very little room (if any) for spontaneity. It was all very ordered, predictable, comfortably uncomfortable and somewhat boring.

I was still looking outside of myself for validation, for the most part living in the feeling of anxiety and in a perpetual state of fight or flight. I was still bending my shape and attempting to fit the proverbial round peg in a square hole. I rarely spoke my truth for fear of judgement or being misunderstood and, therefore, I still felt like an island.

I still had connections that did not serve me, engaged in social pastimes that drained my energy, said yes when I meant no and continually worried about the things that I'd said or done that could be misconstrued. I felt like I was on a knife edge; standing on a crevice, moments away from being pushed over or ousted. I was always anticipating attack. Life was somewhat tortuous – my internal world was in complete disarray.

Daily I would run through my head a list of all the people I had spoken to, reassuring myself I was not alone – counting friends, finding solace in a numbers game. I ran through the events of each day and the conversations I had, ensuring I'd done nothing 'wrong'. If a phone call rang off or went to answerphone, or if a text message remained unanswered, I could read this as confirmation that I was on the chopping-board. Sometimes I avoided messaging for fear of encountering silence, which equalled anxiety. My position in life was always precarious; I was never on solid ground. I could trust no one, not really. Family, friends or colleagues, it was all the same… I was fair game for the slaughterhouse.

I felt that my position in life was under threat. The trauma response I felt on the back of perceived rejection is difficult to describe. My head would pound, I couldn't form any rational thought, my heartbeat would speed up, my breathing became shallow, I couldn't sit still and my legs would shake. I would be unable to rest until the object of my obsession would return my call or respond to me and my fear would be abated. The anxiety would be temporarily alleviated and I would be safe in the knowledge that, at least in this moment and for today, I was still in favour – I hadn't been 'found out', accused or negatively perceived, I hadn't been abandoned. I could breathe again.

Thing is, it's never OK, because when you're running thinking like this through your mind on a continual basis, you train your mind for catastrophic thinking and the targets… well, they're forever moving. No sooner had relief washed over me, than the next fear-based thought had reared its ugly head, goading me to entertain it and I moved into the next round of fight or flight.

And when the grooves in the record have been etched this deep and played this many times, it becomes the default position. The needle will always shoot back to the same dial. This is why it was easier to be by myself. At least if I was outside of a relationship, nothing could go 'wrong'. If I wasn't speaking to anyone, I couldn't say anything potentially catastrophic. I was safe.

I was still inside of many co-dependent dynamics – always people pleasing. I would allow myself to be treated in ways that were less than I deserved, having none or very shaky boundaries. I truly believed that I 'needed' you, that your approval validated my sense of self and my sense of self-worth. There was no way you'd hang around if I became 'difficult' – that is, simply telling you what I needed, speaking my truth and expressing my feelings. Who was I without you? How would I live if you didn't need me anymore? Then what? How would I breathe?

Make no mistake, I was no shrinking violet – people around me would have said I was strong, argumentative, sometimes stubborn, indignant and quick to anger, always believing I was right and straight to the point. Realising that my inside world was so fragile, that I was so scared would have been shocking to those close to me. The external displays of strength were compensating for this internal weakness. My outward behaviour was masking a world of pain.

Away from college, I was always reading, diving into books that cemented my feeling and inner knowing that there was more to life than that which we perceive with the senses. I was subscribed to many mailing lists offering 'alternative' teachings, which allowed me to deepen into a sense of my Self. I was continually signing up for meditations, talks, events, etc.

And so it was, that after obtaining a postgraduate diploma in psychology, I enrolled on a course that had me drop deeper into an experience of my Self and helped me to understand more about the difficult feelings, emotions, invisible belief systems and limited thinking that I'd been inside of.

This course had such an impact on me that I decided to train in this discipline. So, once again, I paid the money, jumped on a plane and went to LA to commence the training that I would offer in client sessions – another string to my bow. It did not disappoint. I loved the depth of this work and the clarity this brought to me and to those who had been at the mercy of their distorted thinking and worldviews, unable to move past limitations and stuck points in their lives. After being so unhappy for so many years, finding work that I loved was the greatest gift, a true blessing and I was deeply grateful.

On obtaining my certification, I registered as a life coach and soon afterwards, clients contacted me. Moving into this identity made complete sense to me – to do anything else felt irrelevant and nonsensical. I was made to do this; I was made to be this. I built up a practice and continued working both with my prior psychology training in mind, together with this new coaching discipline. Then 'out of the blue', my journey took another twist and turn.

Another Step Up the Ladder

My sister was married around this time and, after the wedding, a guest who was a close family friend contacted my father to thank him for being invited to the celebrations and to wish him congratulations. For some reason, he had cc'd me in on the e-mail. The interesting thing was this – I had no need to respond to this message and nothing contained within it was of particular interest or relevance to me, but I found myself experiencing a rush of gratitude for the heartfelt message and felt a strong pull to respond.

I thanked the sender for the message, potentially wished him well and left it at that. He then wrote back to me, asking if I fancied coming to a talk given by a rabbi in a charity local to us. Now, as we know, I am interested in everything 'alternative' and Judaism with its beautiful code of living was of great interest to me, so I found myself saying yes. If I would have given it more thought, I potentially would have bailed. This friend is not someone I had ever socialised with and I wasn't sure we would necessarily hit it off on a one-to-one basis, but it felt 'right'.

So it was, that on a Monday night back in 2011, I had a

quick meal with our family friend and attended the rabbi's talk and, from the second I walked into the building of the charity, I knew something was calling to me – I felt 'home'.

A girl I knew from my local nail salon was working at this charity and I found myself asking her if there were any part-time roles going. As an aside, I had been regularly bumping into her for a while in fairly obscure circumstances, e.g. I had been on the London underground tube when she'd run in at the very last moment as the doors were closing to sit in the only free seat next to me. So, I was not surprised that she turned out to be a bridge between where I was and what was next for me. I have since learned that there's no such thing as coincidence.

She said that no, there weren't any vacancies, although the rabbi's PA may be leaving, so she'd put some feelers out. I had had no prior intention of taking an office job, as I believed that part of my life was over. I was working for myself and felt I had a clear idea of where I was headed – I'd built a client practice and had seemingly moved on.

Regardless, and spurred on by this invisible pull to the organisation, I decided to send an e-mail to the rabbi, making myself and my new-found desire known to him.

Looking back, this is a true case of 'Will before Consciousness' as is taught within certain psychology circles. Our Will propels us forward as we take action in service to our evolution without consciously knowing it. It takes a while for this understanding to 'catch up with us' – when we are able to see the bigger picture and join the dots. Even now, this fascinates me, as from this vantage point, I see the breadcrumbs that were leading me home and this e-mail was just one of them. And, sure enough, it transpired that the rabbi's PA was due to leave on maternity for a three-month stint and he would be needing a replacement. I was offered an interview.

Now, it's important to make it clear that this was an Orthodox Jewish charity and without needing to go into details, there are certain criteria and ways of dressing and presenting oneself that need to be adhered to. I attended the interview in a pair of jeans and cowboy boots. Looking back, I am somewhat shocked that I thought this appropriate – Orthodox Jewish women do not wear trousers, let alone jeans!

I mention this because it is even more astounding that I was considered as a candidate following my choice of dress and the glaringly obvious 'differences' between my secular upbringing and the Orthodox world, both externally and with regard to my religious observance. I was thanked for coming in, told that the rabbi would need to interview more candidates and do his due diligence and they would be in contact. He didn't. They hired me. And a few weeks later I was a member of staff. This changed my life.

It is important that you see how high the odds were stacked against this coming to pass and, if viewed from the rational mind, how unlikely it was that my position in this charity would materialise. What made me reply to the e-mail from the family friend? Why did I apply for the job with no desire to work in an office? Why did they hire me if I wasn't an obvious 'fit'? Why didn't I bolt as I usually did when my start day came into focus and I was convinced I had made a mistake, that I would feel confined and imprisoned again in an office job? Because at the 11th hour, in the grip of fear, I very nearly reneged on my acceptance of the job and was seriously considering offering the position to someone else I knew who was looking for work. As it happened, I sought counsel with a wise friend who told me I must ignore the fear and take the position anyway as I would change the job in time and it would look very different to how it did in this moment. How right she was!

The reason I document the circumstances around my entry into the charity, is because we can only see clearly when we look back. Hindsight is 20/20 and each 'coincidence' and decision made – replying to the e-mail from our family friend, attending the Monday night talk, speaking to the girl, e-mailing the rabbi – contributed to this new chapter unfolding for me. This whole scenario and career move wasn't in my 'plan'; it wasn't in my (conscious) awareness. Simply, it wasn't up to me. I could have chosen differently at any given moment. If I'd ignored the nudge to reply to the e-mail, listening instead to my rational mind or if I had ignored any other of these internal or external promptings, this part of my life may not have materialised and I would not be where I am today. Every event contributed to the 'unfoldment' of this new chapter. Life can only open a door, it is up to us to walk through it.

I loved being a part of this charity, relished being part of this 'family' and, after three months of maternity cover, my position as PA was coming to an end and I was feeling dispirited at the thought of my impending departure. But life was to strike in my favour once again. As the clock ticked towards closing time, another member of staff decided to relocate abroad and I was offered his position! The divine timing!

And when I truly think about this, it's nearly unbelievable, because that three-month maternity cover turned into six and a half years of profound growth for me – it was a game changer. Life was making sense and I had found members of my tribe. I felt I'd come 'home'. The charity was involved in teaching individuals how the human experience is created and this contributed to a change in my understanding and worldview that was beyond anything I had imagined or anticipated up until this point. To be involved in this type of work was a dream come true and I found myself feeling overcome with gratitude countless times during my time there. There were many moments when I simply could not believe that Life had gifted me with this opportunity.

Life does not make mistakes. I knew that I was meant to be there and viewed from where I am today; I see it even more clearly. The time in the charity helped me to build a very strong foundation and platform from which I would springboard into the next chapter of my life. I grew up within this charity – I became an adult. I entered a girl and left a woman – a woman whose eyes had been changed forever and saw the world in a completely different light. This new way of seeing changed the course of my life and it was to continue to deepen, grow and evolve.

And when I look back, I see even more clearly how Life was holding me and keeping me in this safe space, even when the odds were stacked against me. Because when I consider who I was back then, it's incredible that they put up with me – I don't believe any other organisation would have! I did a great job, yes and, at the same time I railed against authority, raged against any perceived injustice and, like a child, I pushed and tested boundaries. At many points, my unprofessionalism was astounding – I stormed out of the office in the midst of an emotional outburst on many occasions. In hindsight, it was just another growth spurt!

But this wasn't any old organisation and I truly believe I was given a safe container to be-come more of my Self within a group of people who had their eye on the bigger picture. I deepened into a greater understanding of who I was, what life is and what it means to be human.

It wasn't all perfect; I bumped heads with many members of staff on numerous occasions. I loathed the job at times and regularly seethed at my manager (who I felt intense dislike towards), but somewhere, on some level, I felt I had permission to spread my wings a little more than I ever had done. And let it be known that my then manager is now one of my closest friends and has helped and supported me in my life beyond measure.

If it were up to me, I'd have left that job and severed my connections there on many occasions. Something 'beyond me' was keeping me there and there is no way I could have told you that one of my dearest friendships would have materialised from such a shaky start. We are always being supported; we always get what we need and some of our best gifts are wrapped in very odd paper! Sometimes we have to dig through the sludge to find the gold.

My colleagues had a very different lens on the world that really wasn't the 'norm' and it was them who planted a seed within me that would grow in time. They alluded to the fact that they strongly disagreed with the term 'addict', that it was simply a misunderstanding and that I was most certainly not one.

With my 'evidence' to the contrary and my conditioning, I continued to defend my 'title' and identity, at times feeling intense anger towards their ignorance of the affliction of addiction and their obvious unwillingness to understand my plight. How dare they comment on something they knew absolutely nothing about! Their lives had been 'simple', I thought – they had no idea what I'd been through and had very little respect for the intensity of the struggles I had experienced. Nevertheless, my colleagues continued to say nothing and simply smiled knowingly.

A New Idea of Addiction

A situation occurred which proved to be a turning point in my life, calling for a re-negotiation of my identity as 'addict'. I was in Tel Aviv, Israel, and on my first night in the city, I had a date. The guy was good-looking and charming and I found myself excited about the possibility of something meaningful materialising between us. We sat in a bar not too far from my hotel and I felt incredibly excited about my impending (imagined!) romance. This, together with the free and easy holiday vibe I found myself inside of, contributed to me saying yes when he asked if I'd like a drink.

I recognised that I'd hesitated, acknowledged the rapid beating of my heart and felt the fear of the consequences, but the adrenaline and excitement had taken over and I simply could not see the harm in a little Irish coffee. It was alcohol, for sure, but with the coffee and cream as an addition, I rationalised that it wasn't *so* bad – more of a dessert, really! And here's the thing, it wasn't solely an act of recklessness, throwing caution to the wind and jumping without a parachute – I truly wanted to learn the truth about addiction vs all I had been told.

I now had a very different lens on the world and a new understanding of how experience (and therefore, addictive thinking/cravings) worked. I had applied the understanding of 'thought creating reality' in many areas of my life with success, but I had, up until this point, remained steadfast in my resolve that addiction was an entirely different ball game, totally outside of my control and therefore dangerous territory to play in. I still believed that I could not partake in anything that altered the chemical balance of my brain, as this would spark an allergic reaction, acting as an invitation for carnage. And so, with trepidation and a beating heart, I once again dipped my toe in the water and sipped the Irish coffee.

With each sip, I waited for the demon to present himself, waited for my persona to change as I morphed into a crazed beast, becoming possessed and losing my rational mind. So far, so good. I was still me, looked like me and felt like me. I experienced the effect of the alcohol, sure, but it was more of a rosy glow than a full-scale anaphylactic seizure! I felt a little tipsy and nothing more. I didn't finish the drink and we left the bar. We moved on to somewhere else, he had another drink and I did not.

Now, this was puzzling to me. Surely, the slogan of 'One too many and 1,000 never enough' had my demise in the bag? This was counter to my expectations, for I had been told that the slope was a slippery and sticky one and one drink (even a sip) could send me hurtling down towards a murky bottom.

The avalanche hadn't occurred, but when I put my head on the pillow that night, I felt sick and anxious as I anticipated the dread I would undoubtedly feel in the morning. Maybe I'd been lulled into a false sense of security; maybe I'd been given a reprieve for the evening and the demon was lurking in the background, licking his lips; maybe it was only a matter of time until I came unstuck.

As I opened my eyes the following morning, I braced myself for the onslaught of anxiety and the dreaded fear I believed would materialise within me, weaving itself around me and holding me in its embrace until it squeezed the life out of me. I dreaded a repeat of that last time, the time when I'd heard those words, "Emma, you've lifted the lid," which, by this point, was some eight and a half years ago.

After that relapse a year and a half into recovery, in late 2007, I had remained teetotal and on the straight and narrow, abstinent from all drugs and alcohol for another eight or so years. The fear had been proficient in locking me straight back into the identity of 'addict' and I'd tightened my belt with absolutely no wiggle room.

As I lay there with the minutes ticking by, the fear did not visit me and the anxiety did not materialise. It was simply the truth that came into view – I recognised that I had enjoyed an alcoholic beverage (left it unfinished) and had remained in my 'right' mind. I had not fallen into an addictive spiral; I'd had no need or desire for another drink. I was 'normal'.

This was a huge revelation to me. No anxiety. No fear. No self-judgement. No headache. The waters were calm. I was somewhat astounded. I thought maybe I hadn't woken up properly and that I should step with caution. Maybe it would look different by lunchtime. Maybe the fear and anxiety were waiting to catch me unawares. But they never showed up. Not on that day and not in the days and weeks that followed. And for the first time in my life, I saw (my) addiction from a completely different angle and through a completely different lens.

I had been told by many people, including family members and colleagues that I was not an addict, but I had been too scared to truly consider the possibility for fear of the repercussions. If I let go of the reins of 'Addict', surely this would cause me to spiral out of control? The negative consequences I had been told would doubtless follow this change of heart had been enough to keep me from exploring the unknown.

I now had a new outlook and a fresh pair of eyes on the past. Emma as addict was becoming an old, outdated story that had been held up and supported by a huge misunderstanding. I saw the truth about the 'disease' of addiction – it was in fact, a lie. I had yet to experience what was possible in this new paradigm. Things could potentially be different now. I could trust myself. I didn't need to be scared any more. I sensed freedom.

Although it was not to be a quick turnaround, the growth period does not happen in an instant. I had lived one way for many years and there would be much to learn. Life was going to keep giving me exactly what I needed in order for me to evolve. I would go through a deep and intense process of unlearning (letting go of all the false ideas I had about life and who I was) before I would truly be able to embody and integrate a new version of myself and be-come something and somebody entirely different. I needed to change the record and this wasn't going to be a five-minute scenario, this was to take years.

I was so used to being in pain, so used to living in worry and fear, that I was constantly (somewhat unconsciously) reinforcing this state of being. My mind had literally been programmed to live this way, my body so used to adrenaline that I was feeding the very thing I wanted to let go of; re-wounding myself again and again and again.

There is an old Native American story. An old Cherokee is teaching his grandson about life:

"A fight is going on inside me," he said to the boy.

"It is a terrible fight and it is between two wolves. One is evil – he is anger, envy, sorrow, regret, greed, arrogance, self-pity, guilt, resentment, inferiority, lies, false pride, superiority, and ego."

He continued, "The other is good – he is joy, peace, love, hope, serenity, humility, kindness, benevolence, empathy, generosity, truth, compassion, and faith. The same fight is going on inside you – and inside every other person, too."

The grandson thought about it for a minute and then asked his grandfather: "Which wolf will win?"

The old Cherokee simply replied, "The one you feed."

This is the conflict that exists within human beings, the 'fight' between right and wrong, good and evil – not only with regards to our behaviour, but also that which comes prior to our actions, our thinking. Which thoughts do we choose to give our energy and attention to? What are we choosing to feed, nourish and keep alive?

Looking back, I wonder how many times the younger me living within, has hung her head in sadness and resignation as I continued to choose thinking that kept her living smaller than was possible, whilst I continued to skip over love and choose fear instead. I wonder how many times she thought she might as well give up – would I ever heed the call to the difference? But she's resilient. She knew that sooner or later I would choose love over fear. She knew that it would only be a matter of time until I opted for a different record. She knew I would hear the call… eventually.

PART III

Relationship to Life

At this juncture, I could continue to dive into more of my 'story' and whilst there is much to say, we are looking for solutions. To regurgitate more of the same may suffice for entertainment purposes, but will prove unhelpful if evolution is the name of the game.

So, that being said and having 'landed' on firmer terrain, here's what I came to know about life and the way it works...

If You Want Love, Give Love

As I said, co-dependency was still rife in my life. I still 'needed' you, needed your approval. At some point along the path, I realised I had no real connections. I liked you, enjoyed you, wanted to be around you, but truly cared? From a heart space? Honest to God cared about your wellbeing? Not really. I was much too concerned with what I was getting (or not as the case may be), too caught up in the fear of you leaving me to actually connect to the feeling of love between us and give of myself unconditionally in care of or concern for you.

I was still acting out friendship, rather than feeling friendship, still playing a role rather than experiencing true connection, letting our relationship organically and effortlessly evolve with me just *being* me. I would cry a river for the suffering of human beings around the world, so deep was my empathy for others' pain, but in my personal relationships my guard was up – you may be too risky an investment and I needed a guarantee that you were safe and secure for the long-term.

Over the years, I occasionally felt a deep love for

those around me that came when my mind wasn't over-analysing and I was present, free from worry with no thought of selfish gain or judgement, when I moved out of my own way. And I loved those moments. They took me by surprise. I was overcome with a feeling of such deep affection for another, seeing them in their truth, outside of my lens. And I'd think, 'Aha, this is what true love for another feels like!'.

It was revelatory. I'd want to call that certain someone and tell them I loved them, just because. I'd want to wrap my arms around them and hold them in an embrace, love them just for being them. I wanted nothing, needed nothing – desiring only to express love. Those moments were so eye opening for me, indeed, heart opening. So, I knew it was possible, I knew I could love – love truly and deeply. There was just this little matter of getting out of my own way, opening the door to my caged heart and up-ending nearly a lifetime of conditioning.

Thing is, as soon as the moment passed and my brain moved into gear, I'd be right back where I started. But I also saw that love is not about the person/the object of my affection, for they were not in my direct company when I had these experiences. I recognised the love was coming from within me, that it *was* me.

Previously, I'd always associated this giving of love as an open door to loss – that had been my lived experience. If I love you and you leave, I'm screwed. But I'm not. Not really. Love is who I am. It's my truth, my essence. No one can take that away from me; no one can take that from any of us. The only thing that keeps us out of love are our judgements and expectations – they act as barriers.

The more love I give, the more love I receive and the more I exist in the energy of love. It doesn't matter if you stay or you go, it's not about you – it's not about the receiving, the gift is in the giving. If you want love, give love. I am interested in living in this space of expansion, expanding my capacity to love. Love is who I am. If I exist in this space, your absence or presence is inconsequential; it is not dependent on my feeling state and sense of wellbeing. I am doing what a human being is here to do – be love, give love.

I can give with abandon, without needing anything in return. I can give from a place of wholeness. What you do with my love is none of my business. I give because it is my nature to keep giving. I don't need you to respond in kind. At my essence, away from the limitation of my identity as Emma, away from my fear-based myopic thinking, away from 'my story' that I *need* anything from you, it is my joy to give. I came here to do exactly that, to share who I am… with you.

Closing my heart and withholding love causes *me* to suffer… and potentially the other. It keeps me living smaller than is possible. Living with a heart wrapped in fear means that I live in a space of constriction rather than expansion, closed down and focused on the tiny (perceived) experience directly within my eye line rather than the bigger picture. This lens is incredibly restricting.

The sun continually provides us with light and warmth. The sun does not give in order to receive; it needs and expects nothing back. It gives because it is its nature to give; to continually emanate and to fulfil its potential as the sun.

It is the nature of water to keep flowing, to bend and mould itself around anything in the path of its flow, to take the shape of whatever it is poured into, necessarily adapting to the situation at hand – no resistance, no pushing, no forcing, no moving back on itself – always moving forward. We are part of nature; we were made to give of ourselves unconditionally and to serve others, to keep pouring, sharing, expanding and moving.

Judgement keeps us out of the heart and out of connection. Expectations cloud our ability to see. Pushing keeps us out of the flow and away from the present. Withholding keeps us locked inside, restricting our natural shape and nature. Connection or judgement. Resistance or flow. Holding on or letting go. The choice is always yours.

In the Beginning

In the beginning, there's you, fresh from whence you came, a blank canvas for life to paint you. You're sponge-like, pure consciousness, ready to become all of who you have the potential to be. Just as an acorn holds the potential of the oak tree, so too is there a far greater and grander version of you residing within your being, ready to become manifest.

So here we are, ready to become our magnificent Selves – radiant, joyful, abundant and free – 'all' we have to do is to be-come. But, with the amount of addiction, mental health issues and record sales of antidepressants currently blighting the landscape of 21st century living, it seems that something may have gone awry. What happened?

Let's go back to the acorn. So, yes, the oak tree most definitely resides within, but there is something fundamental that needs to occur in order for that imprint to become manifest. Conditions need to be ripe. The environment needs to be wholly supportive to ensure the full flourishing of this magnificent tree. The earth needs to hold the seed; it will require water, air, sunshine and oxygen. So too, do we as human beings need the 'right' environment to become fully our Selves. We need loving, conscious parenting, teaching systems upholding the Truth, embracing the whole individual, wise elders, room to grow, room to breathe, space to be allowed to be-come, permission to be our Selves.

I am not pointing the finger of blame at one specific area of potential lack when I talk about the 'right' environment for human growth. For instance, I wholeheartedly believe that the majority of parents love their children dearly – of course they do – and are simply and genuinely doing their best. I believe that most people in this world mean no harm and do not have malicious intent. Yes, there have been many obvious perpetrators of abuse of many kinds, but on a day-to-day basis, the majority of us mean well. It's just that what has been our best thinking up until this point isn't necessarily what's best for the overall healthy functioning and full flourishing of the organism – in this instance, children – who then become adults and therefore, by default, society.

I don't believe any one of us set out to create the mess we seem to be in – with a vast percentage of the population suffering with depression, low self-esteem, health issues and the like. As individuals, I don't believe we would choose anything other than optimum health if we saw we had a choice. But if we survey the landscape, it seems society is riddled with health issues, both mental and physical – we're severely under functioning in the area of optimal psychological health. To my mind, it's been a car crash waiting to happen.

We've been operating unconsciously and somewhat robotically, away from our deeper Truth for eons. How much of the way in which we think is coming from our innate wisdom and how much of what we do comes from a rerun of an old, outdated record, playing over and over again?

We think and behave in the way we've been taught, not stopping or wanting to question, not wanting to upset the apple cart. We comply with rules and regulations even when they make no sense to us. We do what is expected of us by society even when it goes against our inner knowing.

We find ourselves parenting in the way we were parented, even if we found this somewhat lacking and vacuous; we're friends in the way we're taught friendships 'should' operate; we act in the manner deemed appropriate dependent on the situation at hand; and we live each day pretty much the same as the last and, for the most part, on automatic pilot with the same pattern of thinking streaming through our heads on repeat. And really, how many of us actually stop to question this?

How many of us actually pause to contemplate – is this for my highest good and the highest good of all? Is this reality-on-a-loop serving me? Do I actually feel the way I 'think' I feel about life, the situations and people I have opinions on? Do the things I've been taught (religion, dogma, etc) resonate with and serve me? Do I want to be doing what I'm doing? Do I enjoy my current circle of friends? Were these friendships consciously created or have they come about by default? Do I still want to be involved in the activities I'm entertaining or am I stuck in a habitual rut..? And on… and on… We're living a Groundhog Day and it is, quite simply, a travesty.

For the most part, the way we've been behaving and going about the business of living has not, does not and will not support our mental health, our overall wellbeing (individually and as a collective), the full flourishing of the human being and what's possible. The way we've been existing does not constitute or even come close to the truth of what is possible for us as a human race.

Again, it's no one's fault. We have been misled and misguided and in the majority of situations, acted from an innocent misunderstanding. Simply, we have not known better.

We've carried down patterns of thought, behaviour and conditioning from generation to generation which do not create the 'best' environments for human beings to become their 'best' selves. We've believed our 'leaders', trusted in the 'systems', been given a messed up view of what's 'right' and 'wrong' and been drip-fed fear through our TV screens, media outlets and newspapers, which has us operating at a lower vibration and frequency (more on this later). We've forgotten who we are. And now we're in crisis.

Rewind. So here we are as babies, looking for the right environment for our full development and we find it somewhat lacking. We're given rules and regulations, instructed on the behaviours that are and are not deemed appropriate and that will or will not be tolerated and we absorb all the misplaced and unconscious emotion from those around us (unmet needs, suppressed feelings, anger, fear, insecurities… ad infinitum). It's not a party I'd consciously choose to be a guest at.

Regardless of our natural inclinations we are (for the majority) thrown into a schooling system that makes no allowances for the 'differences' in individuals, e.g. the natural leanings and inclinations of a specific child. Thousands of children are being diagnosed with ADHD (Attention Deficit Hyperactivity Disorder) because they simply cannot sit in classroom situations or find themselves totally uninterested in what is being offered. They experience intense internal discomfort, frustration and an inability to concentrate and will therefore 'act out' in their suffering, being labelled as 'odd', defiant, difficult, defective, unruly or badly behaved.

Putting a creative or gifted child in a classroom is like putting a tiger in a kennel, leaving a dog locked up in a house all day or placing a bird in a cage. Of course, the tiger, dog or bird would react – they would roar, bark and uncontrollably flap their wings. These creatures were not made to exist within these parameters and therefore cannot thrive in these types of environments and they will respond to this constriction appropriately.

And if you didn't know better – that the tiger needs the vast plains, that the dog needs the park or woodland and the bird needs the sky – you may view their show of displeasure, their 'acting up' in their confined spaces (rocking the cages or squawking), as inappropriate behaviour and promptly administer a Valium shot or… an ADHD pill.

Thing is, all that was needed was a change of environment. The animals needed to be placed in their correct and natural habitat. Why is a child any different? It's an ignorance that labels these children, not medical science. If you research children currently being prescribed ADHD tablets unnecessarily, you will find the statistics somewhat astounding and heart-breaking in equal measure, as is the age of the kids taking them. If we do not adhere to protocol in any area, we're labelled 'difficult'. I am not suggesting that in some cases, potentially some type of medication is advised, but the number of children being labelled with ADHD and medicated, is a far cry from that which is necessary.

To add insult to injury, sometime in the very near future, we will come to understand that our outside appearance (clothes, weight, etc) is of utmost importance and is representative of who we are on the inside. This message is streamed to us from multiple sources – movies, TV, the media, publications, social media, parents, peers, etc. We're then expected to work in jobs that do not fulfil us in order to make a living (for a life that we do not fully live) and spend much of our time wondering what went wrong – what's wrong with us? Why do we have a gaping hole inside? Why do we feel so empty and unfulfilled?

What's more shocking, is that despite walking around with this hole inside of us, we plaster a smile on our face over our inclination to scream or cry and we look forward to numbing this deep sense of unease by going unconscious in front of the TV screen on a nightly basis, consuming too much food, binge drinking, shopping for those must-haves, enslaving ourselves to our mobile phones or fixing ourselves with that unavailable man or woman.

Listen, there's a long list here, but this is only the tip of the iceberg. We humans are incredibly adept with regard to our avoidance tactics (not to mention creative, as I have documented with regard to my own experience) and there are numerous behaviours we've employed to numb the pain and divert our eyes from the very real work of re-membering who we truly are. We had no control as youngsters and, by the time we're adults, we're stuck in what appears to be a deep rut, our true natures forgotten. We get in our own way – struggling, controlling and pushing, striving to fit a round peg in a square hole, becoming rigid and fearful. We have forgotten that we can stop, relax, let go, trust and yield to the force of life. More on this later.

The words I have considered many times over the years are 'love' and 'nurturing'. There is a huge difference between them. If we look at these in the dictionary, we see love is 'a strong feeling of affection' or 'a great interest and pleasure in something', whilst nurture is '(to) care for and protect (someone or something) whilst they are growing' or '(to) help or encourage the development of'.

To my mind, the absence of either one of these within upbringing (and I refer not only to parenting, but also to the role of society/systems in its many guises) can have detrimental consequences to our sense of self and wellbeing. We need only research the number of antidepressants being dispensed and patient intake statistics in drug rehabilitation centres and psychiatric institutions for evidence. People simply do not know, do not remember, who they are.

One can truly believe they love something or someone (person, thing, animal, plant, etc) but not necessarily know the best way in which to care for it or provide the best chance for its evolutionary growth and flourishing. I'm not talking about survival here; I'm talking about fully flourishing to reach our potential (inanimate object apart).

For instance, not every plant needs the same type of care. If you treat daffodils the same way you do cacti, you may find your gardening skills severely lacking. If you feed your cat the same food you give to your budgie, you'll have one very disgruntled (and potentially emaciated) feline friend and I wouldn't suggest taking your goldfish along to accompany the dog on his daily walk! Every thing and every one needs different types of care, love, environment and nurture. One size does not fit all.

We were all children, yes, but we were and are, all different to one degree or another. We need some of the same fundamental things that keep us alive and kicking, but when it comes to supporting the personal growth and evolution that allows for the full flourishing of an individual to become manifest – for us to become all of who we are meant to be – we MUST accept, embrace and support the differences in each of us. It's crucial.

As human beings and as a society, we've lost our way. We are so far removed from our true nature and the understanding of what life actually is, that the absence of mental health in our society was unavoidable. Indeed, it needed to get to this crisis point in order for us to realise that we may have missed something along the way and come to recognise the intrinsic and urgent need to create a new reality.

We need to re-visit – Who on earth are we? What on earth are we doing? What are we thinking? How are we behaving? What do we really know about life and the way it works? What kind of world do we wish to create and how are we each a part of that? These questions are crucial if we wish to step out of the dark and into the light, creating a 'better' life and a whole new world.

What's It All About Anyway?

What's this thing called life really all about? What does BEing human actually mean? Good questions, quite lofty musings to consider. Bottom line is, I couldn't in total honesty tell you. I certainly couldn't put my hand on my heart and take an oath to tell the truth, the whole truth and nothing but the truth. But, there are some things I absolutely do know – the potential for humanity and what it means to be human resembles nothing like what we're seeing in our current society. Our understanding of the purpose of (human) life is a million galaxies away from the truth, from its actual potential. Namely, it's nothing like that which is currently being played out in 'reality', in the media, on our television screens, within the majority of the conversations we're having and in the way in which we relate to our Selves and to each other.

Being human and living on planet Earth is not what we think it is. It is not about manners and protocol; it is not about striving to make a ton of money to never actually enjoy it. It is not about being pulled along through a schooling system that treats every individual the same as the last. It isn't pretending to be someone you're not in order to 'fit in', to smile over your inclination to cry, to force yourself into a too small pair of jeans in order to concur with the current image of the body beautiful. It is not about entering a stilettoed, fully made up two-year-old child into a beauty pageant in order to affirm your sense of self-worth.

It is not about giving over our power to big businesses, corporations and governments whose only real interest is selfish gain and money. It is not about abdicating our own voices and allowing leaders to lead that haven't got the first clue as to what they're actually doing and who seem totally oblivious (or not…) to the detrimental impact their decisions are having in and on our world. We have fallen asleep. We have gone unconscious to the Truth and to our individual innate power and abilities.

We sit back and observe the absolute pain and devastation governmental actions are causing the world over and shake our heads in total bewilderment. We're in full victim mode whilst feeling powerless to do anything about the carnage unfolding. We are asleep, behaving unconsciously by rote, for we have not consciously understood that we do not have to adhere to nonsense, to that which we know in our hearts to be intrinsically wrong, whilst witnessing crimes against humanity. We've been led to believe that we need to be led! We have forgotten that we ourselves are powerful beyond measure and are our own authority. Each one of us, YOU, has the power to change the world, but you must wake up to this deep truth and move out of the illusion of powerlessness. We must stop abdicating responsibility.

We have not come close to understanding the potential of the human being and what is possible for us individually and collectively. Being human is an awesome gift that hardly any of the 7.8 billion people (and rising) currently residing on this planet are utilising. We are asleep to the truth of who we are. Of course, there are those who have a greater understanding of the human potential, personally and collectively, but they are few and far between. We've been brainwashed, conditioned and mislead – sometimes innocently and sometimes not so innocently.

I will say it again, each one of us, YOU, have the power to change this world, but you must wake up to this deep truth and move out of the illusion of powerlessness. What is happening to humanity and to our planet is a farce and it is the very reason so many of us feel like we're dying at the very same time we're supposed to be living. Of course we're in pain when we see the unnecessary suffering of so many; we know in our hearts, on a visceral level, that it does not need to be this way, we know it's wrong, that something's 'off'. The illusion that we are powerless to do anything about it is just that, a complete illusion.

So much of this 'asleep' behaviour would actually make me laugh if it were not so devastating and painful. Societal rules and 'right' behaviours are happening on many levels (from the mundane to the extreme) and in every area of life.

For us personally, for example, in order to be viewed as a 'civilised' human being, we feel we need to adhere to social protocol and etiquette in order to 'fit in' and be accepted. Some of these rules and 'correct' behaviours may seem irrelevant, innocent and somewhat unimportant, but we're constantly being fed messages about what is 'right' and ignoring our inner knowing in the process; we are constantly being shepherded to 'fit in'. Some of it may seem harmless, but on a worldwide scale, it can be devastating. We bend and distort our natural shapes in a bid to be part of the 'whole' and silence our voices to avoid making waves, to follow suit and to 'do the right thing', thus continuing our asleep behaviour and our abdication of personal power.

Let's look at the mundane. Take 'correct' table manners for instance. As a British society we're obsessed with etiquette, politeness and behaving appropriately at the dinner table – people will actually overlook a potential life partner if they fall short of the prescribed protocol. But in some areas of the world, India for instance, it's acceptable to eat with your fingers. Does this make the Indian culture wrong or perhaps archaic? I can tell you from my perspective; I greatly enjoy eating with my fingers, although in a bid for transparency and honesty, this is not something I currently display in the public domain, as I have not yet reached the enlightened state of 'not giving a toss'. It is also my understanding that the finger was created before the knife and fork.

Let's look at the humble and innocent belch. In some countries it's considered rude not to burp after a meal, but here in the UK, let one rip and you're branded a pig! Being somewhat of a windy individual, I have a vast amount of experience in this area. Should I sit in discomfort because it's not the 'done thing'? Last time I checked, it's a natural bodily function – better out than in.

What about breastfeeding – the most natural thing in the world? Why do we have to fight to make this acceptable in public? It's sustenance for a baby. For many of us, it's the reason we're alive and kicking, potentially even the case for those who feel outrage and petition against it. You see the total hypocrisy here?

It's OK to ogle a pair of breasts in a pornographic magazine or in our daily tabloids for sexual gratification, that's acceptable, but to show a breast in public in the name of feeding your baby – uh-uh, that's inappropriate, a total no-no – it's just not the 'done' thing. And here's the thing, let's admit it – some of us will feel incredibly uncomfortable seeing a woman breastfeed her baby in the public domain. It has become so alien to us that we can hardly look in our embarrassment. On a deeper level, away from conditioning and brainwashing, we know that it's a truly beautiful and natural occurrence.

And what about the world of advertising and brand endorsements? I will usually record the programmes

I'm interested in, in a bid to fast-forward through the abundance of nonsense that fills the screen in commercial breaks. There are a few reasons for this. One being, that life on Earth is short and I'd rather not spend my precious time and energy staring gormlessly at a conveyor belt of consumer goods I'm uninterested in, whilst waiting for my preferred viewing to recommence.

I resent being led to believe that my life is missing something critical and of paramount importance (i.e. the latest hair removal product or the world's quickest and most efficient cucumber slicer) when I'd been quite content and blissfully unaware just 30 seconds earlier. I do OK with an old-fashioned, bog-standard razor and, up until now, I've been pretty proficient at slicing my pickles with the humble kitchen knife.

Let's take it a step further and look at how we're detracted from pain and suffering and uncomfortable truths. I recently saw an ad for pork breasts, featuring a couple sitting in their suburban home eating said meat for their dinner in front of the TV. A man dressed in a chicken outfit sits on the arm of the sofa, arms folded across his chest indignantly, disgruntled and bewailing to the couple that he's not on the menu that evening. Tuesday, in this particular household, is usually chicken night and he's been bumped off the menu for a pig. According to the advertiser, the pork breasts are quicker and easier to rustle up and much tastier.

The ad was designed to make us, the viewer, laugh,

but if you look under the surface it's actually seriously disturbing and masks a disconcerting truth. The majority of chickens served to the population have lived truly awful lives in horrific conditions. These creatures are mistreated daily and fed antibiotics whilst existing in a space no bigger than an A4 sheet of paper. And whilst we're led to believe otherwise, these animals feel pain and emotion, but this seems to be irrelevant as the demand for poultry is high and dead chickens are a very profitable business.

We do not want to know that the chicken suffered its whole life, living in squalor, unable to display any of its natural behaviours, unable to walk around or even spread its wings, never breathing any fresh air, sandwiched in-between thousands of other chickens in a tiny compacted area, stepping over many dead and decaying carcasses on the 'farm' (factory) floor. Many of the chickens are deformed as they are over-bred and therefore lack the calcium needed for the health of their bones; their hearts and lungs simply cannot keep up with their oversized breast muscles and over-rearing and their beaks are clipped to stop them from pecking at one another due to the high stress levels they experience due to confinement and pain.

But, let's sweep that under the carpet. Let's make light of it and dress a grown man in a chicken costume whilst he acts miffed that he's off the menu for the evening. Caveat, he needs to be dead for this to happen. It's just another example of how the public are brainwashed and blinded to an inconvenient truth by the advertising world and big business.

And anyway, we don't want to look at the reality, we don't want anything to unsettle our neat little worlds. We'd prefer to remain in ignorant bliss – it's easier that way. We'd prefer not to own our part in the equation (business meeting market demand) or heed a call to action – we'd prefer to relinquish responsibility. We want to see a nicely packaged, clean piece of meat in the supermarket ready for marinating and cooking, looking nothing like the animal itself – the presentation masking a world of pain and let's not even mention (in many cases) the hormone-drenched flesh you'd be ingesting. Denial and ignorance serve a purpose. Animals are suffering horrifically to feed the population and, in the long run, the chicken will be easier to swallow than the truth itself.

Let's go back to the 'less harmful' lies. Most of the adverts are filled with ridiculous characters (a nodding dog, a talking bear or a group of deliriously happy individuals raving about the wonders of the banking system) and irritating jingles that jangle my nerves. But, more than anything, I find it astounding that we, the public, the human population, are coaxed and (willingly?) hypnotised into purchasing an inordinate amount of products, food, clothing, etc that we do not need in order to keep up with fashion, to be seen to be 'in the know', 'on trend' or affluent or to digest 'food' produce which, in actuality, lacks any ingredient that could be classified as food!

But more than this, we're once again unconsciously filling that gaping hole within us with yet more stuff, pushing down that which is desperately attempting to be seen and heard, attempting to feel internally complete using 'things'/food and striving to accomplish wholeness at the 'wrong' level. The hole of the soul cannot and will not be satisfied via the world of form/matter.

To attempt to pacify this internal void in this way could be likened to wallpapering over a crack or plugging a burst dam with a toothpick – it's simply not going to do the job. In your attempts to pacify yourself in this way, you will simply mask the problem and chances are, that crack will get even larger. The problem will remain; it's merely hidden out of eyesight… for now. The wall will crumble, eventually.

The world of spirit (that internal void) and the world of form (material things) are two entirely separate dimensions. This is the quandary and the paradox, for we are both – human and spirit. You need to be aware of the level at which you're operating at and which part you're feeding – body or soul.

On occasion, I will find myself following the masses and scrolling aimlessly through Instagram or the like, to be further baffled by humanity. We have become obsessed with the world of celebrity and celebrity lifestyle and we buy into this 'shiny', happy and perfect world, viewing it as something worthy to aim towards. We do not realise that nearly all of what we see is a gross misrepresentation of the truth, giving an intentionally distorted and warped impression of what is 'real'. Most of it is a sham. Behind the holiday snaps, the wide smiles, the luxurious lifestyles and the need to share minute by minute updates on the mundaneness of life, resides pain and untold stories.

The celebs amongst us have been paid heavily to endorse products, which they claim to be life changing and are therefore unable to live without. We see the evidence of said product in their thick and shiny hair, their toned bodies and flawless skin (all of which have been photoshopped) or the latest celebrity beauty being pursued by panting admirers who find themselves unable to resist the tantalising smell of the latest Chanel fragrance.

And if we're honest, we know these celebrities and public figures do not subscribe to these products themselves, in their 'real' life, but in our desperation to fit in and attain the 'perfect' life, we've bought in regardless. We've come to believe these 'things' are important, that they truly define us, that these acquisitions actually aid us in our attempt to feel 'whole' and a 'part of', whilst we scramble to cement our preferred sense of identity. It's all smoke and mirrors. Who are you looking to impress? Does it actually matter if anyone gives you the seal of approval or the thumbs up? Do you wish to continue to live life on the 'surface' or are you interested in a deep dive inward?

And what about our own personal Instagram and social media accounts, whilst we're on a never-ending mission for 'likes', 'comments' and short-lived outside affirmation? If you find yourself in this bracket, the news is this – there's no end to this game, there are no winners and you'll find yourself continually chasing the ever-elusive affirmation and connection, leaving you feeling empty, disheartened and ultimately exhausted.

Peace will elude you if you continue to look outside of yourself for the love and connection that you're longing for, whilst ignoring what's calling to you from within. Your ultimate happiness lives inside of you.

If you do not wake up to the fact that you are your best friend and the one you've been waiting for, you will be chasing your tail for the rest of your time here on Earth. You will never know the type of connection your heart yearns for if you think it lives outside of you, somewhere 'over there', with him, her, them or in the world of social media. You're kidding yourself if you think these platforms have anything to offer you in the way of true and personal connection. They do not.

And the Absurdity Continues...

My indignance towards nonsense and adherence to
societal norms has been around as long as I have and I
have oftentimes raged against protocol – although this
energy has not always served me well!

I have experienced hundreds of examples of this
throughout my life and the situations left me feeling
baffled, somewhat speechless and in a state of disbelief,
seriously wondering whether the larger part of society has
indeed lost the ability to discern for themselves and make
rational decisions based on their inner knowing and the
situation at hand.

A few years ago, on disembarking an airplane and
approaching passport control, I saw the winding maze of
rope constructed in order to herd the crowd in an orderly
fashion towards security personnel. In this rare instance,
I was delighted to find the hall virtually empty and could
see no logic in winding myself left to right through the
rope maze as I determined that my destination could
better be reached in a straight line. I therefore ducked my
head under the rope and arrived at the passport window in

record time, saving myself at least two minutes of winding time and congratulating myself on my lateral thinking and on making up good time towards the baggage claim area. Tick for me!

I was more than a little surprised to find that, despite this option being available to all my fellow passengers, everyone else was observing the rope system, twisting and turning back and forth on themselves to eventually arrive at their destination a substantial amount of time after me. I inwardly shrugged my shoulders, but what I found more astounding was the reaction of one of my fellow passengers.

A woman was engaged in heated conversation with her partner, whilst looking in my direction and shaking her head. When she finally arrived within earshot, I asked her what seemed to be the problem. She was visibly disgruntled and more than a little angry as she proceeded to inform me that I had been behind her in the queue, that this was airport protocol and I should observe the rules. It was astounding to me. I informed her (if I'm to be honest, in a not-so-loving manner) that the straight line option was also available to her and her husband and that she had made a choice, but it seemed to fall on deaf ears. Rules are rules, apparently.

In keeping with the airport theme, there's a hilarious scene from the film *Meet the Parents* starring Ben Stiller. His character, Greg Focker, walks through a deserted boarding gate and approaches the stewardess at the desk, handing over his ticket. She looks at it, inanely smiles in his direction and informs him that they are only boarding rows nine and above. He glances around the empty space and at his ticket, points out that no one is waiting to board and tells her he is in row eight. With the inane smile still plastered on her face, she tells him to step aside and wait his turn which he eventually does, stunned and in disbelief as he once again glances around the deserted area with only the sound of a distant vacuum cleaner and tinny airport music to be heard.

After several long moments, with the two of them being only two feet from one another, the stewardess picks up the tannoy and announces loudly (to no one bar him) that all remaining passengers can now board. With obvious resignation registering on his face, he steps towards the stewardess who greets him, as if for the first time, registers his ticket and wishes him a nice flight. This is a comedy, created to make us laugh, but my goodness, it's not a million miles away from what we see in everyday 'normal' life.

I could write a book on this phenomenon. I have hundreds of examples of what I deem to be total stupidity in the name of protocol. I've seen people standing at the sides of roads adhering to the 'Don't walk' sign for minutes on end whilst not a single car comes by, only crossing when the green man signals. I've been served coffee in two paper cups (my pet peeve) to avoid the risk of burning myself when the coffee in question is lukewarm. On stating I'd really only like one cup to avoid unnecessary wastage, I've been told that it's health and safety and I'll not be permitted the drink if I will not accept the extra cup.

What does our blind and robotic compliance teach the younger generation? What message are we sending out when we do something 'just because' or 'because that's the way it is'? 'It's protocol', 'it's what the government says', 'everyone else is doing it', 'it's what's written on the sign/ the paper/it's what the offer states', or 'because I told you so'. I cannot count how many times I have heard these statements and looked at the people around me with another shake of the head and a feeling of resignation as I view another display of blind compliance to nonsense. We should be able to assess a situation for ourselves, apply common sense, think out of the box, discern in a moment and question that which appears nonsensical. It's fundamentally important to model our wisdom-in-the-moment thinking to the younger generation or else we will continue to create more of the same.

Let's go back to the schooling system and curriculum, a system that has treated each individual as the 'same' and graded children in terms of their intellect, encouraging competition and therefore low self-esteem for those who cannot keep up and are therefore found lacking. The success and potential of an individual has absolutely nothing to do with their ability to lock in information, recite history, understand biology or do maths. There is merit in all of these things and some children will thrive in these environments, but not all. Not everyone will have the same ability and natural inclination and we should not be pitted against one another, compared to our peers or graded – just encouraged to find what's right, for us.

With regard to my own personal schooling experience, I will share that it was a hugely frustrating time for me at many points whilst I struggled to 'keep up' and felt forced to comply with an institution that did not feel right to or for me. Yes, there were certain subjects I enjoyed, art and English being two of them and some friends I felt more my Self with, but for the most part, my 'education' felt like a waste of time and the stress I experienced throughout revision and exam time was truly debilitating.

With regard to curriculum content, I cannot bring to mind the last time I needed to dredge up the birth and death date of the inventor of the pottery wheel in order to move forward in my life and I'm not sure where I would be now had I not known the difference between warp and weft! I joke, but so much of our upbringing and stages of our growth (if I can credit it with that term) have been pointless. It has turned us into robots, filling our heads with unnecessary/flawed information and distorted beliefs and worldviews. We're so far away from the magic and mystery that constitutes life that it's frightening – just observe the daily news, it actually is frightening.

I think back to my analogy of the too small pair of jeans that we attempt to squeeze ourselves into – mission, body beautiful. I guess that's what happens when we, this incredible, awesome, beautiful being incarnates on planet Earth and has to pour itself into the constraints of the human body (no wonder a baby cries as soon as it enters the world!), given labels and pushed into little boxes, tiny versions of ourselves that belie the truth of who we truly are. How does the body actually contain the magnificence of our beings? How does the acorn hold the oak? It's pretty mind-blowing, really.

Children come into this Earth full of joy. Everything to a child is new, exciting and magic – children are magic. You only have to watch young children at play to feel your heart swell, because we all know this space, we remember this is how we used to be – running, jumping, laughing, playing make-believe and being in awe of the world around us. It feels good to watch this carefree, present and in-the-moment behaviour, because it reminds us that this is who we are, it's still inside us. This is our essence and who we were before we conformed to social norms and we forgot.

Now, please consider the damage we do when we tell these little beings to 'shush, stop making a noise, be quiet, you have to wear that dress, sit up straight, don't dirty yourself, say thank you, watch your manners, don't speak at the table...' and on and on and on. Could we kick the joy out of these kids any more if we tried? And truly, what a total travesty this is; this open-hearted joy that comes in with these children is exactly the kind of energy that will heal this planet. We should be encouraging it, not denying it, not suppressing it, not stifling it and stuffing it down in order for us to create carbon copies that fit neatly into little boxes that society can accept. We should be looking to them to teach us. They are love, they embody this energy, they live and breathe it and they only want to share it.

Can you imagine what it feels like for a child to be told to stop play? That it's too much, they're too noisy, they need to behave... when in actuality, they are living in the field of imagination and magic, fully *alive* in life, expressing their excitement and joy – they are *living*. It actually hurts my heart when I think of all the disappointment felt by children the world over who have heard the message either overtly or covertly, 'be seen and not heard'. How many children have altered their shapes and denied their truth in order to be accepted? Can you see how this is a recipe for addiction and depression? Can you see how this would move a person out of balance and into dis-ease?

We're given an overview and an understanding of life and of ourselves that is laughable and to the expansive mind of a child who lives in imagination, fantasy and wonder, it must feel pretty restrictive – being told that what we imagine doesn't exist, that we're talking nonsense, that the world of make-believe is just... well, make-believe.

And it's not just a suppression of joy we have to deal with, we also have our reality denied. We're told we're being silly, making a performance over nothing, there's no reason to be upset and given labels we then adhere to – we're not as clever as..., we're the shy child, the pretty one, the naughty one, we're difficult, a nuisance, always daydreaming and labelled in a million other ways that turn us from limitless, boundless potential, being fully in the world and connected to everything, into limited individuals with restrictive personalities and seemingly fixed identities, falling neatly into our little boxes and feeling downright rotten in the process.

How long can a human being deny their truth and live with a closed heart under adherence to protocol? It's a ticket for disaster and we're doing this all the time, programmed to act, speak and think in a way that belies our Truth and benefits no one (at least, not the majority of us) and is most definitely not for the highest good. We need to return to our true nature; we need to be those children again, joyous and free in a world of make-believe.

Why on earth would we have come to this incredible planet to live identified with a list of personality traits we are led to believe constitute all of who we are, to limit ourselves and turn a blind eye to what's possible? We struggle, feel low, judge ourselves and think and feel we should somehow become someone/something else. Does this make any sense? Have you seen the beauty and majesty of planet Earth? Have you seen the beauty and majesty of You? Is it any wonder so many of us spend our lives counting down the days until our annual two weeks away on the beach to escape the very lives we've created?

Question this. Think about it. We've incarnated into human form to LIVE. Why on earth would we want to escape 'life'? Our lives? Who said life on Earth should be anything other than joyful? How sad that we wish our lives away, 'getting through' months of the year for our time 'off' (of life), whilst we take our 'vacation'.

We project forward, missing the moment (namely life and all the magic, beauty, abundance, potential and opportunities this offers us), until our 'escape' day finally arrives. And, newsflash – there really is nowhere to go. You'll always take yourself with you – same head, same mind, same thoughts, same 'problems', same worldview – only to return to the same life you've unconsciously created. Travel for pleasure, travel for culture, travel for adventure and exploration, but to escape life? It's nonsensical. Life is not supposed to be difficult, you are not supposed to feel miserable and wish to escape *your* life. This is not how the human experience is meant to be.

Why not create a life you love so you'll not need to run away from it? I don't believe we set out to create a life of mediocrity. We didn't sit down with our best thinking and brainstorm how to exist in a perpetual state of discontentment and restlessness, it's not been our life's objective or our preferred destination – we've simply not known any better. No one's told us we have the option of living any other way. We didn't think/know this was possible.

An enjoyable, full life has been the exception rather than the rule; it falls outside of the status quo. We've been told that life on Earth is 'hard', it's competitive, you have to fight to win, work hard to get anywhere, roll with the punches, accept things the way they are, follow the rules, live within the system, operate between the lines... Life has been very logic-based up until now, but there's a whole other way of operating which comes from a very different part of us, a part that knows so much more than our brain could possibly comprehend, until it does...

The brain only knows what it knows and if we're playing the same record over and over again, thinking the same thoughts and doing the same things on repeat, we'll get exactly the same experiences and results. How could we not? We literally create and run a programme with the same settings. We're the washing machine – load up, hit the spin cycle, rinse and hang out to dry! We've set the wheels in motion and operate at the same level of consciousness on a daily basis.

It's not the fault of the brain, it's been behaving perfectly, doing exactly what's expected and what it's been programmed to do. It will do what it's asked; it's a masterful slave. We're thinking in a limited way and therefore 'getting' and receiving in a limited way – you get out what you put in and if you're thinking limitation, limitation is what you'll get. This is truly inhibiting for us. We have this incredible apparatus capable of magic and we're underutilizing it in the most disastrous of ways.

We're in desperate need of a software update, a full system overhaul that's downloaded deep within our cells, literally changing who we are from the inside out. We need to break out of habitual living, the outdated ways of being and experience life on a whole other level; if we'd just be willing to look in another direction and get out of our own way.

We've been operating within a very small radius, under a glass ceiling with a distorted view of reality and of what's possible. We're the goldfish in the goldfish bowl, swimming around and around and around in a circle (sound familiar?) seeing and doing the same things, taking the same route, totally (although I'm not sure how blissfully) unaware that there's a whole other world out there.

And again, unlike us, the fish with its three-second memory is content to continue in this way. We humans, however, have been blessed with awareness, with consciousness – we have the ability to remember, think and consider. We have a niggling feeling that something's 'off'. Something's not quite right about the picture we're seeing.

If we're honest, we know there's more and if we're willing to look that little bit deeper than where we've been looking thus far, we'll have a strong sense of our potential and it becomes deeply uncomfortable (and sometimes impossible) to ignore. There's a stunning vista to behold at the summit, but we're only taking a few steps up the mountain, if we attempt the climb at all.

This is no reason for self-judgement, however, for if we knew better, we'd do better and if you're reading this, you're obviously interested in the 'difference' – you're in the right place. And it therefore begs the question, how can I see what I have not already seen? Where should I place my gaze? How do I create a 'better' way of living?

Living From the Heart

There's a very different part of us, a space within us, that can provide us with a very different experience from that which we've been existing within thus far. It's a place of deep knowing and profound wisdom. A part of us that resides only a short distance from the head, although finding our way there can sometimes feel like the longest journey. That place is the heart.

We've not been giving this incredible organ the credit it deserves. Yes, we know it beats regularly and keeps us alive, that without it our blood would not pump throughout our body, that it provides us with the oxygen and nutrients we need, that it expands when we're in love and feels like it's breaking when we're in pain. We see images of hearts in society – they adorn the school books of teenage girls, are used to represent our strong feelings for one another and are linked with romantic love – but the heart is so much more than this.

The intelligence of the heart is astonishing and far superior to the brain when it comes to leading us in the right direction and taking us where we need to go. It has our best interests… well, at heart!

It is not just an organ that keeps us alive in the bodily sense, but it has the potential to allow us to blossom and flourish, living fully in life and feeling vital. It has the power to connect us with our (heartfelt) dreams and our grandest visions… if only we'd let it. To do this, there's an unlearning that needs to happen.

As I have spoken about previously, we have been so conditioned to operate from a head space, understanding that this is the preferred way of 'being', that we have severed the connection (literally 'cut ourselves off') from that which has the ability to truly lead us. The heart is our lifeline.

Through simply living in our current society, within our systems and outdated ideas, we have given too much credence to the intellect and, whilst intellectual knowledge can go some way in guiding us through life, it has its limitations. When we do not use the mind and heart in conjunction with one another, we miss out on so much (we miss a beat!); the heart and mind have to co-exist if we are to truly step into our power and realise our true potential.

The brain was always meant to serve us under the guidance of heart intelligence, but we have allowed it to become our master. It can only go some way in this role, it is not the best leader, for as I said, it only knows what it knows and therefore has limited perspective. It keeps us operating in familiar territory, regurgitating more of the same. The heart, however, sees the bigger picture and provides us with wisdom that is 'beyond' us.

Humanity has not operated from a heart space for a very long time, it's been eons since we as a collective have resided in this place – this way of existing has been forgotten, albeit temporarily, for this is a process of re-membering.

Many philosophies and Eastern wisdom traditions have extolled the virtues of the heart and pointed to the benefit of heartfelt living, rather than living solely from the intellect, which, as I have already stated, can only go so far in allowing us to live in alignment with our deeper truth and all that is possible for us, both personally and collectively. We can learn more 'stuff' and become 'cleverer', but you will continue to churn out more of the same if you rely solely on this one area of your being – it's two-dimensional. Heart living is a different matter altogether, for here lies the doorway to all knowledge and Truth, it knows much more than our intellects can fathom. Fundamentally, it is the gateway to profound universal wisdom that can lead you to your best life.

Many meditations will have us concentrate on and bring awareness to our breath, asking us to divert our focus to the heart space. Meditation, although used as a relaxation technique, is also used to bring us into alignment with our true Selves and open the door to deeper wisdom and Truth.

This is found not by allowing our awareness to focus

on our busy minds, which keeps us existing in a chaotic loop, but to 'drop down' into a space that allows us to breathe easy, relax and let go. This place takes us deeper, into a space that provides us with the answers to the questions of our lives as we listen, becoming able to hear the still, quiet voice within. Questions such as, who am I? What is it that I truly desire? What are my next steps? How may I best serve myself and others? What is life really all about? What does my best life look like?

The heart knows what the brain cannot yet comprehend. It is less about 'doing' and more about 'being' and because we have been taught and therefore come to understand that the way to success lies heavily within the 'doing' mode, we have forgotten that we can trust this place of 'being'.

We are uncomfortable here, we don't know how to be still, it has become alien/foreign territory; we feel as though we are wasting time, not being productive, that we are perhaps lazy. This is far from the truth, for the opposite is true. Research has shown the heart to be an access point to a source of wisdom and intelligence that we can call upon to live our lives with more balance, greater creativity and enhanced intuition. The answers to your life lie in this place of being – you can trust the wisdom of the heart – it knows.

Brain identification is an area I know all too well. For the majority of my life I moved through the 'system' and operated (for the most part) wholly identified with my mind, which brought me little or no joy. I also understood that to gain approval from my elders who prided themselves on intellectual knowledge, I needed to be 'clever', quick-witted and smart. This leap into my mind to become 'clever' (retain and regurgitate facts, figures, knowledge, etc) was unnatural to me, for my natural inclination was to consult my heart for guidance – feelings, visions, intuition and imagination. My creativity, genius and passion emanated from my heart.

As a child growing up in the western world in the 20th century, I quickly understood that the latter way of walking in the world was not 'right'. I was not going to gain the approval I was longing for or the required A grades if I stayed true to my nature and natural inclinations. There are thousands of rules we are told we must adhere to in order to survive – intuition, daydreaming, *being*, allowing, imagining, gazing, visioning, dreaming – wasn't (isn't?) supported in society's understanding of what makes an individual 'successful'; it hasn't been the correct or preferred way to operate. We therefore took a big leap out of our hearts and into our brains, thus cutting ties with our 'deeper knowing' and internal guidance system, which ultimately meant that we cut ties with our Selves.

There's a wonderful quote from Einstein, "We cannot solve our problems with the same (level of) thinking we used when we created them." It's time for a new way of living. If we continue trusting and living within the same ways of being and (outdated) operating systems, we'll continue to create more of the same – personally and collectively.

It's time to stop following the status quo. We're dreamers. Dreamers of our own dream. We have the potential to do anything, to create anything. We are meant to live a life of beauty and joy. We are meant to have loving, deeply connected and rewarding relationships. We are meant to be fully seen and experience deep intimacy with one another – it's crucial for the survival of human beings. We need this level of connection; the absence of which is why we see such high levels of heart disease in the world today – people are lonely, they're disconnected, they're not living their passions or their truth and their hearts are aching.

Within ingenious tribes and in places where people live in close communities, feeling loved and supported, this level of dis-ease does not exist. There have been actual studies on this phenomenon. It's been statistically documented that there are significantly lower (or no) cases of heart disease in the places where people feel supported and forge strong heart connections.

I ask you to imagine a world where we operate from this level of open-hearted connection to our Selves and to others. Imagine what life would be like if judgement of ourselves and others no longer made sense. What would be possible if we operated from a place of love instead of fear, abundance rather than scarcity, where compassion and open-hearted kindness were our default?

Ultimately, we are relational beings. We are not meant to be alone and lonely, isolated, confused and walking a solitary path. Our very nature is love and so it stands to reason, if we are to feel fully alive and create a world that we love being a part of, we need to open our hearts and keep the flow of love moving from us, to us. We need to live, as love. It is our essence. It is, ultimately, who we are.

Listen to your heart.

Just Do You

As I mentioned earlier, I understood from those around me (parents, school, peers) that I was naughty, difficult and a little bit odd. I felt and expressed a lot of anger, even throwing tantrums as a three-year-old that had me pass out. I was fighting against the world from a very young age. Again, I have often wondered what caused this level of rage to surge within me and I do not know for sure, but what I *do* know is that there wasn't and there isn't anything 'wrong' with me. I may have acted out due to something that felt displeasing to me (maybe I was frustrated and didn't have the words, maybe I sensed injustice and it was more than my little self could contain, maybe I needed more of a creative outlet…) but, regardless, my behaviour did not and does not constitute who I intrinsically am – it is not the sum total of me.

I am not difficult. I may have acted in a less than compliant manner, but I am not only or 'just' that, it does not make up the whole of me. I may have had an inclination towards and felt anger (a lot!) but I am not fundamentally an angry person. I may not have been as calm or compliant as those around me, but that does not mean I am defective or constitutionally strange or weird, it means I am me.

None of us are just one thing – there are many parts of us that make up the whole, we can show up in a myriad of different ways, with different identities, ever changing ideas, opinions and unlimited thoughts. We will not remain constant – it's just not possible.

We will all, in our lives, encounter most, if not all, of the vast array of feelings available to us on the spectrum of human emotion. We will 'feel' anger, 'feel' scared, 'feel' excited, confusion, grief, happiness, sadness… but none of these emotions constitutes WHO we are. We experience them. They are NOT us.

We are aware beings having a human experience, experiencing human emotion; we are not the emotion itself. We have the ability to bring these energetic vibrations to life, but they are not us. To label a person as intrinsically one of these emotions (even if they experience one particular emotion more regularly than another) is a mistake. And it's dangerous.

It seems that we have somewhat of an aversion to 'big' emotions, for overly passionate, expressive and vocal individuals. We don't know what to do with 'intense' personalities and strong emotional displays, viewing a show of anger or deep frustration as intense and potentially inappropriate. Highly demonstrative behaviour can take us aback as we find it somewhat unsettling and we tend to shy away, not wanting to look or feel the impact this has on us; it falls outside of the box of what is considered appropriate and we simply do not know how to provide the space for another to be in this feeling state. We do not know how to contain their strong emotion, for we cannot hold ourselves in this place. Why are our emotions and feelings only acceptable when they're packaged neatly and presented with decorum?

It is highly possible that if ADHD had been a popular diagnosis when I was growing up, I could have become another statistic. Highly likely. It makes sense that if we're expecting each individual to be exactly the same as the last, fitting into a specific mould like products passing through a factory line, anything that falls outside of the specifications will, of course, be deemed 'wrong' or 'faulty'. It will find itself cast aside, not quite making the grade, or we may attempt to 'fix' it.

Understandably, there is no room for error when meeting the demands of the consumer market – cars, machinery, packaged food for the supermarket or the latest 'must-have' designer handbag follow specifications, but we are not products or produce moving along a factory line, we were not made to be the same. The world needs 'difference'. The world needs creatives – artists, poets, writers, dancers and magicians. It is understandable that those whose awareness is focused in the creative realm will be unable to concentrate on 'facts', sit cross-legged, straight backed, stock-still or facing forward attentively as they attempt to learn how to 'work things out' and ingest information that truly makes no sense to them. Information that will be useless to the mind of the being who was brought to this Earth to splash colour wherever they go, thus making this world brighter.

G-d/universal energy does not make mistakes and it's absurd to suggest that the divine intelligence that created the galaxies and all of the universes, slipped up when it came to creating human beings, in any guise. Please consider this – who has the right to set the benchmark and pronounce what is 'right'? Who has the authority to question the creative process and find it (a being) lacking? When you truly consider this, it's astounding that anyone (individual or system) has the authority to apply a blanket rule for 'all' and decide what is 'right' for an entire species. What gives anyone carte blanche to judge another? We would do well to contemplate this and question the status quo.

It begs the questions, why is society so concerned with downplaying the human race, suggesting we become carbon copies of each other, replicas of the next, following the same route in life? Why have we been led to believe it is preferable to become the 'same' as everybody else?

If you lived a life meditating on a mountain top, who's to say that this is not a life well lived? Who says it's any less successful or worthy than the billionaire property developer or the individual who's 'succeeded' in creating a chain of world-renowned coffee establishments? Who on earth set the benchmark anyway? Incidentally, there are some who would propose that the former meditation option qualifies as more of a 'success' and is fundamentally more important and kinder to planet Earth. Something to consider.

Differences should be celebrated, not censored. What a boring and uninteresting world this would be if we were all identical. It is our differences that make us interesting, creating diversity, weaving this wonderful and colourful tapestry of life. It's the things that tell us apart that make us unique, special, wonderful, interesting and really rather magical! Our differences are the gifts we have been given to offer into this world and we MUST be allowed to express them and to share them. And what is 'normal' anyway? There's no such thing.

With this divine perfection in mind, how absurd does it then seem that we reach a conclusion that we are flawed and attempt to 'fix' ourselves by swallowing tiny little pills in order to right this perceived wrong – it's nonsensical. I am not suggesting that sometimes, when it truly becomes that dark for an individual, a little medication in a bid to part the clouds wouldn't be somewhat beneficial (for the short-term), but continually suppressing emotion and therefore dumbing down what is in actual fact the beauty of an individual and the wonder of the human experience, makes absolutely no sense.

If we look back at history, some of the most exquisite minds belonged to those who were believed to be odd, crazy and a little bit wacko. There's some mind-bending documentation to be found on the behaviour of some of these great minds and geniuses in both their professional and personal lives, (a proportion of which caused me to raise an eyebrow or two!), but thank G-d for these change makers, for they have contributed to and blessed this world in a myriad of ways.

As Arthur Schopenhauer, the great German philosopher said, "Genius and madness have something in common: both live in a world that is different from that which exists for everyone else." And indeed, it was Steve Jobs who said, "Creation is messy. You want genius, you get madness; two sides of the same coin."

Normal does, as normal is, 'conforming to a standard; usual, typical, or expected'… who's excited by that?!

Let's Go Back

Now, let's go back once again to childhood, to a time before an individual had been assessed and affixed with a label of 'depressed, ADHD, crazy or mentally unwell'. Right back before we felt a need to fix ourselves with prescription drugs, moving further and further away from our true nature.

Enter again the word nurture. To my mind, truly understanding a child and having a heartfelt desire to enter into a child's world (intimacy – into-me-you-see) makes the difference that will make all the difference. We need to penetrate the surface and become interested in understanding another's reality – find out what's going on for that individual and act accordingly. I am sure if I had conscious adults around me growing up (society, parents, teachers, community) – and note I say conscious (aware of what I was feeling and needing) and not simply loving (by rote) – most or all of what I struggled with would not have come to pass.

Our mental health comes from love, nurturing, genuine interest in coming to KNOW the individual in 'truth' (which is forever changing) and creating an environment that allows for growth, an environment that serves the highest good and the full flourishing of the particular individual. As I say, it will differ from person to person and we therefore need to be aware and conscious of what we're seeing, feeling and noticing.

How best we 'take care of' something or someone is crucial. The actual meaning of this word says it all. Care, 'the provision of what is necessary for the health, welfare, maintenance, and protection of someone or something' and 'serious attention or consideration applied to doing something correctly or to avoid damage or risk.' 'Serious attention… to avoid damage or risk.' Says it all, really.

Deeply listening to what feels right and true (for ourselves and for another) and honouring our wisdom is critical. We must be supported in shining our own individual light. Humanity and, indeed the world, benefit when we show up like this. We need acceptance, positive mirroring and unconditional love. We need to be heard, seen and understood. These ways of relational connection lead to a healthy sense of self, a strong identity and crucial self-confidence. We need to know that we are perfect within our imperfections. We are as G-d intended.

I am not suggesting we be allowed to run ragged with no guidelines, causing havoc and acting out our strong emotions on others. We need to learn what it means to be a 'good' human being. We need to learn to treat others with love, respect, compassion and be provided with a 'good' and strong foundation for living life, a foundation that we can extend upwards and outwards and be built upon as we move through our lives, but there's a fine line between guiding a child in the right direction and clipping their wings.

It's a little like the over-bred chickens in the previous chapter. By distorting their shape and over-breeding, forcing unnatural growth at an increased rate, you will still receive the goods (eggs and meat), but the animal will become unhappy, stressed and deformed.

We all need to be allowed to develop and flourish naturally, according to the Divine Plan. Any forcing or pushing will have detrimental effects. We need to be pointed in the 'right' direction and shown the way, whilst being given the room we need to grow and to express ourselves. We must be allowed to speak, make choices, manoeuvre and change direction as time moves on – rigidity and hard and fast rules will help no one. We must be allowed to bend or we will break.

Maybe a child needs a new environment; maybe the education he/she is receiving is too intellectually based and they're needing more of a creative environment and outlet; maybe there's been a miscommunication and the child has been silently but negatively impacted, drawing incorrect conclusions about themselves or a situation; maybe there's been a misunderstanding (verbal or non-verbal) and decisions are being based on limited or inconclusive information; maybe the child needs more or less space; maybe there is a need for a change in routine. Maybe they're struggling and cannot find the courage to speak or the words to express this, it may become obvious that an activity is no longer benefiting them. There are many things that come to light from deep listening and genuine interest and if these findings are ignored, they could have detrimental effects.

We take for granted that what we're seeing and experiencing is the same for everyone else around us. But this is not the case. Each of us is filtering the outside world through our internal lens.

If you interview witnesses of a car crash or at a crime scene, they will each have a different interpretation of the same thing. Some details will correlate, but there will be many discrepancies. It is important to know and understand that we all live in a different experience of the same thing – we each have our very own individual internal worlds. We are all inhabiting the same world, Earth, but we each live in our own separate realities. We all come from the same place, but we see and experience life differently.

Like fingers on a hand and waves in the sea. Each finger is part of and makes up a hand, but will look and operate slightly differently from its neighbour and will have a different relationship to what the hand is holding. So too is each and every wave individual and also a part of the sea itself. Each wave will rise and fall independently from the next, differing in appearance and shape, but they all originate from the same place and are made of the same substance, water. All are the same and all are different. And just like the waves, we too will rise from and fall back into the whole, into the sea of life, but whilst we are here, we must celebrate and honour our differences. I often think how truly shocking it would be if we were each given the opportunity to look through the eyes of another – I bet we wouldn't recognise the world we live in.

So, too, do children live in their own worlds. Indeed, just by the very nature of being a child they are already living in a world that is poles apart from the adult; the eyes of a child perceive a vastly different reality than those already grown. Children, just like adults, can misinterpret what is taking place around them and misread the interactions and reactions of those in their life and find themselves to blame. But with much less experience and therefore ability to discern, it does not take much for a child to conclude that the anger or upset of a parent, a pairing off of friends at school or a disappointment in an expectation is something to do with them – that they're not good enough, are somehow at fault or responsible for 'it'. Even as adults we slip into this misunderstanding more often than is necessary.

The child's false assumptions could be made right and ironed out if the practice to voice their experiences was commonplace for them. If the culture was such that the child felt invited to share in a safe and nurturing space, all manner of misinterpretations would be rectified. When our words are met by an understanding ear and an open heart, we are provided with an opportunity to dispel any misperceptions or misunderstandings.

Untruths

Let me expand a little with regard to meaning-making.

I remember many instances over the years when a situation took place and, within that occurrence, I concluded something about (my) life or who I fundamentally was as an individual. Something occurs (an exchange, someone's misplaced anger, a communication malfunction, the absence of something or someone, a change in plans) and I reach a conclusion that's based on my interpretation formed through the lens of my understanding. 'She's shouting because I'm naughty', 'he didn't show up because I'm unlovable/unimportant/not good enough', 'he's angry because I always spoil things', 'they changed the plans so I couldn't join them', 'I don't understand what's being said, therefore I'm not clever enough'.

These meanings and conclusions become beliefs, albeit incorrect ones and, if not reconciled, they become the (our) truth, cemented in our beings, forming who we believe ourselves to be as an individual and in relation to others. They are the invisible limitations and glass ceilings in our lives. They become the lens through which we view the world. We literally live inside of them and they feel 'real'. We wear them like an overcoat.

If I go back to the memory I have of my sister receiving a gift on my birthday, I made reference to me reaching a conclusion that my sister was special, she was better than me… I wasn't as good as her. As she'd been given the coveted gift, I also deduced she was more important than me and most definitely preferred. When I recognised that I'd never been given a gift from the neighbour on my sister's birthday I felt crestfallen, unseen and irrelevant – it crushed me.

This could be painful for anyone, but as a child who cannot make any logical sense and is totally unable to articulate the feelings (instead, swallowing down the hurt and locking it inside), it's a disaster. The experience occurs, the hurt is felt, the meaning is made and the information is locked into our systems. If we are unable to make any other sense, all avenues will point to the same place; in this instance, 'I'm not good enough'.

This is a moment I have wondered about. Perhaps if the culture was to share and speak, I would have felt I had permission and space to give voice to my emotions, knowing I'd be heard and taken seriously. My upset may have been alleviated and the situation would have passed without incident. Perhaps if I hadn't thought I would somehow be made wrong and have my 'reality' dismissed with a 'don't be silly, Emma', 'here we go again' or 'don't you want your sister to have anything?', impatience or a variation on this theme, I would have shared my internal experience, the truth of the situation would have been explained and the meaning I made would have evaporated.

In this instance, that was not to be the case and so I went about my life with a little more evidence to water the seeds of 'I'm not good enough/as good as' and 'I never get what I want'.

And the thing is this; these belief systems are always looking for evidence to support themselves. We can find ourselves honing in on almost imperceptible occurrences to prove ourselves right. Someone doesn't see us and is engrossed in their own thinking and we conclude, 'she's ignoring me'; a good-looking guy doesn't make eye contact, 'I'm unattractive'; a friend forgets to reply to a message, 'she's annoyed with me/doesn't want to know me anymore' or someone glances in our direction to ensure they can't be overheard, 'they're talking about me'. The list is endless.

The most innocent of situations can look like a conspiracy or attack. The seeds of these beliefs we hold about ourselves grow stronger and stronger as we water them with more and more perceived evidence as time moves on. These strong belief systems operating 'in the background' then become a worldview, a way of believing that there's me, the world, and the fact that 'I don't get what I want', or any other variation of a theme.

These belief systems are the stories we tell ourselves to define our personal sense of reality, they are the narratives of our lives – we *believe* them and we therefore make them a reality. It is through this system, this mechanism, that we 'make sense of' and see the world around us, expecting and anticipating, in my case, inevitable disappointment and evidence that 'I'm not good enough' and 'I never get what I want', feeling as though life somehow skipped over and forgot me.

The part of me that did not feel good enough or 'as good as' became another extension of who I was, as real to me as the fingers that extend from my hands – these beliefs, like my fingers, were a part of me. Another individual will be filtering life through a completely different lens.

Thing is, these belief systems do not live solely in the head. These falsities/woundings can actually be felt in the body. They're visceral. We literally live INSIDE of them when we're feeling and experiencing them. When we're triggered into one of these (through an interaction, situation and therefore an internal narrative/thought) we will see the evidence to support our 'case' and feel a bodily response to this.

For instance, as I've alluded to, a friend not calling me could provoke a train of thought within me that has me deduce that perhaps they no longer want to be my friend, which in turn creates anxiety and fear within me and a sense of panic that runs through my body, causing me to live inside of this experience for as long as I hold on to the thought.

These beliefs are not the 'all' of us, they never are

and never have been, but they run in the background and under the surface and, as I say, we will always find evidence to support them, indeed, we are looking out for it. For me, 'I never get what I want' was a foregone conclusion – and I started expecting it. So life, being incredibly supportive of whatever we expect to find, gave me exactly what I wanted, more evidence of 'I'm not as good as', 'I never get what I want' and other variations. Throughout my life I have seen this over and over again (although it took years for me to see myself as the creator of these experiences).

For instance, in your belief that you are inarticulate, you may attempt to speak and find yourself stuttering or stumbling as your words stick in your throat, you may lose the thread of your sentence or find your voice muted by a louder individual. In your belief that you're unattractive to the opposite (or same) sex, you'll perhaps not be noticed by the guy or girl you've got your eye on, the friend you're with will attract more attention than you and you'll feel skipped over and unseen or you'll home in on someone emotionally unavailable. When deeming yourself not smart enough, you may be involved in a highbrow conversation and find yourself lacking – and all of this (and more) because this is precisely the kind of evidence you're looking for to support your belief system. It's simply what you're expecting.

Ever wanted to buy a new car? I bet you saw the make and model you were interested in everywhere once you'd set your attention on it. It's the same with a new word –

once it's in your mind, you'll hear it again and again. It's not that these things weren't there before; it's just that your antenna wasn't programmed to spot it - it was off your radar. It wasn't in your awareness and you weren't actively seeking it out, unconsciously or otherwise.

What we believe to be true will show up everywhere in our lives – it's been programmed into our brains. In a situation where many things are taking place, you will home in on the one thing you've got your radio tuned into. You're literally a beacon sending out signals to the Universe. You're incredibly powerful as a creator and super sensitive to that which you believe – you're walking Velcro, attracting the fluff of your beliefs!

You'll want to get conscious of the lens you're looking through if you'd like your experience of life to change. 'I'm never part of the cool set', 'people are going to leave me', 'I'm not good enough', 'I'll never be a success', 'you can't trust people – they always let you down', 'if they see the real me they'll leave', 'I can't speak my truth', 'I'm too animated and passionate', 'I'm aggressive', 'I'm difficult', 'I always cause problems', 'the world is a scary place' – the list is as long as your imagination.

I could have given you a list as long as my arm as proof to support my 'case'. I see now, that with a different lens, I would've viewed my 'evidence' in a completely different way. In fact, I may have seen absolutely nothing at all if my radar wasn't constantly seeking the same target.

Not only do we start to see our false beliefs projected

back to us in the world, but we also play up to them within ourselves for we have come to believe the labels hold some truth. They become thought patterns that literally stick and become part of our personality and we find ourselves as actors in our own movie, adhering to the script in our minds, playing it out, entertaining our audience and giving them exactly what they have come to expect.

I was forever rearranging the parts to make them fit my story – we are all doing this more regularly than we'd care to believe. If I hadn't used my magnifying glass to detect potential cracks, I could have enjoyed the bigger picture as a whole. I would not have experienced 'innocent' situations in a way that had me feel wretched. We get exactly what we expect.

For instance, we know that I grew up feeling awkward, unattractive and uncomfortable in my own skin. I looked outside of myself and found my close friends to be prettier than me, more popular, with better clothes and more confidence. I would experience my friends attracting the boys I thought were cute, whom I wished would notice me. It seemed the 'cool' boys that I put on a pedestal simply overlooked me and headed straight for my peers.

I wonder what I would have seen had my radar not been on the lookout to gather evidence that I was low on the pecking order. Maybe 'lack' would have been absent and I would have noticed all the boys who *were* scrambling to get close to me – for they were there, I had simply overlooked them in my disappointment that 'I never get what I want'. I set myself up for disappointment by focusing on the individuals that weren't 'right' for me so I could experience rejection, move into my feeling state of 'less than' and reaffirm my reality. I literally couldn't see the 'other' boys, blinded as I was in my upset.

I wonder how many opportunities I missed whilst my head was turned in another direction, a direction that supported my downfall rather than my evolution. And because these dialogues we hold in our heads are, for the most part, invisible and unconscious, we don't even know we're entertaining them.

These conclusions we arrive at either 'innocently' or from the messages we receive from the outside world either overtly or covertly, lead us to believe we are somehow broken and cause much of the pain and suffering we see in our world today. Many people are walking around with a warped view of themselves and a very limited worldview.

We have glass ceilings on our lives, negative self-talk playing on a loop and a sense of grief for the part of us we've swallowed whole, together with a deep sense of sadness that we are not being fully met, seen and accepted (by peers, friends, spouses, family, siblings, colleagues, etc) for who we truly are – although this 'not being seen' can only be rectified when we see and accept ourselves.

Something happens to us when we're reined in, unconsciously or otherwise. This suppression of our true nature has us exist in the world as a much smaller version of ourselves than is possible, unable to truly express who we are. We operate at a lower frequency, hiding and concealing the 'real' us, understanding that we somehow need to be different in order to be accepted. We close ourselves down in judgement of ourselves, further dimming our light and denying the truth of who we are.

This causes conflict (dis-ease) within an individual. On the surface we feel one way and at a deeper level, we know something profoundly and fundamentally different – namely that there's a grander version of ourselves buried underneath and behind the negative self-talk, the distorted sense of self and our limited worldview. We're playing a game of make-believe and not in a positive way. Instead of allowing ourselves to be-come our true Selves, we're adhering to a finite script, creating and experiencing limitation, lack and the shrinking of our potential.

The irony is, the ways in which we have been investing in staying 'safe' are actually the things that are killing us. It is a false sense of security and, in actuality, it keeps us stuck. This swallowing down of our truth and hiding away, whatever the situation, literally stunts our growth and on an emotional level it lessens our capacity for deep, authentic connection with so much of our energy being invested in keeping up a pretence – upholding a lie is exhausting. The face we present to the world is a mask, which hides our truth and causes a dumbing down of our potential.

Our comfort zones are the things that strangle us, they are the doorways to addiction/controlled and controlling behaviour, for we need some kind of outlet, some way to relieve the stress of holding it all together and the pain of denying our true selves. We need a way 'out'.

You Are Only Ever Feeling Your Thinking

Life is about choices. We pave our path with the decisions we make – who we are (how we show up in life) and what we do (our actions); who do I want to be in the world and what actions do I wish to take in service of that vision? We can make decisions consciously, with awareness and discernment, or unconsciously; by rote, robotically and somewhat automatically, functioning on automatic pilot. The former will enable life to open up to and for you, allowing you to expand, blossom and bloom; the latter will keep you stuck on your treadmill and in the current hell (on whatever level that is for you) of your own making.

But there's something important to know before this, before decision making comes into play – we need to understand how life is happening. We need to understand who we are in the face of life, what is our relationship to and with it? How does this relationship impact us? How is our experience happening? What constitutes our reality? What is true (to be trusted) and where should we err on the side of caution with regard to what we perceive to be 'fact'? What makes us think that our identity and current life situations are static and immovable? How can we trust which of the problems we're focusing on requires attention and action and which, if left alone, will simply disappear?

In order to answer any of these questions, let's consider how the human experience occurs and what constitutes (our) 'reality'. Let's consider the role of thought in our lives.

I would suggest that our ability to discern that we are even on this Earth, conscious and aware, is through our thought process, that is, the power of thought. If we weren't thinking, we'd be flatlining. You'd have no concept of anything, not the you that you 'think' yourself to be, no concept of your life/planet Earth/your friends/family... quite simply, they'd be nothing – not that you would even know this because there'd be no thought, there'd be no you!

Consider how you even know you're reading these words? How are they coming alive for you? How are you seeing, hearing and perceiving them? The words are in front of your eyes for sure, but they are being brought to life through your thinking process. And this is the case with everything outside of yourself – you will be 'lighting up' any external situation through the power of your thinking. How else do you receive knowledge of something 'out there' if not through this process of thought? How else could you be receiving it?

If we are filtering everything through our thinking, I will suggest that absolutely no experience you have outside of yourself has the ability to cause a reaction within you.

Nothing external to you can impact you emotionally. That is, no situation can cause you to feel any specific way; no person, circumstance, movie, holiday, family dynamic, etc. Every situation in life (everything 'out there') is neutral but for your thinking about 'it'.

How then are we impacted by the external situations in our life? We will feel about a situation the exact way in which we think about it. Thoughts that have a positive connotation for us will make us feel 'good' and thoughts that have a negative connotation will create the opposite experience. 'I like her, I'm enjoying this, that's a kind gesture, this is tasty, this is my favourite place, the food here is exquisite, we got the best seat in the house, I love my outfit', etc, will bring about pleasing and enjoyable experiences. Whereas 'it's too noisy in here, she's being so difficult, this is boring, this isn't what I ordered, I miss her so much, I feel really uncomfortable in these jeans, they're talking about me, you never listen to me', will create a less than pleasing experience for you as you filter the external situation though your judgemental thinking (namely, it's not right/not fair, etc) and have that experience within your being. You feel your thinking.

There is simply no other way of having any experience here on Earth, but through thought itself, at least, this is the case for us humans, as we currently know ourselves to be in this dimension in the 21st century! If you're not thinking, you're not experiencing and if you are thinking, you will experience exactly what it is that you're thinking about in each and every moment. It's as simple as that. Thought creates reality. The end!

So, if someone has 'upset you', you will know that it's the thinking you're running through your mind about the situation that is the cause of your upset. You will feel the charge of that thinking and feel the impact emotionally and even, perhaps, bodily. But, when we choose to think differently about said upsetting situation (perhaps, 'gosh, they must have been in a terrible state to be so rude to me, I wonder what's troubling them?' Or 'people act so crazy sometimes, shame for her/him'), we'll change our experience of it. In the above instances, concern for another or bewilderment with regard to the human condition, rather than upset on the back of feeling personally attacked. When our focus and thinking changes, the 'problem' will change or may even cease to exist. As Wayne Dyer says, "When you change the way you look at things, the things you look at will change."

If you are continually pulling to mind the altercation you had in traffic on your way to work, mulling it over, focusing on it and 'lighting it up' over and over again, you will continue to re-experience the event in your mind, which ultimately, will be your reality in the moment and therefore, your experience. How can you have any other experience apart from that which you are thinking about? It's not possible to be fully immersed in the re-enactment of the morning's argument (or whatever else you're holding in your thoughts at any given moment) and have any other experience bar the one you're thinking about. You experience whatever it is that you hold in your thoughts. Period.

And what you focus on grows, so how long 'something' sticks around looking like it warrants attention (and possible action), will be in direct proportion to the amount of time that you spend looking at it – that is, holding it in your mind. So, when some situation looks like it's running on a loop and you can't 'get rid of it', I would suggest that it is, in actuality, the amount of time you're in your thinking about said situation and not the situation itself that's causing the insanity! For, if you're not thinking about it, it simply isn't there – it's not 'alive', it doesn't exist.

For instance, if you see a commercial advertising a new brand of crisps or you flip the station to a cookery programme, you may find yourself 'suddenly' feeling peckish as your thoughts are immediately directed towards food, potentially causing your brain to conjure up which goodies are currently in your larder. It doesn't matter that two seconds previously you were blissfully satisfied and food was the last thing on your mind.

With the thought of food now in your mind and with your focused attention on it, giving it more and more of your energy – 'mmm, that looks tasty! I wonder what's in the cupboard' – you bring it fully into your awareness, 'lighting it up' and making it your experience in the moment. With your thinking, you literally create the feeling of hunger and if you jump on this train of thought and action it, you'll be off! You may get up from where you're sitting and move towards the fridge or cupboard and promptly scrounge around for something to satisfy this newly found hunger.

This whole scenario could take only seconds and you may find yourself baffled as to why you're munching your way through a bag of potato chips on an already full stomach, having felt somewhat powerless as the urge to forage for food overtook you. But, make no mistake; we make a choice in the moment, even if it is unconscious and therefore invisible.

This whole thought-to-action process happens at record speed and, although lightning quick and somewhat imperceptible, we are always making a choice – it's just that up until now, it's gone unnoticed as we have been slaves to our thinking and on automatic to that which runs through our minds. It is up to us to make the invisible visible, free ourselves from victimhood and move into a place of empowerment and conscious choice. We do this when we become interested in understanding how this human operating system (our experience) works.

Now, what would happen if the phone rang as you were moving towards the cupboard in your quest for nourishment and, on answering, your friend imparts some juicy information to you, which has you stop in your tracks as you're gripped to hear more? You will find yourself pulled into this new experience and conversation and you may even forget that you were halfway to the fridge to engage in a snack attack. On hanging up the phone, you find (if you even remember to reference it again) that your prior experience of hunger simply vanished into thin air and the possible follow-on scenario of feeding this (perceived) hunger simply did not come to pass, you did not make it a reality.

On the back of 'forgetting' this hunger urge and the drive towards food due to your attention being diverted, the feeding frenzy did not materialise, it vanished with the dissipation of the thought. What had become your compelling experience only moments ago recedes into nothingness as your attention is pulled elsewhere and, therefore, you are in an entirely different experience which then becomes your reality. So, is life creating our reality somewhere 'out there' or are we creating our lives based on where we focus our energy and attention and with the choices we make?

This is truly fascinating, don't you think? That life is nothing but an experience of thought and action-in-the-moment. Nothing else. Whichever thoughts you follow will determine the experience you have – it will become your reality. At any moment you can change the direction of your thinking and therefore the direction (and experience) of your life. This is incredibly freeing and more than a little exciting, I'm sure you'll agree!

And if this is true, if thought really does create our experience and we only see what we are focusing on and thinking about and this whole human experience is truly happening through our thinking process, then that's really rather wonderful news as we can no longer point outside of ourselves to the cause of our upset.

Where your attention goes, your energy flows. Wherever you place your focus will become your experience/reality. You will illuminate anything that you look at, for it is in the looking that you give it life. How much life it has, will depend on how long you look at it and hold it in your attention. You will only compound something if you chew on it and mull it over – adding thought on top of thought on top of thought… And then, you're in a thought storm!

And it doesn't matter how strong a situation appears to be for you, no matter how compelling and 'huge' it is, when you divert your attention and focus, the thing or situation will cease to exist. It will be nowhere to be found and you'll be in an alternative experience. For remember, we create our experience in the moment and the only experience we can know is our own, so if you're not thinking about something, where is it? If you're not holding it in your mind, does it even exist?

The answer is no… not until you remember and think about it again, at which point, you will find yourself back in your experience – in the case I've pointed to above – hunger – and on 'actioning' the thought, a drive towards food. Life is always coming to you via your thinking and again, if you're not thinking about something, it has no life – it's simply not there. It will not exist in your reality.

Knowing this will give you fundamental and long-lasting change in what constitutes your experience of reality, namely, how you feel day-to-day in your life and even how you view yourself. This shift in your level of understanding, becoming aware and conscious of how the human experience is playing out, is your best bet for living a life you love.

This understanding gives you choice. Where once you lived as an unconscious collaborator/a slave to the thinking that entered your mind, like a puppet on a string, you can now move into conscious collaboration as you become aware of 'the system' and understand the nature of thought. It sticks around when you look at it and it's nowhere to be found when you refuse to pay it attention. This understanding will allow you to sever those puppet strings and become conscious of the choice that is *always* available to you. No matter what.

I have seen this time and time again in my life. Whether it be something someone has done 'to' me, a worry thought that has materialised in my mind gathering momentum and creating anxiety, a lens through which I view life as 'true', a belief system, an addictive process, a way I see myself – anything that has my focus. The second I divert my attention and stop giving it energy is the second it ceases to exist for me.

It's so simple that it's hard for us humans to get our heads around it – we like a struggle! Funny that as it's our head (our thinking) that got us into our current dramas in the first place, so it makes sense that it's our head (our current level of thinking) that's going to be the one thing that stands in the way of us seeing through the illusion of thought. Again, as Einstein said, "We cannot solve our problems with the same level of thinking we used to create them."

The head/ego mind will attempt to block our understanding of the truth of the human experience in its bid to stay alive and have us operate within 'the known', keeping us 'safe'. It will attempt to intellectualise and make rational sense of this understanding, creating even more thought. We need a deeper level of 'seeing', a seeing that is beyond thought and the thinking mind, which can only happen when we stop 'trying' so hard to understand something.

The trick is to take the head out of it. We need to see this new way of viewing the world on another level. We have spent our lives believing that life works in a certain way, namely, that life happens 'to' us. We are now being invited to consider the opposite – that life is happening 'through' us, inside out. We create our experience.

Since we were youngsters, we have been led to believe that something outside of ourselves can affect us – 'you've hurt her feelings', 'he made her smile', 'a cup of tea will make you feel better' – and we're constantly looking through a lens that has us at the mercy of an outside influence. And it continues throughout life – 'she was mean to me', 'he upset me', 'that movie really cheered me up', 'I'm so upset

I lost that job', 'I need a holiday', and on and on. We're constantly giving credit to outside influences as being the cause of our feeling state.

Again, it is never the external situation that causes our upset or happiness – it is our thinking of and our association with the situation at hand that is giving us our experience. Yes, the movie may have cheered you up, but only because you found your viewing choice pleasing and your experience ('cheered up') was determined by this level of 'pleasure' thinking. Your thinking changed and so, therefore, your reality changed. Simply, life is not happening in the way we've been 'thinking' it's been happening. Nothing outside of us can impact us and determine our feeling state in and of itself.

If we'd only relax our grip and our gaze, we'd fall into an altogether different space and a totally different experience of the very same life we're living. We've spent our whole existence in this lifetime using our minds to 'work life out' – micromanaging, judging, over-analysing and intellectualising. We've been playing the game of life, but we've not really understood the rules. We've never been told that we don't need to be so involved in the 'unfoldment' of our lives; we didn't know that it's not up to us.

We trust and accept that the intelligence that created us in the first place can proficiently manage the intricate workings of the body (I've never had to supervise my digestive system – well, maybe a little in my case!), but we feel we can't trust it when it comes to the day-to-day occurrences of our lives. We do not think that this same intelligence can help us 'in the world' in the same way it runs our body. We haven't trusted that if we simply relax and surrender into the great unknown (let go of our thinking), everything we need in the moment will come to pass.

Your body will tell you when you're hungry, when you need to pee, cough, swallow and breathe. This same intelligence/wisdom will most certainly tell you the right things to say and do in any given moment of your life or the best direction/place to go, or not as the case may be. You haven't known or trusted this up until now because it's been outside of your lived experience, you haven't been shown how the operating system works. We need to *listen*. Life has always been prompting us, but we've been tuned out of its radio frequency, listening instead to station me, me, me!

The irony is this, the more we 'try' to push and control, the harder life will feel, the more complicated it gets and the more stressed we feel. But, when we stop, when we surrender and trust that any idea, solution or helpful thought will pop in when the time is right, the more we can relax into life and live in a state of flow, enjoying the journey. We can live in a state of grace.

Have absolutely no doubt that the intelligence that created life itself, the human biology and the intricacies of the Universe, will have absolutely no trouble in working out the best route for you to take in your own life and the best way for you to get there. The quieter and more surrendered you are, the more you will hear the internal promptings that provide you with everything you need in any given moment. Maybe you're pulled to a certain place, feel called to play a musical instrument, dance or paint – maybe it's time to enrol on that course or visit that healer, to stay alone or be in company... who knows what will ring true for you. Trust the promptings, follow your heart – go with what feels 'right'. Only you will know what your 'right' feels like, but you need to start listening in order to ascertain your yes and your no and exactly how that little knowing feels, for you.

How Does the 'System' Work?

This 'new' understanding (this inside-out way of viewing life) cannot simply be understood with the intellect, it needs to make sense on a bodily level, like knowing what a mango tastes like or feeling what it's like to submerge yourself in water. You have to taste the mango and dive into the water to understand the sensation; we cannot simply talk about and intellectualise the taste of a foodstuff or the feeling of submersion in a bid for understanding and 'knowing', we have to experience it for ourselves.

The same is true when it comes to understanding that we are creating our reality through thought, we need to actually 'see' it for ourselves. And how do we do this? First off, we need to be interested – get curious, start questioning and look in a different direction. In fact, even knowing there's a different direction to look in is incredibly helpful – it's a start.

You want to be listening with a quiet mind, listening to what's in-between and under the thoughts, become an observer. At least now you see there's somewhere else to go, that is, apart from the hamster wheel we've been peddling on thus far! There's light at the end of the tunnel. Be open to see how thoughts pop into your mind unannounced, creating a sensation within your body and a feeling state as they come with their own charge, energy and vibration. See if you can correlate your mood or feelings to the thinking you may have been holding in your mind; wonder what you were thinking the moment before you became angry or upset, happy or excited. Be interested to see how the system is working.

Each one of us makes up a part of the whole – we're all part of the web of life. There is an intelligence that far surpasses our imagination; an intelligence that created planet Earth, the galaxies, the trees, the natural world and all the wonders you see around you. This intelligence supports the change of seasons, the process of metamorphosis, allowing a caterpillar to change its form into a butterfly. This intelligence creates the miracle of life, from conception to birth to death. This intelligence makes your heart beat, your lungs breathe, your digestive system take what it needs and dispel what's left over. This intelligence created you.

Each one of us has been given the gift of life/the gift of consciousness. We are conscious beings, we're aware… of ourselves and of the world around us. This awareness means we have the ability to witness. This awareness is our essence – who we truly are… pure consciousness.

To become aware of our existence, we were given the gift of thought, which gives us the ability to experience life. A genius system that allows us to consider ourselves, people and the outside world. We were given the senses – taste, touch, smell, sight and sound – as a feedback loop from external to internal. These senses provide us with an experience of what we come upon – the taste of the food we ingest, the feel of the bark of a tree, the beauty of a sunset or the stars at night, the sound of songbird, a hug, our family/friends/colleagues – all of which are filtered through and felt by us through the power of thought. We are all filtering the 'outside' through our preconceived ideas/thinking (beliefs, judgements, past experiences) and our level of consciousness in the moment. Each one of us on Earth is doing this all of the time, every human being is processing life in the same way.

We have free will and it is up to us how we wish to filter the external into the internal, thus creating and determining our experience in any moment. And in using our free will, we can also change our thinking and therefore change our experience and ultimately, our reality.

For it is all self-created. We are the creators of our experience. We are aware beings moving through life, lighting up and bringing to life whatever we look at, think about and focus on. Thought creates reality. And because we are all filtering our experiences through our minds (expectations, beliefs, judgements, etc), no one person will be having the same experience of the same thing. For as I have explained, our own personal life experiences have given us all very different lenses and filters to peer through. There is no constant, no blanket rule. Nothing is perceived in just one way – each person, situation, sunset, taste of each meal will be experienced differently from person to person.

Think about how many things are happening 'to' you on any one given day, things you feel angry or happy about, things you feel ambivalent about, things you do and do not enjoy doing. You are having experiences ALL the time and if you look around you at a time when you are having a particular experience, or check in with the people you're with at any given moment, you may be surprised to find that everyone is having a completely (or somewhat) different experience of the same thing, or will have absolutely no awareness of it at all.

This may vary only slightly or your reality in a moment could be poles apart from your neighbour. You may find that what feels 'huge' or important to you or that which is 'giving' you a strong reaction and seems to negatively (or positively) impact you in the moment is of no consequence to the person sitting next to you, as they remain oblivious or they have an entirely different reaction or response to the same thing. Every thinking individual is having a very independent and personal experience – we all live in separate realities.

As I write about this phenomenon, I have just had an experience of this. I am sitting in a café, writing. I am here because I expected it to be quiet, allowing for my focus and concentration. Rap music streams from the speakers of the music system and a child has been screaming – it's all I can hear. I feel irritated by this disturbance; I'm in judgement of the choice of music and the seemingly unaware mother of the screaming child in question.

As I scan the customers in the café, no one else is in the slightest bit bothered. They remain very much engaged in what they're doing (chatting, reading or typing on their laptops). I am looking to lock eyes with another disgruntled customer, but there are none to be found!

What is happening? Is the music only playing in my world? Are the other customers in the café hard of hearing or indeed, deaf? No. What is occurring is this… I have a moment's awareness of the music and the child, conclude in that instance that it isn't 'right', which then causes me to feel irritation and I choose to home in on it, thus bringing it further into my awareness, enlarging and exacerbating the problem which then becomes my reality, albeit a less than preferable one, as I continue to feed this level of thinking.

This disturbance is not what I was 'expecting' for my writing sojourn and, the more I think about it, the more it seems to be distracting me and the more distracted I feel, the more irritated I become. Instead of becoming aware, having the irritated thought and seeing it for what it is (a thought), letting it go and coming back to my writing, I give it my full attention and energy, heaping thought upon thought upon thought ('It's not OK, this is stopping me from concentrating, why is this happening to me in my quiet place? Why is the mother not dealing with her baby? This shouldn't be allowed...') and the annoyance I feel gathers momentum and becomes stronger as I become more and more agitated and restless.

In the next instance, my phone rings and I engage in conversation with the caller. I am interested in what is being said and I listen to my friend. In that moment, all that exists is the dialogue. I put the phone down and I realise that for the entire length of the conversation, the music and child ceased to exist – they no longer held my attention and I forgot, until I write this, that I was even the slightest bit bothered by it in the first place. Fascinating, isn't it? How can something that filled my awareness only minutes ago, becoming a mountainous issue, disappear from my world entirely?

I held on so tightly to judgemental thinking that it's all I could see, it became all of my reality in those moments. And here's the thing – had the phone not rang, I potentially would have acted on my annoyance. I may have entered into a heated discussion with the manager or maybe even walked out of the café, but when the call came, I diverted my focus and attention, had a change of thinking and my entire experience shifted – it changed completely and I carried on with the writing. Gone was the irritation that had, only minutes previously, filled my being so completely. The music was still playing, the child was still in the café at varying degrees of decibel, but it ceased to bother me any more.

Now, it may be that following the conversation with my friend, I still hold the music in my awareness and decide to take action, asking for the music to be turned down or maybe not, we have free will. The importance lies in understanding that the 'problem' (if I choose to label it that way) was not the level of noise; it was my thinking about it. It was there one minute and gone the next, despite me being in exactly the same spot with nothing changing externally. We are filtering EVERYTHING through the power of thought.

And this is happening to us all day, every day. If we simply choose to allow a thought to show up and pass on by, it will disappear into the ether, into the place from whence it came. It's only our attention to any thought that shines a magic light on it, making it visible/real and, therefore, a part of our reality and experience. We bring the formless into form with our attention and action.

That is, we make the invisible (thought) visible, when we hold it in our attention and act on it; we're disgruntled and we say something aggressively to the cashier, we walk towards a homeless person, engage in conversation and offer money, we have a hunger thought and we buy food, etc. Namely, we have a thought and we do something with it, which brings it into the world of 'reality'; and consider, we could ignore any one of these thoughts and not act on them, e.g. omit to be rude to the cashier, miss out on an act of kindness, etc.

When we act on thought, we literally pull something

from the unseen world and bring it into the world of form (here on the 3-D plane) with our attention and action and there is always cause and effect – everything we do will have an outcome, good or bad. Doesn't seem like a big deal? Well, consider that we have between 60,000 and 80,000 thoughts every day, each of which would create entirely different experiences, outcomes and realities if acted upon. Your life will take the shape of whatever thoughts you hold and take action on. Every one of us is doing this all the time, minute to minute, and as each of us is a part of the whole, our individual choices will be contributing to and creating the collective consciousness and reality as we know it. We are creator beings, creating with thoughts and actions.

There are an infinite number of responses to the same situation. I could have heard the child screaming and smiled at the mother compassionately and engaged with her. There could have been a lovely connection and in the calming of the mother, the baby may have quieted. I could have signalled for the waitress and asked if she could possibly turn the music down instead of mulling it over in my mind for ten minutes, or if rap music had been my preference of music genre, I may have really enjoyed an upper body bop as I listened to it playing through the speakers, perhaps viewing it as an enhancement to my creativity and writing time.

There are millions of different experiences and outcomes to each situation. Nothing is a given. We are the experiencers of our reality through the gift of thought and can choose our relationship to the external at any time. Is it pleasurable or otherwise? It's whatever you think it is.

Once again, we are never affected by that which happens outside of us, seemingly 'to' us, we are always at the effect of our thinking about the specific occurrences and life circumstances – life is an inside-out job.

And believing otherwise, that 'things' have power over us and the ability to make us feel a certain way, is a recipe for disaster, as we've seen in our lives. You give away your power as a creator and abdicate responsibility when you believe you are at the mercy of outside influences, no matter what that influence is – person, place or thing. It would be a precarious existence if everything 'out there' could harm us or affect us either negatively or positively. We'd have to brace ourselves as soon as we walked out of the front door in fear of what life may throw at us, feeling totally out of control of our experience – that's what's been happening, isn't it? Thought creates feeling and this understanding will make all the difference to our sense of calm – between our mental dis-ease and our mental wellbeing.

We also mistakenly believe that in some cases our reaction to the external is the 'norm' that there is a blanket response, i.e. it rains – we feel miserable; we're offered the job – we're excited. But it simply isn't a one size fits all rule.

Think about it – when it rains, some people feel disappointed about the weather, whereas others may enjoy the sound of falling water on a window pane or live in a place of drought and pray for a heavy downpour.

Take spiders. Some people are scared stiff of them whereas other people keep tarantulas as pets. Therefore, how can either rain or spiders be intrinsically 'bad'?

Apply it to the world of cinema. In a movie theatre screening a specific film, every viewer will have a different experience of the same film, together with an altogether different opinion. I have had a couple of very real experiences of this for myself.

I attended a cinema some years ago with a friend who was passionate and excited about the film being screened. It was a comedy and she convinced me that it was up there with the top ten movies of all time. The film started rolling and I was less than impressed. The more I watched, the more irritated I became, feeling incensed that we, the public, are duped into parting with good money for absolute drivel. I was so displeased that I complained to the cinema manager and asked for my money back.

Roll forward a few months and I'm at home feeling unwell. I'm scrolling through the available films to rent on my TV and I come across the very same movie. For some unknown reason, I decided to give it another shot. As I mentioned, it was a comedy and I was feeling a little dejected and felt I needed cheering up – every other film was either horror, fact-based or the subject matter didn't interest me.

All you need to know is this: Throughout the

entirety of the movie, I had tears rolling down my cheeks as I laughed from start to finish. As the credits rolled I felt decidedly better and did indeed agree that this film deserved a slot in the top ten comedies of all time! I was astounded that this was the same movie I had complained about only weeks earlier. I couldn't wrap my head around it.

Now, what happened to create this 180-degree turnaround? I'm the same me and it's the same film. Nothing changed. What changed is my level of consciousness and thinking at the time of watching the movie. Instead of expectation and an irritated state of mind, on this occasion, I was 'in the moment', interested and 'open' to experiencing the film without a filter of judgement and criticism, which gave me a completely different experience of the same film.

This has not been a one-off occurrence for me. The same thing has happened with a couple of different movies where I have moved from feeling utter dissatisfaction to total appreciation for the genius of both the actors and the script. It was totally fascinating for me to see this. And this is not isolated to the film world. I can do a 180 and have a completely different experience of people, clothes choices, restaurants, food, traffic jams, my regular morning latte, the weather – the list is endless.

And perhaps one of the most enlightening experiences I have had of this phenomenon is with my friend, Julian, whom I mentioned earlier. As my manager in the charity,

I loathed him to such a degree that I resented the air he was breathing! We just didn't see eye to eye and at every opportunity we locked horns and my anger towards him was fierce.

A few years into my job (whilst continually updating a list of all the reasons why I felt he should be removed from the organisation, which I'd intended to present to my boss), I had a thought pop into my head that I should ask Julian if I could be his PA. I have no idea where this thought came from and it kind of shocked me a bit, but after a while I came to think that it was either the craziest thought I'd ever had or pure genius – keep your enemies closer...

Anyway, on putting this suggestion to Julian, he looked like he had eaten something rotten and his body recoiled away from me – not the best start. But, with some persuasion, I told him that perhaps he was overloaded with work and he could do with some help in managing and organising his workload.

Eventually – and he'll probably tell you he doesn't understand why – he agreed to give it a go. Bottom line – fast-forward a few years and he's one of my closest friends. The way I viewed him totally changed as time moved on. The person I once viewed as the spawn of Satan became (a rough round the edges) angel in my life. Did Julian change? No. My thinking about him did. Now, if that's not evidence of a change of thought creating a change of reality, then I don't know what is.

And as a caveat, where did the idea come from that I should offer him my PA services? My rational mind would never have come up with this. At the time, I would have deemed this thought preposterous – which I half did! As I said, life is always wanting the best for us and our job is to listen. Life gave me this nugget of wisdom knowing what the outcome would be – I'm just happy I listened and ran with it.

To sum up, we will always only experience our thinking about the *person/thing*, and not the *person/thing* itself. And in a lower mood, we will have more of a tendency towards low grade/negative thinking, whereas in a 'higher' or better frame of mind, the same thing (person, situation, meal, etc) will look and taste completely different.

The Latin philosopher, René Descartes, said: "I think, therefore I am." We could also reword this to, "I am, therefore I think."

What we feel about ourselves also comes from our ideas of who we think we are, which again, are nothing but thoughts. We're making it up all the time! Our eyes are our lenses to the world and they have been warped. We are seeing only that which we expect to see with the knowledge we have at any given moment, which does not present us with a true representation of the outside world, including the way in which we view ourselves. Indeed, it can even mean that sometimes we simply do not see what is in front of our eyes, as we have no reference point.

The Myth of the Invisible Ships

It is recorded in the journals of early European explorers that the Native Indians were unable to 'see' their large ships approaching them. Having never before seen anything even closely resembling a large object that is able to glide on water, ships were simply outside of and beyond their current understanding and they, therefore, did not have the proper mental receptors to process or accept them. It has been said that, although plain and visible to the eye, the natives did not even glance at the ships that remained invisible or unrecognisable to them.

I wasn't there so I cannot corroborate this story, but it is a great analogy of how we sometimes simply do not see that which is in front of our eyes, as it exists outside of our filter – no matter how large it looms! We can be totally unaware of the stark truth before us (and within us), unable to see the opportunities and blessings in our lives, as we become prisoners to our own thinking, held captive by our own limited worldview and ideas about ourselves.

Thinking Never Stops...

We are not just having thinking about the things we see, hear, feel, etc, or that which happens 'to' us. We are having thinking 24/7. Every moment of every day, thought streams through our minds. It cannot not – it's the way the system works. We cannot stop it or control it. It's the 'trying' to push it away and our judgement of the content of our thinking that causes us discomfort.

There's a constant dialogue happening in our heads. Some of this dialogue/thinking we notice and take action on; some thinking is familiar and habitual to us (making up who we think we are, what we think we know, what we routinely do, our preferences, etc); some thoughts are useful (remember to pick up the kids, don't touch the hot saucepan); some we will remember and some will be of little interest or importance to us and therefore, will have no effect and some thought will come in and invisibly pass straight through, totally unseen and unnoticed by us – red car, blue car, café, woman with pram, white car, sports car, clothes shop, coffee shop... you get my drift.

Whatever percentage of thinking belongs under each

category is irrelevant, the relevance is in understanding and accepting that you are a thinking being and wishing it were different or attempting to force thought away is futile. It's like trying to push a river upstream – it's simply a waste of energy, you'll never succeed in stopping or changing the direction of the flow.

Where does this thinking come from? Are we choosing our thinking? As far as I can gauge, the answer is, who on earth truly knows! And although we consciously choose to engage in some thinking, for the most part, thinking chooses us.

What I do understand is this: thinking comes in from a greater 'somewhere'. The thoughts pop in from the great unknown, Greater Mind, universal consciousness, whatever you'd like to call it. Sometimes it's helpful (an idea, something useful in the moment, a reminder), sometimes it's bizarre, sometimes irrelevant, sometimes familiar, sometimes what we term telepathy or possibly incredible wisdom or whatever – there are lots of different flavoured thinking. What comes 'in' is, for the most part, undetermined by us.

It is useful to know that many of our familiar thoughts come with a 'charge' that causes a feeling state within us. As discussed, the thought of food can bring on the feeling of hunger, the thought of a disagreement with a friend can bring on anxiety or dread, the thought of someone you love can bring with it joy, etc. This felt experience of thought happens almost instantaneously. The thought will pop in and the moment that it registers (consciously or unconsciously) you will feel the charge/emotion.

It is important to understand the power of thought so we do not take our feelings so seriously. Instead, we understand we are feeling the power of our thinking and do not have to act on or believe everything we feel. The opposite is true. We can let it go.

We also need to understand the nature of thought – left to its own devices, thought will leave as quickly as it comes in. It only stays when we lock it in with our attention. If we don't get involved and meddle with the natural flow of thinking, it will pass us by unobstructed. You will keep your thinking hostage with your attention – remember, what you focus on grows.

It is always better to surrender and go with the flow, much less resistance and you'll find yourself carried. There's a saying I love that highlights this: "We cannot direct the wind (our thoughts), but we can adjust the sails (our relationship to it)." If we do not judge that which is naturally occurring (in this instance, a stream of thinking), thus allowing it to flow and observe it with an element of non-judgement, this will create the distance we need between us and 'it' to 'dis-identify' with the thinking. Non-attachment is key. Remember, you are the observer of your thinking, not the thinking itself.

Thought is energy and its very nature is to move and simply flow through your mind, like clouds in the sky. It's the grabbing and holding on tightly to any given thought that keeps it on lockdown and has us feeling chained to and at the mercy of it.

Test it out. Just because a thought flows in, it does not mean you need to entertain it or even look at it. Watch what happens if you see a thought pop in and you choose not to pay it any attention. See what happens when you put distance between you and 'it' by taking on the role of observer. We are not our thoughts, thoughts are not 'us'; they exist in a separate reality. We are truly free when we come to know and understand this on a deep level. Thought is not personal; it's not *yours*. If you don't want it, leave it alone.

If you saw a person you didn't particularly like, you wouldn't beckon them over and embrace them in a hug, or if you saw an item of clothing in a shop window that was not to your taste, you wouldn't walk in and purchase it. Therefore, if you don't like what you're thinking about, don't engage with it. If you see it and decide you don't like its flavour, spit it out and if you'd rather not look at it any further, divert your gaze and take no more notice. You are not your thinking. You are merely the thinker. You have choice. Take what you want and leave the rest. You do not need to buy into the illusion that thought creates – it's in your best interest to know this.

Habitual and addictive thoughts that we have entertained again and again over the years feel compelling and strong. They come with a very strong 'charge' that we feel strongly in our bodies, which we refer to as a craving.

The energy and pull of an addictive thought can feel incredibly real and overwhelming. Indeed, we may feel that we are powerless to ignore its calling. This is another illusion.

Become interested in understanding the nature of thought. Whether strongly charged or otherwise, every thought is made of the same 'stuff'. Again, if you don't want what it offers, leave it alone. Turn your head, avert your gaze and let it go. We have learnt to believe our thinking instead of understanding it to be nothing but energy. It's not yours unless you claim it.

As I mentioned, in understanding life to be thought-created, you cannot simply understand it at the level of intellect – going back to the analogy of submersion in water, you have to swim in the understanding. This knowing must be felt throughout the body as you come to see a deeper truth that life really is happening through you, through the power of thought.

When you see it for what it is and you choose to swim in the ocean of life itself (more interested in what is creating [before thought], rather than what is being created) it will hold you afloat. And if you stop resisting, struggling and pushing, it will carry you to where you need to go. Whether you choose to walk, swim, glide, crawl, hop, skip or jump through life, it's your call. We're all going somewhere but how you want to navigate the journey is up to you. You have been blessed with the gift of free will – make it easy or hard, move with grace or rigidity – the choice is yours.

I want to give you a very real example of what I'm talking about here. I remember when I first started questioning how my experience was being created after hearing this for the first time. As you know, a familiar feeling for me was depression. It was a feeling state I had been inside of many times over the years. In my late 20s/30s whilst I was living alone in my flat, this feeling would 'come upon me', especially when I returned home alone and locked the front door behind me.

Now, up until this point, after the locking of the front door, I would walk into the kitchen and I would immediately feel engulfed by sadness; it felt as though I was enveloped in a dark cloud. I would feel bereft, scared and desperately alone. After hearing people suggest that perhaps this feeling was coming from me, I started to get interested.

On this one occasion, as I locked the door and stood staring at the kitchen floor, engulfed in that very familiar feeling, I, for the first time, questioned it, thus putting a little distance between me and my experience.

So, here I was, feeling wretched and I asked myself, 'What was I thinking directly before I fell into this feeling?' It took a moment for the penny to drop, but when it did, I was gobsmacked and elated! Aha, there it is, I saw it! Like a light bulb, a little flash went off in my head and I realised that as I had entered my home and locked the door behind me, I'd had the thought 'I'm all alone in the world' or some variation of this theme and I recognised that I'd done this nearly every time I turned the key in the door.

I would associate returning home alone with the thought of isolation and a perceived lack of loved ones in my life and, as I moved away from the front door I would lower my head, hunch my shoulders and think, 'I'm alone'. This little invisible thought would pop in, quick as a flash and was imperceptible to me, before I took any interest and the time to notice. It would register in my brain, bringing with it the feeling state of being lost and alone and I would plunge into the experience of isolation and sadness. I also recognised that once I'd felt this, I'd heap more thought on top of it, gathering more evidence. 'I've been alone for years, where am I going in my life? No one knows me; who in the world even knows where I am right now..?' and on and on.

I'd fuel the fire, exacerbating it with my attention, lingering in this feeling state and of course I'd feel wretched – who wouldn't with this level of thinking running through their mind? Bingo! I had seen the culprit. I had been the unconscious victim of and collaborator with my thinking.

This was nothing short of a revelation to me. It was eye opening. It was the first time I'd seen the little blighter (the thought) flash (almost unseen) across my awareness. And that was it for me – the game was up. I didn't need any more convincing; I had clearly seen and experienced that I was feeling my thinking! I saw how incredibly powerful thought is. And the second I saw it, it could keep me hostage no longer. It's like playing hide-and-seek – once you find the hider the game is up. You can't keep hunting for your playmate when they're sitting right in front of you in the clear light of day!

Now, here's the thing with this priceless piece of knowledge. Just because you start to see that life is made up of a bunch of thought, you can't expect for every skittle to fall on the first hit. You may have many areas in life where you find yourself struggling and many things that you battle with on a daily basis and, although this little golden nugget of information may be a life-saver, unless you're incredibly lucky and this knowledge gives you immediate freedom from all your challenges, you'll have to practice patience. With this new understanding of the inside-out nature of life, we don't know what or which area of our life is going to 'pop' first; we cannot know how 'quickly' we will recognise thought to be the perpetrator of our upset in any particular area of our lives.

In the example I gave, I had seen clearly that this experience of feeling alone and this low grade depression was coming from me and then, as life moved on, I saw it in many other experiences and areas of my life, but it wasn't to be a quick-fix. For instance, it would take some time until I could see that my experience of my place in the family dynamic, my friendship 'issues' or my food obsessions/cravings were coming from me, rather than 'out there'. My boat would still bob and dip for a while.

In fact, I'll put my cards on the table – if I'm to be totally honest, life was to resemble less of a bobbing boat on a rippling lake than a few rounds on the big dipper, being savagely catapulted up and plummeted down, whilst I held on for dear life! This understanding of the nature of thought can ultimately work in all areas of your life, but you cannot say how long it will take – the timing isn't up to us – just keep looking in the right direction. But once you see 'it', you cannot 'unsee' it and, although we will continue to buy into the human experience and illusion as we move through life, we now do so with a priceless piece of information, which certainly takes the edge off.

Us humans are adept at remembering and promptly forgetting. We can have an insight so profound that it knocks us sideways and then find ourselves totally unable to bring it to mind a half-hour later! And that's the thing, thought is constantly flowing through our minds and even our 'aha' moments can disappear in a moment when something more compelling, or even mundane, catches our attention. The deeper you see this, the more it will help you in your 'madness' (anxiety, addiction, fear, paranoia, upset, etc) and ever changing human experience.

Take oxygen or gravity. You're not always conscious of their presence, but you know you can rely on them for breathing and keeping you connected to the Earth. You don't panic about running out of oxygen or falling off the sidewalk – you take it as a given that you will breathe and remain upright. It would be a very odd sight to see folks clinging to the pavement for dear life or leaving their homes with heavy weights around their ankles, just in case gravity decides to up and leave! And the same is true for the nature of thought – it's always supporting you… if you let it. Stop fighting with it – take the weights off. Again, what you resist persists.

When you see the truth of this, you can be slap-bang in the middle of a meltdown and still be able to rest a little in the knowledge that you're in a thought-created-reality of your own making. It's not real. It will pass. Once you see how thinking operates and you know it to apply across the board in all areas of life and in all circumstances (all the time), you can relax a little in any experience you're having, for you know it's your thinking that's creating the experience – even if you cannot, in that instant, let it go. The system is always working in the same way.

Whatever experience you're in, whatever you're thinking, it will pass as soon as you choose. The minute you cease entertaining the dialogue in your head, it will do what thought does, promptly move on to make way for the next.

Think about this gift of thought on another level, away from the mundane and the day-to-day experiences. What about the role thought plays when it comes to our identities? Is who we are static and immovable? The answer is, absolutely not. You are what you think you are, in exactly the same way that you experience whatever it is you're thinking about. You can have new thought in any moment and change your thinking, even about yourself. It's all up for re-negotiation.

In every moment we have the choice to be born anew, but, as humans, we're like dogs with a bone, we refuse to let anything go… and this includes our memories and our identities. We continually lug our past mistakes, misdemeanours, pain and memories of yesterday into our todays.

Each night we sleep and, whilst dreaming, we are fully immersed in our dream. We live in the dream world, we become the dream – it's all we know. Our ability to fly without wings over a mountainous region, hanging out with your celebrity crush, communicating perfectly with the family dog, comfortably living in a house which is not your current home – it's all acceptable and very 'normal'. It's only on awakening that you find it all a bit 'odd' and questionable.

Where was the 'you' that you know in your waking life whilst you were dreaming? What is the nature of reality if your dream felt so 'real', if it became all of who you are for a stretch of seven to eight hours, a third of your life? Which is real?

We wake in the morning and sometimes our dreams have been so powerful, so real to us, that it takes us a while to 'shake them off'. It takes us a moment to come to and re-member (in both senses of the word), as we bring ourselves back together from slumber.

As thought fills our minds, we remember who we are, what's on the day's agenda, the to-do list, what bothered us about yesterday and what may happen in the future etc and we bring our memories back into this moment of newness and potential and our present moment is immediately filled up and consumed, no room for the Now.

We are no longer here, no longer present as we are swept up in thought, whereas moments ago we were oblivious to all of this, consumed in our dream. We're so quick to insert the record from yesterday and re-load the programme of our self-identity – now we're back operating on automatic. Again, our reality will depend on our thinking. When dreaming, you become the dream. On waking, you experience the thoughts that fill your head.

All we ever have is this present moment and we constantly taint it with our memories and projections, clouding our vision and ability to see the new. The past is gone; the future is yet to arrive. Why obscure the opportunity of the now with thoughts of yesterdays and tomorrows?

Instead of embracing each new day with open arms, as the gift/the present that it is, open to the blessings that surround us, we stand in our own way, denying ourselves the beauty of the moment, blocking our potential. We literally cannot see what lies in front of our eyes as our view of the world is obscured by memories and streams of thought, not only of recent times gone by, but from the distant past also.

We are stubborn creatures. We insist on holding grudges, dragging resentment and anger with us, even pulling to mind our happy memories of distant times gone by and long forgotten (if not for us) romances into our now, to be re-experienced again and again, existing only in our obstinacy to let them go. Whatever we are keeping in our mind from the past will keep us out of the present, holding us hostage to the old story – whether the memory has you feeling 'good' or 'bad'. Memory is just a thought, too.

And Why is Any of This Helpful?

1. *Knowing this means we do not have to take every, or any thought that enters our minds seriously.* Scenario: we're holding a baby and we have the intrusive thought of 'What if I drop him/her down the stairs?' Knowing that this is merely thought in the moment means we do not have to scare the living daylights out of ourselves into thinking we'd actually do it, judge ourselves as being some kind of psychopath or give the baby a wide berth from now on, as we clearly cannot be trusted with such precious cargo.

It's just a thought. It popped in unannounced and was not of our making. If people were truly honest, you'd see that everybody has totally oddball thoughts popping into their minds... a lot! If I made a movie of what streams through my head on a regular basis, people would potentially raise an eyebrow or two!

For instance, I'm sure it's incredibly common to walk past a bank and wonder how great it would be to have all the money stored inside. The difference between you and the person in jail doing time for the crime? They had the thought and ran with it.

We're no different from each other. It's just that what looks crazy to someone (the thought of stealing and the immediate disregard of this train of thought) looks like a reasonable option to someone else, namely, the person currently incarcerated and doing the time. We all have free will – we get to choose where we put our energy and attention. We don't have control of the first thought that pops in unannounced, but from there on in, it's up to us.

2. *You have the ability to be free of your unhelpful thinking, behaviours, patterns, addictions and anything else that does you no favours.* If you truly come to know that everything you're feeling originates from thought (that you are a thinking being), it means that you do not have to pay a modicum of attention to any of it. Really, that's what's on offer here. See your part in it and stop playing the game.

If you're constantly feeling 'less than' and finding yourself lacking, you can continue down this road of pain or notice in the moment that you're creating it, you're at the control panel (having and engaging in unhelpful thinking). Become aware of this and choose to pay it no attention whatsoever. You'll know you're in the grip of crappy thinking because you'll be feeling crappy – we feel what we think. You cannot have a 'happy' thought and feel 'bad'; the system doesn't work that way. Your feelings are always an indication of what you're thinking. Think 'bad' – feel bad. Think 'good' – feel good.

As I say, you don't automatically receive a 'Get Out of

Jail Free' card and an instantaneously joyful life experience by knowing any of this intellectually. This type of seeing doesn't happen in the mind, you cannot 'get it' with the workings of your brain. You have to become interested in seeing something new and looking in a different direction – stay open and curious.

I say new, but once you truly SEE this for yourself on a deep level, you'll realise you've always known it, you've just taken a little sabbatical from your Self, a detour from the truth. If you're committed to looking in this direction, you will truly understand the nature of thought – that it is energy and that we are living in an illusion of our own making most of the time. You are not your thinking. You are pure conscious awareness.

We've been taking our thinking incredibly seriously for most of our lives, at least since we moved on from the baby and toddler stages. It's the deeper knowing that's important, for if you 'try' to push thought away whilst your whole body is in fight or flight mode and the fear of the current situation is visceral (i.e. you believe that which is occupying your mind), you'll find it impossible to stop or change your thinking.

You cannot simply have an intellectual understanding of this process, repeating 'it's just a thought, it's just a thought' if you don't really believe it (that is, you're believing you're being affected from the outside in – you're in danger, suffering 'loss', etc), you need to *understand and know* the nature and power of thought, again, in the same way you know you're supported by gravity even though you cannot see it.

It's the deeper knowing and understanding of the nature of thought (that thinking is separate from you and will keep on moving if left undisturbed) that will make the difference that makes all the difference, creating distance between you and 'it' and therefore, change.

Understanding that you're simply scaring yourself when you're inside of a thought storm and *knowing* this with all of your being, is the way out. You have my word. If you take the time to truly see that thought comes in, that it's made up of energy that is forever moving and you make a conscious decision to allow it to move through, you will no longer hold on to that which causes you pain. You will no longer live in an experience that causes you heartache.

More than this, you will know that you don't have to do anything about what you think bar diverting your attention from the unhelpful thought itself. As I have said, it's your energy and attention to the thought that brings it to life. It cannot hang around if you do not look at it. If you cease to entertain the thinking, it doesn't exist. But – and I cannot repeat this enough – you have to actually see thought-in-action and its resulting effect for this understanding to have a profound impact in your life. It is not an understanding of the intellect, but a deeper *knowing*.

Consider this for a moment. If you are not thinking

about something, does it even exist? There is drought and famine in the world, but in this moment and in the reading of this book, were you thinking about it? And if not, where was it? Were you feeling affected by it? Was it part of your reality? And seeing as all we truly have is this moment, which is your reality, it means it didn't exist for you. At all.

Stop giving life to that which causes you suffering. And on that note, how much good are you actually doing if you bring thoughts of human suffering to mind (i.e. drought and famine) and simply linger on it, mulling it over, thus causing you to feel more and more upset?

I am not suggesting we become unfeeling human beings, quite the opposite. For we are here to help, to serve humanity and relieve suffering in any way possible, but continually ruminating about that which causes you distress, is helping no one. Heaping more upset onto an already difficult situation is only adding to and compounding the problem, not dissipating it. We are looking to become part of the solution, not the problem. If you'd like to alleviate world suffering, then do whatever your heart calls for you to do in service to this – take positive action, surrender, become joyous in your heart – adding more light into the world. Simply thinking about suffering and feeling sadness for the plight of others will help no one.

Apply this understanding of the nature of thought to addiction, any kind, but for now let's consider food. If you've felt like a slave to the fridge, totally powerless when it comes to saying no to a snack attack, knowing that even a craving is only a thought with a powerful charge that you give your energy and attention to, means you can treat it the same as you do any other thought. I know a craving feels visceral and compelling, like it's 'bigger' than you and it can 'take you over', creating a physically overwhelming pull to engage, but it's still only a thought, just a very convincing, familiar, 'feels like I gotta do it' kinda thought.

I want to make it clear that I am absolutely not making light of addiction and addictive behaviour. As you know, I personally understand the strong and compelling pull and the very real consequences and immeasurable pain this causes. But I have come to see and understand that although we oftentimes feel powerless and feel like an addiction 'has us', it's simply not the case. It's never 'out there'; the craving is coming from within us, from our thinking. It's an internal activation.

We act 'out' in our sense of powerlessness. It's an abdication of responsibility (albeit an unconscious one), an avoidance strategy. We'd prefer to hide away and cover up all the stuff we don't want to look at within ourselves. The feelings we harbour deep inside feel too difficult to shine a light on and we're well practised in pushing them down. We would rather eat, take pills, have sex, become unconscious or go shopping rather than actually *feel* our feelings, but still, in our pull towards addictive behaviour, we are dealing with the same stuff – thought. The reason why you're having the thought in the first place is another conversation altogether. Regardless, it's still just thought.

3. *You get to choose a new reality.*

Your best thinking got you to where you are in this moment and if you're finding your current reality less than appealing, change your thinking. It's so simple that it looks difficult.

The way we are and the way we feel looks so ingrained and embedded in us that it seems like it *is* us. We imagine it will take years of therapy to release 'it'. This is not the truth. You could see something so profound, so deep and so true about the way the human experience is created that it would become nonsensical for you to continue in the same vein. You could see with total clarity that you are creating your reality in every moment that it would permanently erase the old lens and therefore change your perception and you would refuse to continue on the train to 'more of the same'. Definition of insanity? Doing the same thing over and over again and expecting different results. Freedom is on offer with this type of knowledge.

4. *We can at last take some responsibility for our experience and exercise a level of control over our internal worlds.* If that same familiar scenario pops up, *again*, you have the opportunity to graduate from it, to smile as you see the thinking pop in and allow it to pass through, like a cloud skirting across the sky. We are no longer at the mercy of a negative train of thought. We no longer have to collaborate, play the victim and the blame game. We get to choose how we wish to feel. If you're thinking and

entertaining low-level thought, you'll feel less than joyful and the opposite is also true.

5. *You can relax and take your foot off the accelerator.* You do not have to worry about life. You do not have to worry about your 'stuff'. Whether you have witnessed it or not, currently believe it to be so, or not, life has all the answers you need. There is a greater Mind 'out there' – universal wisdom – that far surpasses your ability to work stuff out. And I know it looks like we have to get involved with our 'problems' and our circumstances and attempt to control them, but it's simply not the case.

We think that if we relaxed and let go there would be catastrophic consequences, huge fallouts, that it's irresponsible to do nothing when life looks like a mess. But here's the beauty of the set-up – the intelligence that created you is an incredibly wise companion and will do all the sorting for you.

We exist within and are held and supported by a body of energy and love that wants us to live our best lives, it wants the best for us, namely, our full flourishing. Once you get out of your own way and stop trying to 'think' your way out of things, choosing instead to surrender to the divine intelligence that surrounds and supports you, you will be given the answers to all your 'problems'. You make space for wisdom to pop in. You will be given solutions to the issues facing you that feel insurmountable and impossible, but again, you have to let go of control, get out of your own way and cease fighting. Let the Universe give you the answers by stepping back and taking your small self/mind out of the equation. If you already knew the answer to your 'problem' you would have come up with it by now. Surrender the 'issue' and allow the solution to 'pop in'.

Once again, if this intelligence (God, life, universal energy – whatever term you're comfortable with) created the galaxies, supernovas and this awesome planet you're inhabiting, you can bet your life it has the answers and solutions to your (perceived) human problems.

The intelligence of life can, for sure, work out how to smooth out the differences between you and your boss, present you with the best work opportunities and find your perfect place to live. If you already knew the answers, you'd be making different choices – know there's greater wisdom 'out there'. Let go and make space in your mind and in your being to hear the wisdom that is always available to you.

You need to listen and you simply cannot do this with a full and busy mind. We're so caught up in 'doing' that it's pretty hard to hear the internal whispers with the noise in our heads turned up to full volume – it's impossible to pour into an already full cup. Wisdom is always flowing through you – it's always here. Your job is simply to make space to hear and then you have to listen. Make room in your cup to receive.

Trust the wisdom of life to give you the best outcome in any situation, at the very best time. And, if it doesn't pop in immediately, trust that it will come, as I say, at the right time. When you receive a 'knowing', act on it. It could be as 'big' as a move to a different home or location or a nudge to attend that yoga class, but whatever the situation, life has the answer.

There is a divine plan and divine timing. You simply have to surrender your plans – your ideas and beliefs about when something 'should' happen. It's impossible for us to see the bigger picture from our human perspective. Let life lead you, it knows what's good for you far better than you do.

I understand that this way of being is alien to us. We've been taught that it's all 'up to us'. We've been led to believe that we need to push the river upstream, that without us at the control panel, on the lookout and steering the ship, continually shifting gears with our octopus arms, it would all fall apart, but we've been trying and 'efforting' this way all our lives and our best thinking has got us here. So, why not give another way a shot? We are human beings, not human doings. We have to remember there is wisdom in the silence, riches awaiting us in the stillness. We need to slow down.

This may look irresponsible when life looks like it's screaming at you to 'do more', 'be more', whilst you battle through your days and to-do lists, but it's not, it's the opposite – your gifts lie in the quiet. You need to allow yourself a re-charge and the irony is, the more you slow down, the more you'll get done and the better you'll feel.

We've had it the wrong way round. Our understanding has been backwards and inside out (although inside out is exactly how life works). Trust life. It has your back. You will always get what you need. Get out of your own way.

The £10 Note

I'd like to share a little story that once again affirmed my belief in a greater wisdom. Someone had owed me money and had given me a £10 note to settle up. I had slipped the note into the back pocket of my jeans and carried on with whatever I was doing. A few minutes later, I distinctly remember thinking that I should transfer the money to my purse, otherwise I'd forget about it. Looking back, I was pretty sure I'd done this.

A few days later, I'm immersed in my morning routine and getting ready to leave the house when I kept having the thought that I should check my jeans pocket for the £10 note. This came out of nowhere. A few days had passed and it really wasn't on my mind and, anyway, as I said, I was convinced I'd transferred the money to my purse.

I ignored the thought the first time around and carried on getting dressed, but there it was again – 'Check your jeans pocket for the £10 note'. When it 'popped' into my mind a third time, I decided to double-check (as I've come to trust these promptings), even though I was certain the money would not be there.

The jeans were now in the washing machine ready for the next wash, so I opened the machine, pulled out the nearest pair and found nothing in the pockets. I reached further in to retrieve another pair of jeans, put my hand in the back pocket and, to my surprise, there was the £10 note, about to be swallowed up in the wash! I was gobsmacked.

This may not sound so astounding to you, but I was truly amazed. Why on earth did this thought pop into my mind right before the wash was to be switched on? I hadn't considered this money since the moment it was handed to me. It was simply not on my radar. So it begs the question, 'who' or 'what' kept prompting me to check my jeans pocket? It wasn't me thinking about it, it wasn't something I'd told myself to remember or even thought I needed to follow up. 'Something' was bringing my attention to the jeans.

On this occasion it was 'just' a £10 note – it wasn't a huge deal and probably something I'd never bring to mind again (although I may have wondered what all the white, tissue-like paper was covering my clean wash!) But it isn't the situation in question that's important, it's the fact that something was prompting me, giving me information that was helpful.

This is the intelligence of life. We are being guided all the time. We must take heed of the promptings, for this intelligence has our best interests at heart. It could be as 'small' as rescuing a £10 note from the clutches of the washing machine, or the guidance could be directed towards a much 'bigger' life issue.

Do you see how reassuring this is? The burden of control need not rest on our shoulders. We do not need to create endless to-do lists or feel we must attempt to remember every last detail of our lives. The irony is, the more we attempt to control, the fuller our minds will become, the more stressed we will feel, causing life to feel like an uphill struggle. With busy minds, there will be much less room for us to hear the quiet whispers within and, therefore, the more we will trip up. We're wanting to get out of our own way in order to hear the wisdom we are being offered and notice the gifts of life when they present themselves. We simply do not know better than the intelligence of life – is it you who is currently making your heart beat? Are you, right now, supervising the digestion of your last meal?

We really can trust that if we stay present, trust this intelligence and move out of our own way, we will be given everything we need – information, contact with the 'right' people, situations that benefit us, the books we need, remembering the things that need our attention, gaining the answers to our questions and, in my case, even rescuing a £10 note before its untimely demise.

This occurrence really made me smile. We do not know how this system of thought/life works, but do we need to? Again, we do not understand gravity or oxygen, but we know we can depend on them. It's our relationship to 'it' that's the game changer. This little incident of the £10 note was yet more confirmation that life has my back. My job? Trust and heed its guidance.

What Does This Mean for the World? What's Possible?

In answer, what's not possible? Change starts with us. Our world seems like it's currently being run on fear-based thinking. We view the world through a distorted and warped lens at the level of the personal, which then ripples out into the world, creating more of the same.

What we create at the level of the microcosm will become the macrocosm. We cannot live in scarcity and fear-based thinking as individuals and within our relationships (co-dependent, riddled with expectations, desperation and need) and expect to create a world based on acceptance, wholeness and love. We are all part of the divine matrix and each one of us (our part) constitutes to and becomes the whole. As I said, it starts with us.

The majority of people are existing at a very low level of vibration and frequency. Our focus has been on fear (either instigated by the media or in our innocence from learned behaviour) and lack as we entertain worry-thinking in our minds and live in the world predominantly for selfish gain within an ego mind. We have been in protection mode, looking out for our own needs. We see ourselves solely as individuals instead of understanding that we are all connected and our thoughts, actions and behaviours will affect those around us, contributing to the overall functioning of humanity.

There is always cause and effect – we simply cannot work in isolation. We have not understood that what we create personally will have an effect 'out there'. Remember, just like each wave behaves independently from the others and will appear as an entity unto itself, it is still fundamentally part of a body of water and its rise and fall will affect the overall flow.

We are all part of the same web. Every choice, thought and behaviour has an effect – nothing is for nothing. It is said that something as small as the flapping of a butterfly's wings can cause a hurricane on the other side of the world. Everything we do, big or small, makes a difference and if the majority of people are living in fear-based/scarcity thinking, away from the truth of who they are and operating from small-mind mentality, how can this not play out on a larger scale? The world is made up of human thought, which affects our level of consciousness.

Everything is energy and if a high percentage of thinking individuals are thinking 'small' and 'sending out' negativity, we will see evidence of this present itself on the larger playing field, namely, in our world. This vibration is the basis for war, disruption, criminal activity, separation and apartheid, etc.

On a worldwide scale we are killing each other,

witnessing corruption within systems, businesses, governments and between people of 'power'; we're fighting over land, convinced our way is better than the 'other'. We make up our minds (solidify our thinking) from a place of ignorance and come to preposterous and erroneous conclusions – 'my religion is better than yours', 'this is the only way to do something', 'this law applies across the board', 'this substance/behaviour is illegal', 'women must look this way', etc or else it's 'off with their heads'. We've become obsessed with money and power, we're full of ego and totally unconscious to the damage this is doing and how our behaviour is contributing to the whole. We're seeing horrific consequences play out on a very large scale – a worldwide scale.

It seems we're not content with destroying ourselves so we're destroying our planet as well, the very thing that gives us life. We're so incredibly ignorant that, for the most part, we're totally unaware or even more abhorrent, we don't care – we think we're invincible. We take far more than we need as we're led to believe (by those who profit) that there's always more, more, more, as we're pulled along on a consumer conveyer belt.

We strip the Earth, abusing resources, always taking – taking away from the very thing that unconditionally keeps on giving; raping our Mother (Earth), attacking our provider, desecrating and burning rainforests, chopping down trees – givers of the oxygen we need to survive, the lungs of the planet, destroying that which gives us life, gives us food, allowing for our survival as a human race. This is pure insanity, total madness. We are waging war on that which loves, supports and sustains us. It's ignorance on a profound level – we're burning our own home.

We are not separate from the Earth; we need her for our survival. We must ask ourselves, is this what love would do? Is this what sanity would do? We're clearly out of our (right) minds, for even the rationally conditioned mind (away from all things 'woo woo') can deduce that this simply doesn't make any sense. That is, if survival is an important factor.

Understanding the way our experience is created will allow us to stop taking our thinking so seriously, pitting ourselves against one another. Deepening into this understanding will give us the space we need to move out of our heads and drop into our hearts, choosing love over fear.

It's not just useful for us personally within our lives and in our relationships with our Selves, family and friends, but as you may be realising, it has incredible implications for the way humanity relates to one another and how we operate in the world. The potential for the 'difference' in our world with this understanding becoming widespread is exponential. And more than anything, it's crucial, for we are living in worrying times.

Simply, we cannot continue in the same vein. It's as if we've got suicidal ideation, obsessively committed to killing ourselves and we're facing possible extinction as we continue to pollute our air and drinking water, poison our food and bulldoze our way through nature – we're extinguishing the basic needs for human survival. The way we're functioning is not supportive of or conducive to our survival as a race. It does not support the evolution of humanity. If we continue, what will be left? It's an unsettling thought. There needs to be a fundamental shift of consciousness – and yesterday!

What would happen if all the people on Earth understood that they were thinking beings experiencing their thinking? That scarcity thinking and lack mentality was a bunch of made-up erroneous thoughts, that the 'divide' between people (countries, governments, businesses), the differences between you and me, the need and greed for money, exist only in our heads as a warped and distorted belief system (namely that there is lack and we have to protect what is 'mine'). These beliefs have been passed down from generation to generation, borne from a misunderstanding and, when we become riled about something, stuck on the way something 'should' be or scared there's 'not enough', we're just giving a certain train of thought a lot of attention and taking it incredibly seriously.

Would there be an all-out war for what is 'mine' and what is 'yours' if we truly understood the nature of thought and knew life to be abundant? Would the colour of someone's skin mean anything at all about the person apart from the area of the world in which they were born?

Would 'I' need 'you' to believe my religion is better than yours? Would we feel that the accumulation of money and power meant that I'm worth more than you? Would we need this external 'wealth' and 'success' to validate who we are? Wouldn't that be nonsensical? Before the creation of this ego, we knew we were not separate, born as we are from the same energy and from the same place.

The dialogue that fills our heads is an illusion, it's nothing and it's make-believe. It's responsible for all the pain, all the suffering, greed and the loss of Self. We've bought into the small mind for millennia, now it's time to let it go. We no longer need to be slaves to our thinking, but our thinking can be in service to the greater good. Our true nature is love and our true state is joy and abundance. It's all around us. We've just been conditioned not to see it.

We deny the truth of who we are when we buy into the illusion of thought. The more we let go and make space, the more room there is for the Self to show up in the world. When we strip away all of the layers of illusion we have lived inside of for most of our lives, we find us, in our essence, incredible limitless beings. No fixed identity, needing nothing, but desiring only to show up fully as the Self, to be of service to others, to be Love and live in a peaceful world, part of the human family, amongst brothers and sisters – for we are all part of the same family. We are connected more than we know. We share this world, we live in the same home, under the same roof, coming from and returning to the same place. The 'other' is an illusion, a cosmic joke.

When we let go of our habitual thinking and move into a place of love and understanding, taking care of and celebrating one another, we create an altogether different energy – the energy of love – and we cultivate true and authentic connection, compassion and understanding. It is precisely this type of energy that will ultimately solve our problems, individually and collectively. We were not made to kill, maim and hurt each other; we were made to love each other. Love the Self and love the 'other', for we are family – we must love and care for each other as brothers and sisters do.

Do you know what lies underneath thought? Behind everything that stands in the way of us, seeing the truth of the present moment? Love. Love is all that exists when we relax and let go of our thinking and quiet our minds. Underneath all the busyness, behind all our ideas of who we think we are, behind all the judgements of self and others, there's Love.

Underneath the thinking that keeps us divided and disconnected, our thoughts about all the things we think we want, need, prefer, deserve, behind all the incessant chatter of this monkey mind, is us, in our very 'being-ness', in a state of grace. And we will show up in this state when we *know* we are not our thinking, when we let go and fall into our true nature, into our Selves.

We have remained unaware of our power and potential for far too long. The news, media, our newspapers and a lot of what we see on social media is promoting and compounding this state of fear. It stops us from seeing the truth and the truth of who we are. The truth is that there is more than enough to go around. Just because someone seemingly has what we want, it does not mean they've taken our slice of the pie. We live in an abundant, limitless and ever expanding Universe, our every need has been catered for. There is no need to worry. The only thing that stands between you and abundance is… you.

At this point, I'd like to make reference to the media and how damaging it is. Wouldn't you agree that it is somewhat 'interesting' that the news is continually bombarding us with negativity and reasons to feel scared and fearful? Isn't it somewhat questionable that when we tune in to see 'world news', we see stories of politicians and governments in battle with one another, fighting between man, terrifying images or war torn countries, horrifically injured men, women and children, drought and famine and local news reporting on stabbings, gang culture, 'hoodies', crime, break-ins, carjackings, etc. All these disturbing images are being beamed through our TVs and delivered through our letter boxes, landing straight into our homes. It's really important to question this. Do you want to live inside of and feed off this kind of energy?

There are currently around 7.8 billion people inhabiting planet Earth, most of whom are loving and well meaning people. How is it that we only get to see atrocities reported as 'world news', when in actuality, on the ground, most people are loving and caring for one another, people are looking to extend the hand of friendship, offer their help and, for the most part, are interested in doing 'good'? If the news and the papers reported on all the beauty, altruism and care that fills this world, there wouldn't be enough space to cover all the incredible acts of human kindness, generosity, courage, connection, partnership, compassion and service that take place each and every moment of each and every day.

So why, when we are interested in 'world news', do we only see projected back to us, images and information that causes us to move into a place of fear or shake our heads in hopelessness? These images and information exacerbate and keep us in a fearful and low vibratory feeling state, whereby joyful stories (and they are aplenty), would raise the energy and vibration of humanity. Really consider this: what we see on our TV screens is a tiny portion of 'reality' and, therefore, an incredibly small representation of humanity; it scarcely resembles any type of truth. World news? I don't think so. Something to consider.

And what would happen if we didn't buy into the media? What if we switched off the 'news'? What would happen if we were discerning about what we viewed and what we allowed into our hearts and minds? What would happen if we turned our eyes away from the reports of raging wars and bloody images and chose instead to fill up on all the good being done in our world? What would happen if we shied away from fear-based information and, instead, made a decision to see the other side of the coin? What would life look like if you made a conscious choice to surround yourself with uplifting conversation, positive people and solution-based dialogue? This change in direction would raise our vibrations, shift our frequency and our consciousness and allow us to live as G-d intended, open-hearted and in love. Fear keeps us living small and love allows for expansion.

With this change in direction we would move into a place of power instead of existing under the thumb of the media and in a perpetual state of fear. We wouldn't be so compliant and pliable then, would we? This turning away is not avoidance, it is the exact opposite. It is choosing to look in the direction of love to become an integral and crucial member of the human race.

When we move away from fear and back to love, we are able to serve ourselves and humanity in a much bigger and better way – we turn off (outside) to tune in (inside)… to be of greater service. I refuse to watch the news but I am in no way blind to the suffering on this Earth, I am all too aware. But I am useless as an emotional mess, which is what I would be if I fed myself with this level of negativity on a daily basis. I refuse to be blinded and held hostage by fear and the 'powers that be' that pull the puppet strings of the media. I consciously choose to divert my gaze in order to be of service. I consciously choose to see the best in people and the incredible potential of humanity. I consciously choose love. I deplete my ability to serve when I allow fear to be present in my being – it saps my power and dilutes my strength. I am unwilling to live in this space. Be discerning about what you're willing to let into your space.

If we recognised how wonderful, awesome and powerful we are, that we are each a spark of the divine, would we feel jealousy and covet the belongings of another? Would we allow a third party to dictate to us and strip us of our human freedoms, causing us to live out of alignment with our truth? Would we comply with nonsense, just because 'the government says so'? Would we think something is missing and seek something outside of ourselves to make us feel 'better', to fill us up? Would we actually need anything at all if we knew we were already whole, divinely perfect just as we are? Would we need to compete? Be right? Have more? If we realised we inherently knew what was best for us, would we give our power away to an external source? We have all the wisdom we need inside of us.

I would hazard a guess that if we truly came to understand our beauty, our infinite and innate potential and understood our capabilities and limitlessness, we'd want for nothing at all. If we lived in wholeness, truly knowing our nature as love, I believe we'd only want to give and share the love that we are.

I cannot imagine war breaking out in a world where we were all living this way – loving each other, caring for the welfare of one another, extending the hand of friendship, displaying kindness, helping, showing compassion and open-heartedness, knowing that we are all responsible for G-d's children, understanding that the problem 'over there' isn't somebody else's issue, it's ours, for we are all part of the equation, each and every one of us. Living together and serving in this way is built into our DNA – this is who we truly are. We are love. Our nature is to give. Our part matters. We matter. We are all connected. We are all One.

When we transform ourselves, we transform the world. Change starts within, *with* us. When we move out of fear and into a place of love, showing up in this way in each and every moment, it ripples out and changes our circumstances and relationships – it changes our world. It cannot not, for, as I say, we are creator beings – part of the whole; what we project out with our thoughts and behaviours will be exactly what manifests.

So ask yourself, from which foundation do I wish to build – fear or love? The choice is yours. And as an aside, showing up in this way is infectious and others will want in! *Be* the change. When you shine your light and live your truth, you give others permission to do the same.

I'll use the words of Carl Sandburg in answer to what's possible:

"Sometime they'll give a war and nobody will come."

Amen.

Your Feelings Won't Kill You

I spent my whole life running away from myself, running away from my feelings. And I get it, it makes sense to me that I behaved this way – anxiety isn't fun, paranoia is hell; walking in the world feeling like I'm somehow broken, 'wrong' and defective doesn't make for a joyful existence. Feeling caged is uncomfortable and micromanaging my words and behaviours is altogether debilitating. So, yes, why wouldn't I want to run away from my feelings?

And for years I did just that. If it felt uncomfortable, I'd bolt, sever the connection, drink alcohol, take drugs, fall asleep, leave the job, walk away or get on a plane... I was always on the go. And this wasn't just a physical running either, my mind was in a constant spin, continually churning, giving me absolutely no rest – just another reason why I felt the need to get 'out of my head'. Why on earth would I want to be in it?!

And here's the thing, I've learnt something priceless over the years, which I know to be true beyond a shadow of a doubt. Your feelings won't kill you. Just because it feels like hell and appears to be bigger than you, has your heart racing, your body shaking, your mind whirling and threatens to swallow you whole, it does not mean this is the case. Looks can be deceiving. We're only in an experience (of thought) which is transitory and your willingness to bring (your) presence to your experience (in non-judgement and non-attachment as the observer) is the one thing that will help you to transform those feelings that have been all too familiar to you for far too long, choking you and holding you prisoner, causing you to live smaller than is possible.

I wonder what would have happened all those years ago if I had sat with myself when my stomach was flipping over and I'd be bracing myself for the onslaught of intense anxiety and the accompanying bodily sensations. What would have happened if, for the first few times, instead of resisting it, swallowing down the rising panic and pushing it away, I'd have listened to what was calling for my attention and sat with myself in compassion and love, undisturbed with eyes closed, bringing my presence and awareness to my experience, bringing my full attention to whatever was taking place within me?

I wonder what would have happened if I'd been willing to stay still until I'd moved through my internal experience, allowing it to be fully present, giving my feelings the room they'd needed to move through me. What would I have heard if I'd listened to the words they wished to speak? Was there a message in there somewhere? Was there something I needed to know, something I needed to see? Something that could have helped me in my distress? I was self-abandoning all the time in my constant running away.

Can you imagine if your child or a loved one came to you in pain, on their knees, begging to be heard by you and you pushed them away and turned your back on them? This is what we do when we self-abdicate and deny ourselves the attention we're crying out for. This is what we do when we ignore our feelings and skip over ourselves in avoidance or for something 'more important'. Nothing is more important. We must love ourselves as much as we do that which is precious to us and shooing our feelings away in fear and judgement of ourselves is anything but a loving act.

I understand how debilitating feelings of depression and anxiety can appear. I understand that hanging out with your internal experience can feel like the last thing you want to do, but I am saying that it's necessary.

As you know, when I experienced 'depression', I moved through a very dark night of the soul that brought me to my knees. I was engulfed in profound feelings of grief and loneliness. It felt as if the lights simply went out in my life. It was black. No joy. No point or purpose to anything. I can't even say I was scared. I don't think I cared enough about anything to feel fear. I wanted only the sanctuary to be found under the duvet or anything that could numb out the pain. I wanted out. So please know that I do not speak lightly of the human experience for I have been in company with it.

And I understand that a little retail therapy or a trip to the movies looks more appealing than hanging out with your old friends – trauma, anxiety and paranoia – but, I am saying that the only way out, is 'in'. Through the dark there is profound beauty, I truly believe there always is. There was more my soul wished to express in the world, through me. I had to come to this place of break down, in order to wake up. Grief and pain are signposts that there's more of you, more *for* you. This is why we need to go inside and listen.

I wish I would have known back then that I didn't need to run away, that I could become the observer of my experience; that it is possible to be still, right where we are, even in our messiness, to bring our presence and awareness inside and feel our feelings without fear. I wish I had known that there was (there always is) a bigger picture at play, that our personal experiences are deceiving, that the gifts in life aren't always packaged nicely, that truly, there is exquisite joy to be found on the other side of a breaking heart. In my case, in doing so, the darkness would have abated somewhat as those heavy clouds would have rolled on by.

My presence to and non-judgement of my experience would have given my feelings the space they needed to move, making way for a clearer sky. My in-the-moment experience would not have become my everything and, even if the clouds hovered for a while, I would have understood that this too was transitory, that this too shall pass. This knowledge would have permitted me the freedom I longed for.

As an aside, I experienced another Dark Night of The Soul very recently to the time of writing. And because I now know differently, I was able to move with it, move through it – no resistance, no judgement. Just allowing, knowing something was changing, something was calling me deeper. Because here's the thing, if you're on the path of evolution, you better get comfortable with death – those things that no longer serve us will leave us and fall away. There is always a greater version of ourselves, wishing to be birthed into the world. In this instance, there was another level of my identity whose time was up.

This sitting with myself is something I have grown used to doing over the years. We are human and, at times, we will be triggered. We'll find ourselves in a misunderstanding, a feeling of upset or trauma. We may feel lost, confused or dejected or perhaps experience an old, painful and familiar pattern or dynamic and this level of presence and attention to my experience of these things has served me well.

When I find myself in an anxious or chaotic space and I have lost my ground, I will go inward. I will turn off my phone, sit on my sofa with eyes closed and turn my full attention inward, feeling my feelings and observing the emotion. I allow my awareness to travel to the places in my body that are holding onto and reacting to old pain and trauma and I give myself permission to 'go in'.

I allow my consciousness to move into the discomfort, the pounding head, the constricted stomach, the tight chest, the racing heart or the tightness in my throat, whilst I witness my response to the trigger – the stuck energy (the difficult emotions I swallowed down and suppressed that were too painful for me to feel) – and I sit, with awareness and interest, giving space to what is calling to be felt, allowing what *is*, to be. And I hold myself here, lovingly, with forgiveness and compassion.

This observing creates the space needed between me and 'it' and, as the observer, the one who sees (in a space of non-attachment), I understand that these feelings are not me. I understand that I am having an experience, for I am not the experience itself. It is not who I am and therefore it no longer overwhelms me and holds me prisoner.

I am able to separate my Self from my experience and it becomes exactly that, an experience that can be observed – it is not the sum total of who I am. And I continue to observe, just feeling, feeling and feeling some more, until it moves, until it passes, until I can breathe easy once again, until I re-member... and it will pass, because each and every experience is transitory – nothing stays the same.

Sometimes it may take only a few seconds or minutes and sometimes it may take a good while, but we must care enough to sit with ourselves in this way and give ourselves the love, care and attention that we need. And I can pretty much guarantee that within this 'lighter' relationship with our experience, it will move on pretty quickly.

As Hermann Hesse says so beautifully:

Suffering only hurts because you fear it. Suffering only hurts because you complain about it. It pursues you only because you flee from it.

You must not flee, you must not complain, you must not fear. You must love.

Because you know quite well, deep within you, there is a single magic, a single power, a single salvation, and a single happiness, and that is called loving.

Well then, love your suffering. Do not resist it, do not flee from it.

Taste how sweet it is in its essence, give yourself to it, do not meet it with aversion.

It is only aversion that hurts, nothing else.

All of our journeys differ, they are never identical, but whatever is presenting itself is wanting to show us something – our feelings are signposts, they have something to say and a story to tell. As the saying goes, 'The darkest hour is just before the dawn' and, again, it is Rumi, the great Sufi poet, who said, "The wound is the place where the Light enters you." It is through our suffering that we will find our bliss, that is, our freedom. Our pain is the doorway to our greatest growth.

Everything has an opposite. Up, down, yin, yang, black, white, happy and sad. Everything has its converse. How would we know daytime if we did not have the night? We would simply have no benchmark. So, too, do we appreciate and understand joy when we have moved through the other side of the coin.

In your attention and awareness to your feeling state, to what is trying to be seen and heard, you may be faced with trauma, with old memories that feel too difficult and painful to sit with and experiences you'd rather keep buried. With your attention to what is calling to you, you will absolutely be faced with yourself. Head on. It won't feel great. It may be shocking to you and you'll have nowhere to run. But who cares? Run in anyway and run in full throttle. Face it all. Have a head-on collision with all the parts of yourself, sit in your mess, bloody and bruised, then pick yourself up, move on through and reap your rewards, for they are aplenty.

I saw this on a deeper level on a holiday abroad in December 2019. I had been triggered on a deep level and was experiencing an old, familiar story once again and I was in pain. It became crystal clear that I was being presented with another opportunity to relinquish and evolve this pattern. I knew that the story was never going to leave if I didn't face my worst-case scenario (abandonment) head on and see it for the liar that it was. If I truly wanted to let it go and be free from this story, I would have to face my fear.

I would have to stop checking my phone, controlling, believing my thinking, calling friends obsessively in a state of fear, responding immediately to messages, re-checking, over-stretching myself, people pleasing, saying yes when I meant no. I was going to have to truly risk on the deepest level to teach myself, body and mind, that fear is an illusion. It's always an illusion. I was keeping it alive with my allegiance to and compliance with it.

I would have to be another type of mess, an internal ferocious inferno of tumultuous, wild, unruly mess as I sat in a whirlwind of fear, feeling it, observing it and laughing in the face of it. I was going to love my fear to death. And you know what? If my worst scenarios came to pass, every single one of them, if I was thrown out and exiled, I would still be here – I would still be OK. I would have my Self; I would survive. In fact, I would *more* than survive. Without this suffocating and choking noose of fear around my neck, this constriction around my throat, chest and heart – I would thrive.

In our unwillingness to dive right in, we put a cork in that which is wanting to bubble up and out of us. Rest assured, when you show up with this type of commitment, commitment to your evolution, saying a hearty YES to life, whatever you commit to move through, will move and what lies on the other side of this type of commitment and intent towards your freedom, is nothing short of miraculous. All that is old, all the illusion of the small self (the personality construct with its twisted and distorted beliefs, built on a foundation of lies) is looking to be relinquished in order for the true you to take centre stage.

When you expand your desire for greater expression,

experience and visibility in your life, your consciousness will expand and therefore life, as you know it, will become a whole new (awesome!) ball game. The True You will shine through.

Again, let us remember that feelings can be signposts to massive breakthroughs and awakenings. We do not need to be defined by our experiences, but each and every one of them can bring us into a deeper level and depth of understanding. We are being given the gift of experiencing the full spectrum of the human experience. To know deep pain means you can know deep joy. To feel the depth of heartbreak allows you to love ever more deeply and ferociously. To feel confusion and find clarity gives you the ability to empathise and help others on a similar path.

We do not need to carry heartache or pain as a burden, but we have felt it, we have experienced it, we know it and we are richer for it. It will not always feel that way in the moment or as you are moving through it, but once you allow it, witness it, let it move through you, let it *move* you, you will deepen into a more profound experience of your human story.

Bad Can Be Good

And this human experience can, for sure, feel tricky. To fully immerse ourselves in this incredible experience, we have the ability to 'enjoy' the myriad of all human emotions. I put the word 'enjoy' in inverted commas because life experiences and feelings do not always feel pleasurable or comfortable and our beliefs can inform us that feeling 'bad' is not 'good' – it is not our preference. This is a dangerous and limiting belief as it brings us into a place of judgement of what 'is'.

Not only do we move through life labelling ourselves, putting ourselves into little boxes of limiting identity, but so too do we label our feelings and our human life experiences. We have preference and, therefore, judgement when it comes to our feeling state. We have come to believe that feeling happy, joyful and excited are good and right emotions and to feel sad, upset, confused or angry is wrong and undesirable – they are emotions to be avoided, suppressed or 'fixed'.

We do everything we can to steer clear of the latter, oftentimes denying our feelings when we have veered over to the 'dark side'. We're not really sure how to handle messy emotions when we're in the thick of them, emotions that are not deemed 'right' or 'acceptable', emotions that may be 'too much' for us and potentially for others. We believe we're better off feeling them privately; they're most definitely not for the public domain.

Problem is, we've become so scared of our less than appropriate and difficult feelings that depression in our society is rife. We push our feelings away, running marathons to avoid them, which ironically causes them to stay as we suppress them further – for what we resist, persists.

Please consider what happens to us when we medicate ourselves and stop the natural flow. I truly believe we stunt our growth. Consuming copious amounts of antidepressants on a daily basis in a bid to keep us at a constant, in a perpetual state of the 'same', thus numbing out an essential part of what it means to be human, is at odds with nature. We will come a cropper if we attempt to fix ourselves in this way – it's not sustainable.

We miss out on the incredibly rich human experiences that are on offer when we set our sights so low, entertaining only specific situations and accepting only certain feeling states as appropriate. In this way, we deny ourselves profound spiritual and emotional insight. If you're going to pay for a trip to an amusement park, go on every ride. You're here on Earth, don't limit yourself and don't opt out. Are you truly content to keep the needle on only one dial? Wouldn't you love to have a truly awesome adventure with all the trappings of the human experience?

Sure, it'll be difficult sometimes, often challenging and, at times, it will feel downright crappy as we look to the heavens and ask, "Really?? Are you serious?!" But the upside far surpasses all of this. The rewards on offer here are far-reaching and without limit. Let's not cut ourselves off from the potential that lives within us and the blessings that life has to offer. Let's say yes to the whole shebang!

When we opt out, we exist and we function (on some level), but we're not truly living, we're not fully *here*, we're not flourishing and working in partnership with life, present in the moment and flowing with the river. We fall short of the depth of growth and connection that is available to us and deny ourselves a part of the rich tapestry of the human experience. It's the difference between thriving or surviving.

If we'd only been told that feelings of grief, sadness, loneliness, etc were 'normal' and part of the human experience, that they are transitory, to be embraced and moved through as the messengers that they are (rather than denied and avoided), we'd be much healthier as individuals and as a society. Denying whatever it is that is presenting itself to you (in whichever frame of mind you're in) is denying your moment to moment experience, denying your *now*. You aren't living in your present moment if you're wishing it to be different and pushing it away. For it is what it is, regardless.

We tend to feel low or upset over something or someone and judge ourselves for having the experience (keeping it alive with our disappointment and resistance to the situation), which causes it to hang around, gather momentum and overwhelm us and we can find ourselves frozen in the middle of the overwhelm. And as 'it' seemingly envelopes us, it most definitely looks as though something 'out there' has 'got' us and we will, for sure, deem this experience 'not right'. No one has told us that it's OK and natural to have low moods, difficult and painful feelings, that it's part of the human experience. It is our judgement of feeling 'low', the over-focus and, therefore, stimulation of this experience and the thinking itself that creates the monster, enlarging the experience beyond all proportion.

The very meaning of stimulation points to what we do when we entertain anything with our attention: 'encouragement of something to make it develop or become more active.'

We go to a doctor, we tell them we're depressed, we explain our symptoms and we're promptly prescribed the necessary happy pills, for in our suffering it most definitely looks like something needs fixing, doesn't it? But what if our relationship with our less than preferential feeling states was altogether different?

As human beings we are not always operating on a high level of consciousness, that's just the way it goes – sometimes we're 'up', sometimes we're 'down' and sometimes we're somewhere in-between. If only we knew that there was nothing to worry about, that it's simply part of the human experience, part of the human spectrum of e-motion – energy in motion. It would be totally against nature if we were always operating in exactly the same frequency, in the same feeling state and living our lives in a state of delirium 24/7. I am always highly suspicious of individuals who display no fluctuations in mood.

It is our resistance to what is, the pushing and forcing of something to change its shape and make it into something it's not, that's the problem. 'I wish she were different', 'I'd have preferred coffee, not tea', 'why is the traffic so heavy?', 'I wish it would stop raining', 'why am I like this?', 'I shouldn't feel this low, maybe there's something wrong with me'… When we judge ourselves, our feelings and our experiences, wishing we/they were different, we're in trouble. I repeat, it is what it is and wishing it to be otherwise in the moment is futile and a waste of energy. Once again, it's pushing the river upstream. Potentially you can do something about a situation, take action when action is needed, but judgement and denial are dangerous games. Love and acceptance are your healers.

A low mood is a low mood, nothing more, nothing less. And if left alone, it will pass. There's nothing to do apart from (as lightly as you can) experience it. Let the experience move through your awareness and allow it to become something else.

But we just cannot leave it alone. We feel at a low

ebb; imagine there's a dark cloud looming overhead and we immediately panic and make it wrong. We look at it through a magnifying glass, we pick it, scratch at it, irritate it and make it bleed, causing it to grow larger and redder. We assess it and dissect it, wanting to find out what's caused it. What's happened? Is there a chemical imbalance? Is something wrong with me? And the more we look at it, the more we poke and prod at it, the further we lock it into our awareness with our unwillingness to let it go and we're left wondering why this 'problem' feels bigger than us. We created a mountain!

It makes sense, it's logical. What you focus on, grows. We haven't been told that it's natural, that if we simply felt the low mood and did absolutely nothing about it, it would move on by and go on its merry way. It may last a minute, it may last an hour, it may last a day – the timing is not up to us, but regardless, it's all OK. You *know* it will leave (everything changes, it's the way of nature), so why worry about it when that's the very thing that will prolong its stay?

There's a teaching that goes something like this, 'If you have a problem, ask yourself, can you do something about it? Yes. Then, why worry about it? And of the same problem – can you do anything about it? No. Then, why worry about it?' Either way, if you can or you can't, why worry? Worry will do nothing but exacerbate and deepen the experience of stress and dis-ease, causing 'it' to stay, clouding your judgement, prohibiting discernment and, therefore, your ability to act accordingly and appropriately.

In the barren moments of winter, the trees do not panic and grip tightly onto their leaves in fear that they will never grow again. They trust that when spring arrives, the leaves will once again make their appearance. Whether summer, autumn, winter or spring, the trees will respond to their environment, they do not resist the change of seasons – they exist within the flow of life.

Consider the animal kingdom, they move with the seasons – no resistance, no struggle – with many species hibernating throughout winter. We do not see animals resisting the urge to sleep or necking a few amphetamines to keep them going! The winter calls for a conservation of energy, this is just the way it is. As humans, we sometimes need to bow out too – honour your cycle, respect your natural rhythm, for we all dance to different tunes. Pay attention to where you're at and to what you need.

We are all part of nature and we are therefore influenced by the very same natural laws. Things change. There are cycles, phases and seasons. Things will come and things will go. Sometimes you're up and sometimes you're down. Why is one way any better than another? By *allowing* what is – whatever 'it' may be – to be, we give it and our experience the room it needs to move. We stay stuck when we hold on. To anything. We take our human experience incredibly seriously. Someone wise once said, "The path to enlightenment means lightening up!"

We miss out on so much when we're only looking

to have one type of life experience. I'll reiterate: it is our constant and immovable preferences of right and wrong that keep us locked into a cycle of judgement that will not allow for the natural flow of life to occur. Let it be.

Re-parenting Ourselves

The understanding that our upset is not welcome has been taught from very early on. For instance, in our distress as children, many of us would have heard (even if lovingly), the words, 'don't cry', 'stop crying, it's not necessary', 'you shouldn't feel upset' or 'you don't need to get so emotional'. Who's to say if we should or should not feel something? For isn't any and every emotion we have in a moment simply our own individual human experience? The irony is, if we were given permission to *feel*, it would quickly move through, leaving us unscathed.

We feel upset, have strong emotions, the tears start rolling and those around us are quick to tell us it's wrong or immediately jump to make it better and 'fix' it, halting the e-motion that is looking to be felt and expressed. We're told to 'stop being silly', 'be brave', 'big girls/boys don't cry' and we're led to believe that crying is not OK or our feelings aren't right or acceptable. Our response to our feelings can be met with a level of disapproval and we therefore suppress our emotions, interrupting the natural flow.

I understand that kids can cry at the drop of a hat, but something has hurt their heart. It may not make obvious sense to us, but that child is making meaning about what is occurring in their reality and something in the moment feels painful or unfair to them.

I understand this is not always the case and in some instances children cry as a learned behaviour to get exactly what they want, but there are many moments when what is needed is a level of compassion, a desire to understand what is happening in the child's world to help bring them to a different understanding, when it seems obvious that the meaning they are making is not representative of the intention or the situation at hand.

And watch how quickly a very young child will move through an emotion or feeling state if left unhindered. They are always in the moment, totally present to their experience. They haven't yet understood that these feelings are not OK and so (if given permission) they will fully embrace them and feel them fully, allowing them to move quickly through their experience, promptly forgetting it and moving on to the next.

They can be raging one minute and playing joyfully the next. We should heed their direction and unspoken advice in this matter as they silently model to us how to be with our feelings. Allow e-motion to do its thing, free from our meddling. When we stop the flow, we stay stuck and we miss the beauty in the expression and the growth that is available to us.

Allow a child to cry. Teach them that it's OK to show emotion. Tell them 'I understand that you're upset, in pain, angry'. Tell them and help them to understand the 'truth' of a situation. Be with yourself in this way also and give yourself permission to *feel*. Affirm and validate their (your) reality and experience, even if there is a misunderstanding to clear up or a course correction to make.

For instance, in cases of divorce, so many children grow up thinking they had a part to play in the parents' split, that they were somehow 'not enough' or 'not good enough' to keep the parents together. They may feel like they could have done something to avoid the separation or perhaps they weren't wanted. They have assessed a situation, given it meaning and concluded something, which becomes locked inside, becoming their truth.

They may not speak this out loud, but it will become a lens through which they view the world, to be carried with them throughout their lives, unless they are helped to understand the 'truth'. They need to be encouraged to express what is taking place within them in a safe and unconditionally loving space, being met and embraced with a deep level of genuine interest, care and concern.

As adults we need this too – a non-judgemental place where we feel we have permission to be ourselves, open with our feelings. The child needs to be helped in letting go of self-judgement and misunderstanding – they cannot do this by themselves, they look outside of themselves for affirmation, to gather information of who they are.

They will do anything to be accepted and be a 'part of'. As adults, we are able to parent ourselves back to health, but as a young child, this is not possible – they do not yet have the capacity for discernment within their experience and do not have the ability to self-reflect.

We've become so busy and distracted in life that we're not aware of what is taking place inside of those around us (not to mention within ourselves), simply because we are not taking the time to understand.

For instance, if we're in an irritable mood and on being asked a question we snap back in response, it's incredibly easy for the 'other' to conclude that our reaction and irritation is about them as they may feel personally attacked. It's an easy mistake to make and much of the time we are not taking the time to clear up the miscommunication and misunderstanding, if we even notice it.

We're so absorbed in our own worlds and up in our heads, slaves to our phones, technology, a to-do list that snakes ever onward into the future and worry-thinking, etc that we have almost cut ourselves off from our emotional radar, unable to detect nuances in those around us, neglecting to listen out for that which is not being said, oblivious to an atmosphere or an energy in the room.

These subtleties and oftentimes, not so subtle signs, are being missed in our preoccupation elsewhere and we're missing out on human connection (our lifeblood) and opportunities for healing. We have become emotionally illiterate. We're constantly looking out for our own individual needs and hot spots and, whilst caretaking another's anxiety brought about by a misperception is not your responsibility – clearing up any misunderstanding within those you love is of importance.

If you desire to be known and to know another, to be seen, loved and accepted for who you are and to extend this to another, you owe it to yourself to show up, do your inner work and risk transparency and authenticity. This is the doorway to connection.

From my vantage point today, I see the irony in my own life. I'd been hiding to keep myself safe, shrinking myself and wondering why I felt so alone and, the truth is, if I would have shared more of myself, my truth and my version of reality, had I not been so guarded, I would've forged stronger connections, the very thing that I was crying out for. Regardless of people agreeing with me or not, my authenticity would have given others in my life the chance to really know me. Intimacy - into-me-you-see. Their reaction to my truth is not my business. Showing up fully and authentically, is.

This way of being is a new language for many of us and you'll trip and fall. But watch a child learning to walk, they don't just rise up and take a brisk walk around the block – they try, they fall, they try again, they stumble, they fall, they bump their head, they cry, they're flat on their face, but one day, in the not too distant future, they're up and away. Walking for the baby is a new language for the body. Indeed, when we learn anything that brings about change and insight, we are learning a new way of *being* in the world, which is in itself a new level of identity.

And once they've 'got it', the child will stay up, ready to face the world within this whole new way of being. Their body now knows a new way of being in the world – upright. And showing up on two feet instead of crawling on all fours will give a child a whole new perspective and outlook on life, a whole new range of abilities. A new world of opportunity will open up for them. They can reach heights they never could before and will experience a whole new level of independence – just with this one new skill of standing up straight and walking (instead of crawling) in the world. This new-found freedom is worth the frustration, the bump on the head, a fall on the face, a few tears and a stumble, because what's on offer far surpasses the 'down' side, excuse the pun.

So many of us move through life on our hands and knees when we have the ability to walk tall. If we'd just raise our heads and put a little effort in the right direction, we'd be upright very soon, giving us an altogether different vista, causing life to unfurl and spread wide open for us in response to our new way of being. But you must be willing to keep walking in this direction of change.

It's time to give up the blame game – it's over now. We're no longer children and, as grown-ups, it's time to take responsibility for our own lives, giving full attention to our inner and outer worlds. It's time to re-parent ourselves.

We cannot continue to point the finger of blame, for when we do, we have one finger pointing at the 'other' and three fingers pointing back at us. The work/the difference (in us, in our experience of life) starts with us.

Blame will keep you stuck. It will keep you locked into the old story of victimhood, a perpetuated negative loop. It will do you no favours whatsoever. Wherever and whenever in your life you choose not to forgive, instead holding onto anger and resentment, you are hurting yourself.

This energy will be held by you in your body and mind, proficiently eating away at you. It is not the other who will feel the effect of this level of disdain, for they will be totally oblivious as you seethe and writhe inside. But you, you will feel the repercussions of this type of negativity, it will leak into your veins and poison you, bleeding into your relationships and into your life. The other, in their ignorance, will remain untouched.

We have to consciously choose to let go of all judgement, anger and fear-based emotions and instead look within and use our energy to re-build the bridge back to our Selves, building a strong foundation, cultivating love and creating a loving relationship with ourselves. Judgement and anger are the breeding ground for dis-ease – they are malignant.

Your choice is this – live fully alive or half dead. It's time to get real and authentic and speak your truth. Give voice to that which is in your heart and on the tip of your tongue. It's time to risk true connection. You need to. It's life or death. Not embracing this way of being should scare you more than the alternative – the thought of moving through life as a watered-down version of yourself with fair-weather connections should terrify you more.

You must dare to risk. It is in risking that your life will change. Again, you'll stumble, fall, stutter and get hurt along the way and not everyone will stick around, but so what? Some will and, let me tell you, each one of those deeper connections will be worth all the pain and the battle scars. Every heartfelt connection will be worth a million of those that operated on a surface level. I assure you, as you start to up-level who you are in the world, the relationships around you will also move up a notch, a substantial notch. As you change, that which is in your life and around you will also change.

We are meant to show up fully, in all our messiness, with all our imperfections and quirks – it's what makes us uniquely and beautifully us. We are meant to shine our individual light. Life wants us to live expansively, with fully loving hearts and boundless energy, with passion, joy and vision.

We are not meant to hide that which lies buried in our hearts, bow our heads and shy away from expressing fear, hurt, sadness, grief or anger, we were made to show up fully, as the glorious and magnificent sparks of light that we truly are… No judgement, no apology, just simply and fantastically You, in all of your splendour.

PART IV

Living the New Worldview

Everything is Happening Perfectly

Everything in your life comes about in order to support your evolution. You can either be aware of this or not. You can live your life unconsciously, seeing yourself as a leaf being blown about on the breeze (therefore missing out on golden opportunities), or with awareness as we see ourselves as conscious collaborators with life, aware that we are partnering with a force that holds our full flourishing in potential and of paramount importance.

And if somebody/something was willing you forward and holding your full flourishing as a priority, 'it' would do its damnedest to show you everything that stands in the way of this – everything that needs to be transformed – all your beliefs, behaviours, limitations, etc that are keeping you living smaller than is possible and that do not serve this greater version of you. Life will continually show you what's up for re-negotiation, but you must be a willing participant, with the eyes to see and the ears to hear.

There is growth in every circumstance and situation. In every challenging occurrence, there's something to be seen. In each difficult relationship, person and situation, there is a nugget of gold. Nothing is for nothing and everything that rattles your cage is an opportunity for growth.

Watch what's familiar. Your challenges are your friends and you can either wail uncontrollably at the feet of difficulty or you can stand back, reflect and consider why this scenario and your reaction to it has shown up in the movie of your life (again) and what it is that you need to do to (re)evaluate. We must always be asking ourselves, What do I most need to learn? What is my part in this dynamic? What do I need to see about this person/situation/myself? What is life showing me? What do I need to let go of? How can I graduate?

You will be shown all the ways in which you are keeping yourself small, Self-abdicating, denying your truth, settling for less and guarding yourself against Love. You will recognise the beliefs you hold which no longer serve you and all the ways in which you judge yourself and others, which keeps you separate, but you must be interested in making the space and taking the time to see.

I have had more than my fair share of difficult relationships and incredibly familiar, co-dependent dynamics playing out again and again in my life. And for years I pointed the finger outward, outraged at the behaviour of another, incensed at someone's ability to cruise through life seemingly unscathed as they left a wake of carnage trailing behind them (my upset). And although, on an intellectual level I knew this was happening perfectly (coming up for re-negotiation, transformation and healing) on a human/feeling level, I still felt acute anger and the anxiety associated with co-dependency. I needed to claim responsibility for my part/my reaction.

Recently, I 'got it' on another level. I actually found myself saying 'thank you' out loud in the acknowledgement that a certain individual had been my teacher. In my experience of our 'difficult' dynamic, I saw that she had helped me to see all the ways in which I was keeping myself small (outdated beliefs and behaviours), showing me all of the parts of myself that needed healing, thus allowing me to deepen into my Self and stand for my Truth. This was very different from the way I had previously thought about this person, as I had, for the most part, run judgmental thinking about them through my mind. How would I have known the things that still needed attention if they weren't (I wasn't) triggered?

I won't say the change happened instantaneously or that the charge left me immediately, but in this 'seeing' on a deeper level, something shifted. Namely, I saw this was my deal (familiar to me) and I took responsibility, which brought me back into my power and allowed me to make different choices, so I no longer felt at the mercy of another's behaviour. We need people in our lives as mirrors – we can only grow in relationship to others.

There is a story of a monk, meditating deep in the Himalayas on a quest for enlightenment. One day, when he feels he has achieved this great feat, he starts to wander back down the mountain on his way back to integrate into society. As he descends the mountain, he comes across some highly animated children who, in their play, obstruct his path. He becomes immediately agitated at this unexpected turn of events, feeling anger rise within him and, no sooner has this reaction occurred, than he recognises the 'problem' and promptly does an about turn, making his way back up the mountain and back into his cave. There was clearly more introspection and internal 'work' to be done.

We are not islands. We do not operate in isolation. It is not enlightenment if we keep ourselves separate and find peace only in solitude. It is not evolution if we can only find stillness and quiet once we're alone. Evolution happens in relationship – to people and to life. So, when we think we're 'there', destination attained, life will give you reminders that there's more that needs evolving, there's something you're not seeing, an avenue you've yet to explore and many of these reminders come in the form of people and dynamics.

Therefore, love the people and situations that cause you frustration, anger, upset, sadness, grief, irritation, annoyance, etc, for these are the gateways to your liberation. Thank those individuals who trigger you and burrow right under your skin for there is something here worthwhile considering – they are your teachers; they are showing you something that you need to look at.

I know this is not always easy and in the grip of strong

emotion it's sometimes just not possible to see outside of it and hold the bigger picture, but always know, 'everything is happening perfectly' and when the strong 'charge' has left you (which it most certainly will), you can do your work, remember and re-member.

And forgiveness is key. We do not always do this for the 'other', we do it for ourselves. Resentment keeps us stuck, forgiveness sets us free – free to be our Selves, to make our contribution to the world, free to move into a place of compassion and into our natural state of love.

Shakespeare alludes to life being a dream, an illusion and, as I see it, a set created for our evolution:

All the world's a stage,
And all the men and women merely players;
They have their exits and their entrances,
And one man in his time plays many parts.

We are all merely playing our necessary roles in this divine production called Life.

Everything is a mirror, reflecting back to you your current belief systems and that which needs attention. Look around you. Who's/what's in your life? What does it look like/feel like? What have you created for yourself? What's familiar? The people/situations in your life can only show up if you've invited them in and written them into your script.

What is it in you that is triggered by an individual or a situation? What's your part in the dynamic? Where's the hook? For someone can only hang up their coat where there's a peg and in your irritation, you are that peg!

You are a magnet/a vibrational match to this occurrence – your belief system literally willed it into existence. Although it would be convenient to point the finger of blame, you cannot deny that your feelings are familiar to you – you recognise them, you've had this reaction and 'response' to life many times before and felt the exact same way. Therefore, this experience simply cannot be 'out there' if you are always present when it's happening – you are the common denominator in the story of your life. You are the one who witnesses and experiences the 'thing'.

How is it that others in the same situation do not 'suffer' or react in the same way you do? This is why the same familiar stories and patterns will come up again and again, on repeat, until you no longer embrace and entertain them. You need these experiences. They are here to show you which beliefs are old and need graduating, what is no longer serving you. They will continue to recur until you recognise and understand that it is indeed you who is creating them through your beliefs and expectations – we are all always living in our story. 'Own' it and take responsibility – this is the doorway to change.

Watch what occurs within you as you're triggered. Reaction is unconscious and comes from history, whereas a response in the moment comes from being present. We are looking to respond to life, not abdicate from the present moment, as we become slaves to the past (experiences), going asleep to our Now. You cannot be 'here' if you're living 'over there', that is, looking through the lens of the past.

Whatever difficulty you're faced with, life is giving you another chance and opportunity to transform those less than desirable feelings, emotions and occurrences from your experience. Life is tapping you on the shoulder to take notice – it is urging you to evolve, to become more than this, live greater than this. There are always messages in the struggle.

It can seem that the moment we breathe a sigh of relief that 'that' is over, we come across another little (cataclysmic!) bump in the road. We are here on planet Earth to evolve, to remember and re-member who we are. Whether you believe it or not, you signed up for this, so life is always going to show you where your edges are and where your growth lies. Your reactions and your ideas of yourself are all part of an old story that will continue to play out until you let them go.

Sleepwalking through life, unaware of your creative contribution in any given situation, means you'll feel like a victim. But as an awake individual, interested in and focused on your evolution, you'll look at the same situation with curious awareness, with a level of detachment as you view 'it' as separate from you, interested in your creation, interested in what's being shown, interested in seeing your part in the story (what in you, pulled this into being?) Take a good look at what no longer serves you and become willing to let go of that which is ready for the off.

These 'negative' feelings, thoughts, limitations and behaviours (as we stifle our voices, hold back, reinforce the lies, live up to the labels and resist or go against the flow) will cause dis-ease within us that will not remain on the mental level, but will manifest as physical illness if we do not pay attention to the messages. If we ignore the nudges and the gentle tapping at the door, Life will knock harder and give us messages on the physical plane in a bid to further grab our attention. Life is saying, "OK, we've tried to grab your attention the easy way, but seeing as you've ignored the whispers, we'll shout a little louder!"

Your growth lies in the graduation of your patterns and behaviours (internal and external) and this includes moving past the old story(ies) and freeing the stuck energies and emotions that are keeping you experiencing Groundhog Day.

Can you imagine what 'you' exists on the other side of the anger, the hurt, the pain, the grief, the irritation? What do you suppose the You who is free of this stuff, would do? How would you feel and behave if you shed the old patterns and behaviours, no longer weighed down in fear and limitation, instead showing up as your best self? Could you imagine how freeing it would be to let go of the lower vibrational reactions to 'life' and have an altogether different relationship to the same stuff? It's possible. Very possible.

Before I end this chapter, I would like to make

something clear in reference to the perfection of life with regard to my own journey. Although I no longer view myself as Victim but as Creator, I want you to understand that I wouldn't change a thing that has led me to this moment. I see the perfection of all that has gone before. I see that I would not have the depth of empathy, compassion, level of understanding or wisdom that I have been blessed with if I hadn't walked this path.

It is precisely because I have moved through these life experiences that I am able to enjoy a very deep and rich experience of life with the ability to identify so closely with (and to help) others. The 'mistakes' I have made and the depth of internal suffering I have experienced has given me the capacity to 'see' more clearly than I could have before. My experiences have allowed me to sit with others in a deep space of care, attention and connection. Had I not travelled this path, I doubt this would be possible.

So, yes, I see that I have created my life; I see that potentially much of my suffering could have been avoided and, at the same time, I see the perfection. I trust life and I trust that I needed all these experiences for my evolution. I am deeply grateful for this journey. I see that life has a plan for me (indeed, it does for all of us) and in order to be here now, I needed to move through all that has gone before. As I say, the best gifts are often wrapped in suspect packaging. I thank God that it all came to pass.

Questions Open Doors

The questions we ask are more important than the answers. This is something I've been fascinated with over the years; it's one of the most important things I've learned and utilised. If you're wanting to understand more about yourself, life, the world, how to (do anything), where to find an answer, then you'll need to start asking different questions. If we're doing the same thing every day and processing the same information on a loop, where's the entry point for something new to pop in? Where's the difference that makes the difference? Again, the definition of insanity – doing the same thing over and over again and expecting different results.

Questions are hugely powerful in that they start a ball rolling in an entirely new direction. Considering something 'different' allows your brain to go 'in search' for answers. Questions that we currently do not consciously know the answers to – for example, 'What does the grandest version of my life look like?' provokes interest and allows the mind to wander, to venture out of its familiar surroundings and comfort zone to go looking for the answer.

We're intending to put our heads above the parapet and stretch ourselves out to grow more, do more; to look outside the parameters of the current reality we're living in and make space for something altogether new and wonderfully unexpected to flow in. Looking in a new direction with interest will allow your brain to contemplate and make space for things you haven't yet seen and, as thoughts create reality, different thoughts will create a different reality.

Questions bring things alive. If you're unsure of what you want to do in your life, you'll need to start asking questions – open questions – questions that truly allow the mind to wander and imagine. You're looking to STRETCH your mind, expand and grow, peer around the corner of the street you've always lived in and get interested in who and what lives outside. What new things are waiting for you there? What new experiences and opportunities live on the other side of the fence? What is it that you've not yet seen? Asking new questions moves you from the same small, suffocating four walls and into an entirely different domain – somewhere 'out there', where the You that you're interested in becoming already resides.

The greater and grander version of You currently exists in the world of potential, the place where all of your dreams are not only a possibility but are already manifest and if you desire to bring this version into your now, you'd do well to re-focus your gaze and attention to 'higher' planes (outside of your 'known') in order to see it, show up and claim it.

The only things that are limiting any of us in any moment are our beliefs, our ability and willingness to imagine – there are absolutely no limits apart from those we place upon ourselves. We need to 'think outside of the box', that is, the head on our shoulders that has given us our version of reality; namely, what we think we know.

Looking for the answers from the 'known', from within the same four walls is futile and keeps you stuck. You're been locked in this same room for years, you know this room by heart – you've already searched everywhere. Every crevice and corner is familiar to you, yet you continue to search for the 'new' in the same place, scrambling in the dark, looking for something that lives outside of this space, going over and over old ground and repeating more of the 'same'.

The you that lives 'out there' doesn't live 'in here', otherwise you would have already bumped into him/her. Wouldn't you? For the room you have occupied has been very small. Move out. It's akin to misplacing something precious and searching in the same drawer day after day, year after year, wondering why it's not showing up, wondering why it doesn't simply appear. If you at least want to give yourself a chance of finding the lost article, you'd better widen your search.

You can get really specific here too; you can set your brain the task of finding any type of answer by asking better questions. For instance, 'If I knew what my next step would be, what would that look like? What would I know? What would I do? Where would I go? What would I say and to whom?'

These questions are full of creative juice. Feel into them. The more specific you are, the more information you stand to gain. Imagine throwing out a fishing net – the wider the net, the further the throw, the greater the distance and the more substantial the catch.

You move into uncharted territory when you 'throw out' a question you've not yet asked or considered as your brain goes off to find the answer. When you truly start imagining who this 'new you' is and take the time to *feel* into this being, you give your brain a mission, setting different wheels in motion, wheels that will take you to your preferred destination.

Think about your brain as a book of knowledge that you have accumulated over your life. If you keep searching in the same book, you will keep referencing the same information. If you want to expand your knowledge, learn an instrument or research a new subject, you would have to reference different material – buy the instrument or purchase a book on the subject of interest. Searching for the 'new' within the 'already known' is not going to enable you to grow.

Consider a dog with a stick or a ball. The further you throw, the further the dog will run to 'fetch', for it has its eyes on the prize. You can continue to throw the ball within the confines of your garden area or you can open the gate and take aim into the land that surrounds the fence. No matter how far you throw, the dog will give chase and will always come back with the goods, for the aim of the game is to 'catch' and your canine friend will not come back without the prize.

Your brain is a powerful tool and the more you stretch it, the further you 'throw', the more you'll learn and grow. Your brain will go looking for answers until it comes back with 'the ball', but you must do this with genuine interest, knowing that it's possible to be-come something and somebody different, that the answers you need are 'out there' (in actual fact, they are within you… somewhere yet unknown). Look with curiosity and intrigue, committed to your intention and evolution, knowing that 'somewhere' this new you and your best life, exists.

If you reside in the energy of lack, showing up half-heartedly and somewhat disbelieving that you can have or do anything, you will block the energy of abundance from entering your life and you will create more of the same. Knowing that you already are the best version of yourself (in the realm of possibility), holding a strong belief and conviction that somewhere in the world of potential you've already achieved your goals, you will make space for this new you to materialise into your now. Know this to be possible, keep an unwavering commitment to this path, regardless of how quickly this new you manifests, knowing that it is not a matter of if, but simply a matter of when. Remember, the timing is not up to us.

Impossible is, in actual fact, 'I'm-possible'.

Close your eyes, ask your questions and allow your mind to wonder and wander, to go fetch. *Feel* who you are in your new life, *feel* who you are when you show up fully, unlimited, in your power – radiant, transparent and on purpose. *Feel* who you are as you embody this new you and show up in this way, shining your light and doing your precious work in the world. *Feel* what it's like to be in partnership with others and with life, surrounded by deep, authentic and nourishing relationships, surrounded by your tribe. Care enough about this version of yourself to embody this new You every day, bringing this new idea and upgraded version of yourself into your body, feeling it and making it your reality now.

The brain doesn't know the difference between reality and imagination. We create from our level of vibration, so consider and meditate on what you're wanting to manifest once or twice a day, taking as long as you can to imagine who you are at your 'best'. Get really specific. Imagine what you would be doing on a day-to-day basis if you were living your best life and showing up as your best self. Imagine what you would be saying to people as this version of you. Imagine how you would feel if all of your dreams had become manifest. Imagine the friends you would have, the colleagues you would be working with, the people you would attract into your life, the area/house you would live in, the pastimes you would engage in. You can get really specific here and *feel* it, with all of your being

– *feel* it.

If you feel into this new you as if it already exists, bringing this knowledge deep into your cells and into your body, your brain will think this exists in 'real time' and life will organise the external events and circumstances to support this vision and version of you. Remember, you are a creator. Your job is to imagine, then let it go, knowing it is done. Release this into the Universe and surrender the results. Amen – so be it.

And you can't do this just one time. You've been living in habit patterns of thought and behaviour for years and years; one attempt at changing your brain chemistry so that it literally creates a different reality, isn't going to do it – just like one visit to the gym will have little or no effect; one meal a week won't keep you nourished and one shower every few days won't keep you smelling fresh. If you care about change, you'll want to reinforce this intention every day and create an entirely new habit and feeling state with a strong commitment to the 'difference', deepening into this new way of thinking and *being*, as a daily practice.

If you do this regularly, feel and *believe*, it is not a case of *if* this new life will find you, but simply, when. Strengthen this feeling state, raise your frequency, make this your truth, show up in your everyday life as if all your dreams have already manifested, embody this version of yourself and make *this* your new default, make this your every day and watch your life change as it mirrors back to you your commitment towards expansion and possibility with your upgraded level of vibration and change of feeling state.

We are energy beings and our vibration will attract in that which has a resonance to it. Like attracts like, we attract from where we're at. It is absolutely possible for you to become a completely different human, an entirely new being. Imagination is the key.

Imagination is real; it's not the stuff of fantasy. Well, in a way it is, but it's a fantasy that exists in another realm, which can become your reality right now. Anything is possible. Do not limit yourself. If your negativity, worry, limiting beliefs and thinking brought you here (for is this not imagination, also? Just from a low vibration of fear-based thinking) then so too can the higher vibratory thoughts borne from love, expansion and joy take you somewhere altogether different and create a totally new reality.

We are partners with the creative force of life, creating with our thoughts – our beliefs, our ideas and our vibration. Do not look to the external for a shift in consciousness and reality.

In summary, your only limitations are your ideas of who and what you can be. Bigger and better thinking creates a bigger and better reality. You can create from fear or love – the choice is yours – but know without a doubt that you are always making a choice in every given moment, whether you know it or not, for even no choice is a choice in and of itself. Instead of fear, let's default to love.

I'll end this chapter with one of my favourite quotes:

"Who looks outside, dreams; who looks inside, awakes."

Carl Jung

Trust in a Higher Power

This human condition is tricky and no sooner have we learnt something helpful to our evolution here on Earth, than it's moved right on through and we find ourselves, once again, in an all too familiar place, bewildered and scratching our heads, nugget of wisdom nowhere to be found.

It's simply not enough to hear something once and hope it sticks for the rest of our incarnation. We are constantly in the process of remembering and forgetting, slipping in and out of our 'aha' moments and higher levels of consciousness, right back into our humanness. This is exactly what happened to me when I found myself bemoaning to a friend, fighting against what 'is' as I moved through some seemingly challenging times. My friend who, at that moment, was a little less caught up in human drama and the emotion of upset, considered my woes and promptly offered the following:

"Emma, you need to start trusting in G-d."

Me: "I do."

The response: "Obviously not enough…"

These few words were enough to stop me in my tracks as I quickly realised that I had moved out of a place of trust. In that moment, I saw my thinking and recognised I'd slipped right back into victim mentality. The thoughts I had been running through my mind were anything but supportive of my wellbeing, acceptance of what 'is' and surrender into the Great Unknown. I had come to view the circumstances in my life as 'wrong'. I felt stuck, nothing was making sense and life seemed unfair. I believed that life had forgotten me and I was walking this road alone, needing to take control of the wheel... and the pedals.... and the oars... and the sails....

Now, we know that I'm aware that there's a power greater than me, greater than all of us, a power that accompanies us on our journey and knows what's best for us and I realised in that moment (and some of the moments that preceded it!) that I had 'forgotten' and I was in the market for a reminder. We will find ourselves in this place many times on the journey. As I say, it's a hazard of the human condition!

I had forgotten that everything happens perfectly, despite it looking differently to how I'd imagined or preferred. I had forgotten that what I thought I needed and what I believed to be for the best was a long way off from the truth and is, in actual fact, simply a bunch of ideas borne from small mind mentality which absolutely cannot know (from my limited viewpoint) what's in the best interest for my highest evolution and the greater good.

This brief communication with my friend caused me to see that, once again, I had slipped into the old story and had bought into scarcity thinking, entertaining fear and worry. I realised I had neglected my daily spiritual practice (a necessity if we wish to embody a new way of being) and fallen back into old patterns. In my resistance to the circumstances in my life (forgetting to trust), I was causing my own distress.

If I'd relaxed and remembered that what was occurring was 'meant to be', I could, however challenging, accept whatever was taking place in my life and trust that, although it looked a little suspect from my perspective and I had moved into upset and disappointment, I would understand the 'why' a little further down the line. Maybe something better was coming my way; maybe a relationship dynamic needed to be evolved or let go of; perhaps I needed a reminder there was still work to do in a particular area of my life… perhaps, perhaps…

In my tunnel vision I had forgotten that it is not me alone conducting the many musicians that make up the Great Orchestra of Life, it is not up to me to weave together this great tapestry or pull all the pieces of the jigsaw together. It's timing. There is a bigger picture and the pieces come together when the time is right and when I'm slap-bang in the middle of a 'crisis' (that is, triggered and buying into my thinking) or unsure of which direction to move in, it can be challenging to keep my ground and trust in the perfection of the journey and it's nigh on impossible to guess what the finished canvas will look like.

I needed reminding that I am not the controller. Indeed, I work in tandem with life, within a field and force much greater than me, in conjunction with 'something out there' that knows what's best for me, knows much better, in fact, than I ever could from my limited perspective.

I also recognised that I had not been reaching out to others for support, but instead I had viewed myself as a one-woman band, thinking I needed to pull everything together alone. I had forgotten that life is about relationships and, as a result, I was struggling – not an easy or comfortable place to reside in and an awful burden to bear.

I have learnt over the years that to live a life of freedom, joy and abundance, it is absolutely necessary to hand our troubles over to something bigger than ourselves, to place our trust in a greater force and then surrender. Whether you refer to that 'something' as G-d, the Universe, The Divine, The Field and Force of Life, Great Spirit, the power of the group (for there is more power in 'we' than me), or whatever works for you, we need to cultivate a deep knowing that even in times of turmoil and struggle we have support, both seen and unseen, that there is a bigger picture at play, a path unfolding for us that is absolutely in alignment with our highest good. Life knows better – it is not solely up to us.

When we pray and ask for what we want, let's leave our prayers 'open' for that, which we cannot yet see to materialise in our life. Instead of asking for one particular thing (that may or may not benefit us in the long run), why not ask for that which is for the (our) highest good and the highest good of all? I tend to end my prayers with, "this or something better," to make room for that which is not yet clear to me in the moment. I acknowledge that my perspective is limited; that I cannot see further down the line to determine what is for the best. I put a cork in the creative flow with fixed ideas of the (my) future, leaving no room for the alternative – that which is 'better'.

Life is awesome, anything is possible and asking for only one thing or looking in only one direction is like visiting a theme park and going on only one ride again and again and again or visiting a new country and staying only in your hotel complex.

You'll only know what's 'out there' when you go to explore, you'll only have the full experience of a country/ culture when you move outside of the hotel gates, mix with the locals, sample the food, go on a tour and take in the sights and scout around for interesting things to do. Bottom line, get interested in what you haven't yet seen and, in this way, your life will take an altogether different turn – you'll widen your vista.

I had this very experience. I'd been working in an area for a few months and when the weather was good enough, I liked to take a walk in the park. The little bit of green situated opposite the office was nice enough, but it wasn't so big. On my way back from buying my lunch one day, I realised that I wasn't quite ready to sit in front of the computer so I carried on walking, down a different street, but still right next to the office block. And after taking no more than five or six steps, I came across an opening to another park. I was more than a little surprised and carried on down the path, which in no time at all, led me to a huge expanse of grass, playing fields, a restaurant and a children's playground.

This park was literally behind the office I worked in and the opening was directly next to the place I parked my car. But because I had neglected to move out of the 'known' (same lunch spot, same walking circuit, same direction), I hadn't raised my line of focus and seen what was right in front of my face. It took me six months to 'discover' this!

The things we desire are right in front of our face, we're just inside of so much routine, habit patterns, conditioning, judgement and old thinking that we literally cannot see them. There are doors to walk through and places to discover all around us, if only we'd raise our heads, open our eyes and look.

This trust in something bigger than ourselves allows us to relax into a space where we can rest assured in the unknown. We come to understand that the openings are 'there', that we will see and discover what we need when the time is right; that even when we don't know, when we're lost in confusion and when things seem to be moving in the opposite direction to our desires, there is a larger plan in action. We need only trust and 'go with the flow' instead of pushing upstream, 'efforting', controlling and struggling to divert the flow of water. There's really not much of a choice in this anyway – have a go at pushing a river upstream and let me know how you get on! Life has your back – make this your mantra.

Remember, life is always wanting us to evolve, to be-come more of our Selves, so it will always set up the perfect conditions, circumstances and opportunities for this to take place. As I said, it won't always feel pleasant or comfortable, but that's not up to us – growth is growth. Sometimes it's painful and sometimes it feels as if we're walking through treacle and we may feel as though we've taken a step backwards. There will be times when it seems as though we've moved through the same thing thousands of times before and, if this sounds familiar, life is showing you that there's still something you're not seeing that needs evolving. Life is giving you another opportunity to let go by presenting you with yet another situation in which you have the option to choose differently.

Be genuinely thankful for your difficulties. As I have said, these are your biggest teachers and if navigated well, they will be fundamental in shaping who you are and creating your best life.

Life is a jigsaw puzzle and unless you have seen the picture on the box, you cannot know the finished image until most of the pieces are in place and maybe even then there'll be some surprises. And this is life, we create and pave our path with each step we take; with each stitch, we pull the fabric of our life together. Even when we are unclear on our next port of call or where exactly we are headed, just taking steps in the 'right' direction, towards that which we desire to create (holding it loosely to allow for an upgraded version to take its place) puts a statement of intent out into the Universe.

Life will absolutely reward your effort. Sometimes we cannot see the wood for the trees, we cannot see the 'how' and our next steps are unclear to us. In this case, *knowing* that clarity will come when the time is right is, in my opinion, the meaning of trust and surrender. Yes, there needs to be action on our part, but sometimes, when you simply do not know, 'action' simply means a commitment to trust and to letting go.

Do not measure your success in terms of what you see; the five senses are not a good indicator of your 'progress'. Trust that with all your effort, even if 'it' hasn't shown up on the 3-D plane as yet, life is working on your behalf behind the scenes – you're being supported in the unseen. Your intention and forward movement puts a very strong message out to the Universe, it shows that you are committed to the path – life will recognise and reward this level of commitment. Life is not about the destination; life is about the journey. Effort in the right direction and surrender the results. Your intention is always planting seeds.

And sometimes those seeds will need a few hours, a few days or a week or maybe they'll take years to fully blossom. It's OK, your journey is your journey – trust it.

We need balance, the yin and the yang, the action and the non-action. And make no mistake, non-action isn't nothing, it's not no-thing. It's a very necessary place of rest in-between the 'doing' and for optimal health – we need this balance for both body and mind.

In the words of Chinese philosopher, Lao Tzu, "By letting go, it all gets done…"

We've been so busy planning, scheming and 'working things out', we've operated as a full cup with no room for life to pour in. Life needs a gap to gain entry and letting go (of some thing, person, thought, idea or even clearing your physical space) creates an opening; it provides an 'in'.

On all levels and in all areas, letting go is what is going to serve us. Even when our physical bodies are hurting, if we relax and breathe into the pain, it eases. When babies fall, they bounce in their relaxed state – they have no idea or awareness of any impending danger and, therefore, do not constrict and tighten their bodies in fear of the fall. Whereas, us, we brace ourselves and hold our breath as we fear the worst – we become stiff and we break, we're injured. Bend or break – any kind of rigidity, inside or out, will work against us.

And what a relief all this is. From a place of surrender, trust, allowing and letting go, we realise that we do not have to do everything or control the outcome. We can give up on 'efforting' in the wrong direction. We can learn to relax into the knowledge that life is taking care of the details and trust that we are being held and guided, for we know that life is absolutely on our side.

Surrender is not an act of weakness, it is not laziness, but is in actuality, a great act of courage. Having faith, letting go and choosing to trust is a statement of intent and an active force – there is strong energy behind this commitment, together with willingness to release our grip, allowing the Greater Mind to lead us and bless us. We will experience riches far beyond our imaginings with this type of intention. Again, effort in the right direction and surrender the results. We can always trust life to carry us, even when we feel alone – we are always being taken care of.

And so the story goes:

Footprints in the Sand

One night a man had a dream. He dreamed he was walking along the beach with the Lord.

Across the sky flashed scenes from his life. For each scene he noticed two sets of footprints in the sand: one belonging to him, and the other to the Lord.

When the last scene of his life flashed before him, he looked back at the footprints in the sand. He noticed that many times along the path of his life there was only one set of footprints. He also noticed that it happened at the very lowest and saddest times in his life.

This really bothered him and he questioned the Lord about it:

"Lord, you said that once I decided to follow you,

you'd walk with me all the way. But I have noticed that during the most troublesome times in my life, there is only one set of footprints. I don't understand why when I needed you most you would leave me."

The Lord replied:

"My son, my precious child, I love you and I would never leave you. During your times of trial and suffering, when you see only one set of footprints, it was then that I carried you."

Once again, there is an intelligence that runs life, all life, including yours and we are being supported in every moment of our lives. Like the footsteps in the story above, we are never alone and just because we cannot see this intelligence and support (at least, not with our current powers of perception) it does not mean it is not there, guiding us, in every moment.

We have come to place so much emphasis on the five senses to provide us with evidence of the truth, that at many times in our lives it appears we are going solo, but we have so much unseen support around us, cheering us on, urging us towards our growth and evolution, whispering to each of us in all our moments and throughout our lives. If only we'd make space in our lives to notice and teach our ears to hear and listen.

"Every blade of grass has an angel that bends over it and whispers, Grow! Grow!" The Talmud

I wonder what it must be like to observe us humans from higher dimensions, watching as we struggle and attempt to control our circumstances, holding on for dear life, taking life so incredibly seriously, totally unaware of our innate potential, our beauty and our gifts and the power that lies in letting go.

And what patience Life has, always supporting us, committed to our evolution, whilst we, for the most part, remain deaf to the promptings, failing to heed the call. Still we continue to be supported, still our support system refuses to abandon ship, for our potential is known and it is only a matter of time until we re-member.

And how truly wonderful to be able to trust in this support, knowing that we are truly loved and are being held and guided always. Life/God loves us in the way we love our children and no matter how our offspring play up, drive us mad, make the wrong choices, remain stubborn, defiant and ignore our pleas; we never give up on them. We continue to embrace them and hold them in our hearts in love, urging them forward, supporting them, hoping they will realise just how beautiful, wonderful and precious they truly are, hoping they will heed our guidance. We want the very best for our loved ones and so too, does Life, for us.

This understanding – letting go as opposed to holding on, surrendering instead of constant 'efforting' – may very well be a complete change of worldview for you, but really, it's about accepting that there is more to life than meets the eye, looking in another direction and seeing something that's previously been under our radar. It's noticing the unnoticed and making the invisible, visible. Everything we need is within us and right in front of us, but as I've said many times, we need the eyes to see and the ears to hear.

When the lights go off at night, you may claim it's pitch-black, that you cannot see anything, but give it a few moments and shapes will appear – you'll be able to see a little as your eyes adjust, there are always things that will become apparent from within the darkness. There is always knowing in the unknown. Not everything is as it appears at first sight. If you wait, with trust and patience, things will take shape and become clear. Things will change.

No matter where you are in your life and no matter what situations you find yourself in, everything is happening perfectly. You must trust this. Even when you find yourself on your knees and bewildered, give yourself permission to be right where you are and remember the external is illusory. Remember that you cannot see the full picture from your limited perspective, remind yourself to stay faithful and trust, safe in the knowledgethat there is a bigger picture at play and your job is to deepen into this knowing… all the time. This too shall pass.

"What things soever ye desire, when ye pray, believe that ye receive them, and ye shall have them." (Mark 11:24)

Remember, the timing's not up to us.

The In-Between

"If you're brave enough to say goodbye, life will reward you with a new hello." Paulo Coelho, *The Alchemist*

So, what do we do when we do not know? What do we do when the gap looms large and we're not 'there' yet?

In our preoccupation with being human 'doings', busying ourselves in life to the point of distraction in our endless quest to…. well, who knows? We've found ourselves lost. As I have said, we have become resistant to doing… nothing. We are scared of the nothingness, scared of the gap, scared to stare into the void. We are scared of being idle, not just because we have been led to believe this will lead us down a path of destruction, but also because we cannot bear to see ourselves, to stare the truth in the face as it screams loudly at us. We know that when the rollercoaster stops, we will be faced with ourselves and we may not like what we see.

We may have to admit that where we are in life feels way off target, that the relationships in our lives are not nurturing us and our dreams (if we can even remember them) feel far, far away and unattainable. We may then have to accept that things need to change and this truth may overwhelm us.

So, we keep the rollercoaster moving, we stay on the treadmill. We are forever moving from one thing to the next, running from pillar to post, wasting time, wasting energy, depleting our inner resources, remaining asleep on automatic, each 24 hours running into the next whilst our dreams hang lifeless somewhere in the space between.

We're making choices unconsciously and in service to what? Which direction are we headed in – do we even know?

We've forgotten to make room to breathe. We have forgotten to stop and take stock, to rest, to simply *be* and see what evolves from the space. For how can we truly know what we want, what we truly desire, if we haven't taken the time to consider this, if we haven't checked 'in' and asked those very important Questions that unlock the doors to a new reality? When was the last time you took a deep dive inside and asked, 'What is it that I'm desiring to create?', 'What is it that I want to do in the world and to be in service to?', 'What would I like my life to look like?', 'What would I like my life to stand for?' or 'Who am I?'

We think life is in the doing, but truly the good bits, that which is golden, the magic, can be found in the stillness. We must become quiet and present to ourselves in order to come to know who we are under the noise we experience both internally and externally. We need to listen deeply to what our hearts are urging us to see. We can only hear this when we stop, pause or take a breath.

For me, this place where I've stopped (doing, being) something and not yet started something else, is known as The In-Between. It is a place where I have experienced an ending and the next beginning is unclear. It's a place between death and birth, death of the old and the birth of the new – a place where I rest in-between growth phases.

I have moved on from the me that was and am moving towards and growing into the me that will be, the me who beckons me forever forward. I have made inroads, I have navigated hurdles, I have grown, I have become a little wiser and I have arrived at a place, sometimes in a place of calm and gratitude, sometimes a little battered and bruised, but with a renewed sense of self and a vision of where I'm headed.

Between these two places, I must rest and take stock; consider the 'unfoldment' of the journey, view the bigger picture, notice what is calling to be seen and integrated and notice what's urging me forward. Who was I? Where was I? What have I learnt? What has changed? And the all-important – where am I going?

And then I stop and I listen and I *allow* myself to simply *be*, trusting that in my 'beingness' and in my commitment to up-level and move forward, the next 'right' thing will be along very soon. My job is simply to show up, keep deepening into faith, keep trusting and take the next step that feels right, for me. No comparisons, no benchmarks, no adherence to an old, outdated script in my head, just listening for my rhythm, dancing to and honouring my own tune.

Prior to my interest in personal evolution and all things 'spiritual', I didn't imagine this place worthy of consideration; after all, it looked like an empty space and if I did not know what was next on the agenda – it provided a good reason to fret, worry, berate myself for being here yet AGAIN and procrastinate – it was definitely not worthy of my time, energy or heartfelt contemplation.

Over the years, I have come to see that The In-Between is a very real 'thing' – it's a place in and of itself. It is most definitely not an empty space in which 'nothing' happens. On the contrary, The In-Between can be incredibly rich, rewarding and full of potential for both personal and spiritual growth. It is fertile ground, a time for planting and if the ground is cultivated consciously, you'll reap rich rewards. The In-Between can lay a strong foundation for the next phase of your life… if you'll let it.

I have found myself in this place many times over the years. A phase of my life has naturally and organically come to a close and the next phase has yet to make itself known. One door has gently closed and the other is opening, but I have yet to locate this opening and see where it leads… destination still unknown. I know it's there, I can feel it – I can feel the potential of it all around me – it's in the air… it just hasn't arrived… yet.

And here's the thing about The In-Between – it can feel scary – a credible justification as to why I should chew my fingernails to the quick, pleading distress to all who cross my path, worry myself into a stupor and generally exist in a low grade depression and a deep sense of unease. But, now I understand this place better, I have the exact opposite response. I embrace The In-Between.

I understand that things take time and there's a time for everything. No matter how much I wish for summer in wintertime, it just isn't going to happen and water will boil at 100 degrees, no matter how much of a rush I'm in... stuff happens when it happens. It's just the way life is.

If you're looking to bake a cake, you'll need to gather the ingredients, mix them all together in the correct quantities and place the mixture in the oven for an exact amount of time. If you remove the cake before the cooking time is up, you're unlikely to win first prize at the local bake off – it won't rise, it may still be sticky inside – you hadn't given it the time needed for the alchemy to happen ('the seemingly magical process of transformation, creation, or combination'). Simply, its time hadn't come.

The caterpillar in the chrysalis is another example – if you disturb this process or harm its cocoon in any way, the caterpillar will die. If it is left alone to form into its next stage of evolution – enter the butterfly. So too, do we rise and step into the next stage of our life (be it relationship, job, opportunity) when the time is right. We're ready when we're ready and not before.

I am not suggesting for one moment that we sit around passively and do nothing (although there is a time for that too), twiddling our thumbs and looking to the sky for the penny to drop, but I am suggesting that you give this space the respect it deserves and embrace it as the enormous opportunity that it is. There is potential for something totally wonderful to materialise.

Once again, the timing is not up to us and when that something that we have our heart set on doesn't arrive as quickly as we like, our job is to continue to cultivate trust, deepen into faith and let go.

It's important to find and stay in the stillness; fretting or worrying will do nothing but cause you to miss the beauty of The In-Between and possibly push away that which life is desiring to give you, for there are gifts far greater than you have imagined waiting to be handed to you, if you'd just open your hands to receive them. You cannot receive with hands which are holding onto the past. If you're rushing around unconsciously and on automatic, there's not much time for the creative process to take place – you'll just be creating more of the same.

The thing is this: not only does The In-Between offer you a possible change in direction – a path leading to more joy, creativity, love and fulfilment, it is also a time to consider whether you want to keep creating in a sidestep motion with no forward movement – same job/different company, same relationship dynamic/different person, same style of house/different street – you get my drift.

For life is always guiding you. Listen carefully for its promptings – the impulses you have towards certain activities, a need to be quiet and alone, seemingly synchronistic meetings with people able to help you on your path, an urge to turn a corner or enter a particular coffee shop, a book that comes your way, a film that inspires you, a song on the radio with a message especially for YOU (we all know that one), a 'coincidence' too uncanny to ignore – there are millions of ways in which life speaks… to you. But, you'll be hard pressed to hear or see with the volume turned up high in your head as you run worry-thinking on a loop.

This is why you'll want to befriend The In-Between, because it's here to help you step into the next stage of your evolution – the version of you that's living the life you've always dreamed of and has achieved all the things that make your heart soar. That version doesn't have to remain in your imagination as something unattainable, a pipe dream – that version of you can become your reality if you'd just believe it possible and know that life wants those things for you too – it's here to help.

As I've said, from our limited perspective, we cannot possibly know what is best for us, which is why you'll need to allow life to show you something you've not yet considered. Be open, be interested and be curious – these are the ways of being that will allow you to receive.

The golden words (as ever) are trust and faith. These are not feelings; they are commitments. Just like visiting the gym to build muscle, you have to keep working your faith and trust muscles to build them up and make them strong. The more you do it, the more faith and acceptance you'll cultivate, the more open you'll be to possibility and the more you'll receive. Don't take my word for it – try it. It's a shift in worldview and a new way of showing up. You're either open and receptive or closed and shut down – it's a simple choice. And make no mistake, it IS a choice.

In closing – nature abhors a vacuum. Something will always flow in to fill a space. If you're in The In-Between, you're in it – like it or not. But how you navigate it is entirely up to you. Will you allow circumstances to materialise based on worry, fear, lack mentality, negative self-talk and limiting beliefs? Or, are you committed to trusting the process, preferring to create your next phase from a ground that's been fertilised with unwavering trust, belief in your vision and faith in life?

So, I know it's only my personal and humble opinion, but when faced with the two options on offer, it's a no brainer for me. I know which one I'd choose.

Keeping an Attitude of Gratitude

One of the most important things I have learnt is the importance of keeping an attitude of gratitude – it's a game changer. As I have said, we are vibrational beings, creating from our feeling state. Every feeling and emotion has a vibration that can be measured.

Every emotion is vibrating to a greater or lesser degree. So too, does every thing have a vibration. So, if you're wanting to attract the good stuff, to become a magnet to those things, you'll want to become a vibrational match. Your very being is a tuning fork that will resonate with everything on the same frequency – people, places and things.

Some feeling states have a low vibration (fear, anxiety, anger, resentment, etc) and some are 'high' (joy, appreciation, love, empowerment, etc). And as we create from where we're at, attracting in from our being state, if you're having low thoughts and feeling 'crap' you will be creating from this feeling state, whereas, if you're feeling 'good' you will be creating from there. Like attracts like.

Feeling gratitude is like announcing to the Universe,

"Thank you for blessing me." You can imagine how 'high' this frequency is and what you'll attract in if you remain in this feeling state. You're sending out a message that says 'life is great, I expect abundance, I expect miracles'. More than this, you actually *be-come* the energy and frequency of gratitude when you're in it, *knowing* that life will support you and gift you with all that you need for your best life.

You send out a beacon, which calls forth your desires… and more. The Universe hears your call (feels the vibration) and responds in kind. Again, we always get what we expect. You will be supported in your beliefs and if you're walking in the world grateful (for that which you have and for that which you know is on the way – that which you *expect*), the Universe keeps providing. This is how life works.

Liken this to how you feel when listening to music. Sound is vibration too. Some types of music make you feel 'good' and other types can grate on your nerves or even cause a state of internal disturbance – you know you 'don't like it'. We are responding to the vibration. And the more you keep listening to music that upsets your internal state, the more dis-ease you'll feel, whereas the more you listen to the good stuff, the better you'll feel. Your thoughts are your music.

Walk into a room where there's been an argument and you can 'feel' it. Speak with an angry person and see how you feel after the communication. We're picking up on energy and vibration all the time, whether we know it or not. And it's up to you if you want to carry this anger or upset into your day by holding onto it, thus creating more of the same/more disturbance, or whether you desire to switch your feeling state to a higher vibration so you'll experience life from there. As always, the choice is yours.

Notice how the world looks when you're in love. Notice how the world looks when you're angry. Same world, same circumstances but different experience. Makes you think, doesn't it? Is it truly 'out there'?

Trust the Journey

When you show up as your true Self and commit never again to self-abandon, it's truly amazing who and what will show up in support and resonance with this 'new' up-levelled version of you. It is not possible from our level of consciousness to work out 'how' this will occur (the 'how' is not up to us), our job is to deepen into our sense of Self, live from this space and leave the details to the Universe as it works its magic!

My time in the charity (Chapter: Another Step Up the Ladder) is an example of trusting in the invisible hands of life to hold us and steer us in the right direction. It was a six and a half year phase of my life, which although at times felt like a backward step, laid a foundation for the next stage of my life. This phase was understood more fully by me only in hindsight, which of course, is 20/20.

To my senses and logical mind, this was all 'wrong'. I did not know back then what the invisible hands in my life were weaving together for me and what they had planned for my life. I didn't have the sense or the worldview to go this deep; my whole outlook was restricted, with the onus lying heavily on an idea of 'success' and career advancement that I had been taught within the structure of society. My outlook progressed on a linear timeline; I had no idea that one could circle back around to deepen into another (stronger, 'better') way of being.

Seeing the whole picture and just how many things had to come into play in order to create this opening and opportunity for me and just how much had been stacked 'in my favour', could only be viewed from a distance. Clarity sometimes comes when you're on higher ground, standing in a place that allows for a different perspective. The bigger picture can be perceived from this vantage point.

Your life is made up of millions of little dots that form the most beautiful picture when you join them up, but whilst you're moving through them, they're just a million little dots, seemingly random and unrelated. And as long as you live, there will be more and more dots, creating a bigger and bigger picture, with the story forever unfolding and evolving.

Some of these dots are painful, some disappointing, some can be regarded as detours and some of them feel downright unfair, but despite the 'evidence', they are the making of you and contain a much bigger purpose – they form the tapestry of your life. Fundamentally and without question, life is benevolent – it always has your back regardless of what your eyes are seeing and your ears are hearing and, most definitely, despite what your thinking is telling you. The door to your evolution and freedom lies in your understanding and *knowing* that you are always being led by invisible hands. We can always trust the journey.

Again, it was the remarkable, even miraculous events leading me to my time in the charity that deepened this understanding for me. I look back and I am astonished and humbled that such a wondrous time of my life came to pass. At the time, what was best for me was way beyond my comprehension and this period set the tone for the rest of my life.

The same is true of all that has occurred since my departure – those same invisible hands are still at work.

Leaving the charity was divinely orchestrated. It was time. It was my manager and close friend, Julian, who nudged me to leave. I think he saw that I had outgrown the place, that I had done all I could do there, that the organisation was moving in a different direction and I should spread my wings further. The energy had changed for me. Being at the charity started to feel old and 'dead' and there is nothing wrong in this – it was life telling me there was more and it was time to move on – my only job was to listen and to jump… into The In-Between, into nothing and no thing and watch the net appear.

I remember sitting on a bench in the sunshine of summer 2016 and how I felt as the realisation dawned that I was to leave. Who would I be without the embrace of the organisation? What would I do? I was so full of fear with the idea of leaving the 'home' I had become such a part of.

I honestly could not see past the charity. I could not see how I'd be OK. How would I ever find anything this good again? It had become my safe haven, such a huge part of my life and my identification. I couldn't believe how lucky and blessed I'd been to find this place and this new worldview and I simply couldn't fathom how anything as good could exist.

Still, I couldn't deny that Julian was right; I couldn't deny the truth in my heart and soul. I'd been thinking about leaving for a while. I see now that I wasn't going to do it off my own back and I'd needed a little shove – Julian provided that for me. And of course I was scared, but this was the same fear I had when I'd taken the job some six years earlier and I have come to understand that fear is never a reason not to jump – it's simply False Evidence Appearing Real.

Fear wants to keep you living small and sometimes it shouts louder than the still quiet voice within, but as I've said, the roar of fear doesn't mean it should be trusted – quite the opposite. Stillness speaks.

Those who feel the need to scream, rant and rave are potentially the people you'll want to avoid in life and the same is true with the (sometimes debilitating and excessively noisy) voice of resistance to change which is always borne from fear – desperate as it is for you to stay put in the same familiar (confining and restricting) known.

Follow your heart. Listen to your truth.

Let it be known, that I didn't fall into trust immediately and completely on my exit from the charity. At times I allowed fear to trip me up and there were a few moments when I tried to muscle my way back into the charity – some part-time work here, a little event help and PA support there – but I simply was not 'allowed'. I finally had to concede (although not always gracefully – at times I was dragged, arms flailing in protest!), but regardless, the energy had changed, I had changed and my time there was over. A line had been drawn in the sand and life had other plans for me. I was off to pastures new.

I had no idea where I was going, but I'd have to trust the journey, regardless. What other choice did I have? The decision had been made. And if I were to be totally honest, with no job to move to and no real plan, from a logical point of view, this all looked a little dubious. But I couldn't deny the silent knowing in my heart that everything was happening perfectly and all was well in the world.

I had cultivated something more important than intellectual knowing and that something is trust and faith. I felt the nudge, sensed the change in energy and knew that life had more for me; all I had to do was heed the call. And that's the beauty of trusting life, you don't need to see the path to know it's there – each of your steps will pave the way.

Traveller, your footprints
Are the path and nothing more;
Traveller, there is no path,

The path is made by walking.
By walking the path is made
And when you look back
You'll see a road
Never to be trodden again.

Antonio Machado

Our job is to listen to our knowing, take a step in the right direction, surrender the results and watch the path unfold and, although waking up the following morning with no job to go to was testing (I felt lost, with no idea, no inkling as to what I'd do next or, more to the point, 'for the rest of my life'), I continued to build my trust muscle. Whenever doubt would come in, I'd see it for the fear-based thinking that it was and I'd let it go, knowing there was more to this than met the eye.

I was in the nothingness, in The In-Between, and so I'd have to walk my talk and, despite feeling trepidation, 'out there' in alien territory, floating in a boat with invisible paddles, I kept trusting. I continued to feel my feelings, remembering and re-membering and trusting, following my heart and keeping faith – faith that all was happening perfectly. As I've said, the path is forged with each step; the picture will become clearer as time moves on. And so, I listened to my knowing, to the inner calling and the only thing that made any real sense to me in that moment and in the moments that followed, was to write. And write I did.

And the Journey Continues...

I'd always loved to write, even back in school when I rallied against the status quo. I had always loved English, I had always enjoyed the process of story-telling and essay writing and I believed I was good at it.

At points I may have felt there was a book in me somewhere. Indeed I had heard there's a book in everyone, but actually creating this and making this manifest had always felt 'beyond' me – how on earth would I do this? Write a book?! Wasn't this reserved solely for the likes of Stephen King, Ernest Hemingway, Virginia Woolf, Jane Austen and the literary greats? Who would want to read about my life? Was there even a story to tell?

I hadn't built a rocket ship, hadn't run for president, I wasn't sitting on a property empire or making a name for myself in the financial markets and I most certainly wasn't made of the same stuff as Shakespeare, unable even to comprehend his level of genius. I'd had a 'normal' life – what's newsworthy about that?

But here's the thing: it's not up to us to know who will benefit from our personal life stories, it's not up to us to determine who we'll serve when we show up and speak our truth (we cannot know what will be of value to another) and it's most certainly not our job to work out the 'hows, the whens and the whys'. What *is* our responsibility is to sit up and take notice of The Call. If we have even an inkling that there's a forum for us and that what we have to say matters, we must take to the stage and show our face, ready and willing to open our mouths and let our hearts speak. This is of paramount importance.

If there's a desire to do something and a nagging that won't go away, we must trust that there's work to be done, that something is calling to us to move towards it. It is our responsibility to show up. If life is wanting your contribution, it will not stop prodding and pushing you in the direction that's calling to you – there's a shape that only you can fill and life is waiting for you to take your place.

We're so self-deprecating (and taught this is somehow admirable), so conditioned to believe that we 'can't', so incredibly unaware of our own personal genius and our very much needed contribution to this world, that it is sometimes hard to move past these limitations to believe that we can be (we are) great, that who we are and what we have to say matters. More than that, it's *needed*.

Each of us has a seat reserved just for us and a mission that only we can realise. And so, with this new-found desire to write that came with a heartfelt love for this endeavour, I put fingers to keyboard and I let it flow. I did my best to take my head out of the equation and allowed my heart to speak and it felt 'right'. It felt more 'me' than anything else I had done up until that point. It opened the door to another version of myself that had been waiting silently on the sidelines, waiting patiently to be called into play.

I remember sitting in a restaurant and having a chat with a lady seated at the table next to me about publishing. I can't recall the exact content of our conversation – possibly she was telling me she had a daughter who'd had a book published – and at that moment I decided that I'd put it 'out there' and try to find a publisher.

I paid the bill, packed up my laptop and was on my way to another coffee shop when a message came through on my phone. The text was from someone who I knew, but who I was not in regular contact with and with no context and no message – he'd sent me an ad from a publishing house who were looking for new authors.

I had to check this message a few times to make sure I wasn't imagining it, as the timing was astonishing. I called the person who had messaged me to enquire as to why he had sent this to me and he simply said he thought I'd be interested in writing for them. That's it. No more to the story. It was astounding to me. So I called the number and chatted to the guy from the publishers who said he'd like to read some of my work and I was off.

Once again, life was nudging me towards my purpose and mission, organising the conditions and creating the necessary support and environment for the writing of this book. The conversations with my contact at the publishing house gave me a platform that felt 'real'. I wasn't just writing into the ether, I had sent my work in, had received a positive response and a framework had been created in which I could write… my story.

Looking back, I had needed this level of connection and holding to keep me going. If it had not been there, I doubt I would have had the impetus to keep going. Someone was waiting for my work, I had a deadline (albeit a moveable one) that I wanted to meet and it gave me something to move towards. Someone had read my words and had found them worthy of publication. Writing my book became real.

The book moved from a distant thought in my mind to something that took up residence in the minds of others too, which propelled it forward into the world of form, into this 3-D realm and it became 'something'. Life knew I needed this launching platform and it provided the very necessary support structure to keep me going. Again, life is always wanting your full flourishing. Look out for the signals and those invisible hands that are always providing you with exactly what you need – in my case, a deadline and someone holding me accountable for delivering my writing.

It wasn't 'easy'; the writing process was challenging to say the least. I pulled a long forgotten story from the past and re-lived it in my now. I was up against old and painful feelings and emotions and it hurt. I continually fought against the urge to hide the truth and soften my words. I struggled with the urge to edit, re-edit and edit again.

I had to work against the part of me that judged my writing, deeming it unworthy and the feeling that this was an incredibly difficult endeavour, that I was being too transparent, inviting criticism, offering myself up as a target to be shot down. I also made procrastination an art form – in the history of writers, I'm not sure anyone has ever matched me!

But through it all, there was this knowing deep inside me, that what I had to say was needed, that my story and my words mattered and, regardless of the outcome, I had to write. And when I found it more important to clip my toenails, scrutinise my skin or scrub the kitchen surfaces, leaving my laptop further unattended, I felt that nagging, that tap on my shoulder and that little prod that wouldn't let me rest. And when the process was underway, when I was immersed in the writing, I moved into another space, another dimension and the 'little me' disappeared, making way for and allowing that girl who was waiting on the sidelines to come to the forefront and speak.

And this is how you know you're onto something, that you're doing something you were born to do. Because time stands still, you're in 'the zone' and everything outside of this space becomes invisible; you're in love with your moment and you feel alive. So when doubt creeps in, I remember this, I remember that this comes naturally and effortlessly to me (once I move past procrastination) and I know beyond a shadow of a doubt, that this is who I am and life is calling me to deliver this book to you. And because of this, because I know deep down in my heart that this is what life is asking of me, doubt doesn't stand a chance in the face of this undeniable and unwavering knowing. Doubt pales into insignificance in the light of Truth.

And now I know I don't need to be Stephen King, Shakespeare, Jane Austen, Virginia Woolf or the like, because I am Me. I have a story to tell. I am in this world, which makes me just as valuable and as important as anybody else.

Life gave me a story, life gave me my struggles, my pain, my joy, my bliss, my heartache, my passions, my truth, my depth, my eyes that see and my ears that hear and my own precious version of this beautiful thing called Life and it matters – I matter.

So, for that reason, I follow the call and I write. I share my experiences because I know I must. I share who I am in order for you to open into who *you* are. I write so that you may hear something that makes sense to you, something that helps you see the world a little differently, something that helps you navigate life with a little less struggle and a lot more flow. I share because I want you to know just how precious and valuable and awesome you really are. Listen. Listen to what life is calling you towards, listen to what you are being shown. Show up. Claim it. Do *you*.

And So to End...

I pray that you wake up from the slumber of the false self. I pray that you become conscious and know your Self as you truly are – an awesome and magnificent being, limitless and joyful, powerful beyond measure. I pray that your desire to live bigger moves into the forefront and becomes your priority, that the dreams you've held in your heart are given the attention they deserve and the space they need to manifest.

It is my wish that you look in the mirror and love the person staring back at you. May you wake each morning and love the life you're living. May the old story be no more and the distorted lens be discarded and may your ears hear the Truth and your eyes see the Truth; the Truth of life and the Truth of who you truly are. May you know deep and abiding joy. From my heart, I wish this for you.

It's been hard existing within a society that sleeps, when I knew in my heart that there's more. And now I understand this to be the cause of the rage I felt from such a young age, raging against the machine, demanding justice, screaming for freedom and for liberation.

And so it is… the search has been long and arduous and it seems I have been looking in all the wrong places. My longing was not for a romance, not for more friends, not for more of anything or even for a partner. My longing has always been for Home, for wholeness, to come back to my Self, to re-member who I am. This is the journey, coming back home to me.

I have been searching to be seen. And here I am, I see me. I have been waiting for permission to be me; I now give myself that permission. The journey has been a return to love – remembering this is who I am, right before the lies filled my head and I forgot. Remembering this is who you are, right before *you* forgot. We are powerful. We are magical. We are awesome. We are love.

There was never anywhere I needed to go – I see that now. Indeed, it has been right in front of me this whole time. I've been here all along and, as it turns out, it's me – I am the one I've been waiting for.

Finally, at long last, I am home.

ABOUT THE AUTHOR

Emma Eker is a life coach and author from London, UK. Trained in Psychosynthesis Psychology (PG Dip), amongst other disciplines, Emma has worked as a coach for over 14 years.

Emma is passionate about all things related to the human experience, evolution and helping people to thrive in life. It is her mission to help individuals remember how powerful they truly are, moving them out of and away from restrictions in order to fully flourish.

This desire has been with Emma since she was a very young child and she is committed to this path of evolution and 'awakening'.

You can find her at www.emmaeker.com

Printed in Great Britain
by Amazon